# Homer

# Homer

## THE VERY IDEA

James I. Porter

The University of Chicago Press
Chicago and London

The University of Chicago Press, Chicago 60637
The University of Chicago Press, Ltd., London


Published 2021
Paperback edition 2023
Printed in the United States of America

32 31 30 29 28 27 26 25 24 23     1 2 3 4 5

ISBN-13: 978-0-226-67589-3 (cloth)
ISBN-13: 978-0-226-67590-9 (paper)
ISBN-13: 978-0-226-79007-7 (e-book)
DOI: https://doi.org/10.7208/chicago/9780226790077.001.0001

Library of Congress Cataloging-in-Publication Data

Names: Porter, James I., 1954– author.
Title: Homer : the very idea / James I. Porter.
Description: Chicago : University of Chicago Press, 2021. | Includes bibliographical references and index.
Identifiers: LCCN 2020056575 | ISBN 9780226675893 (cloth) | ISBN 9780226790077 (ebook)
Subjects: LCSH: Homer—Influence. | Greek literature—History and criticism.
Classification: LCC PA4037 .P645 2021 | DDC 883/.01—dc23
LC record available at https://lccn.loc.gov/2020056575

∞ This paper meets the requirements of ANSI/NISO Z39.48-1992 (Permanence of Paper).

# Contents

# Note on Translations and Abbreviations

Translations from the *Iliad* and *Odyssey* are by Richmond Lattimore unless otherwise noted. References to other translations, philosophical fragments, and more frequently consulted works, both ancient and modern, appear in the text and notes with the translators' or editors' names, followed by book, fragment, section, line, or page numbers. Bracketed names—for example [Plutarch]—indicate uncertain or spurious attestations. Full documentation for works cited may be found in the bibliography. Translations without attribution are my own.

## Abbreviations

| | |
|---|---|
| Allen | Thomas W. Allen, ed., *Homeri Opera*, 2nd ed., vol. 5 (Oxford, 1912) |
| DK | Hermann Diels and Walther Kranz, eds., *Die Fragmente der Vorsokratiker, griechisch und deutsch*, 3 vols., 6th ed. (Berlin, 1951–52) |
| fr./frr. | Fragment/fragments |
| *HE* | *The Homer Encyclopedia*, ed. Margalit Finkelberg, 3 vols. (Chichester, MA, 2011) |
| *Il.* | *Iliad* |
| *Od.* | *Odyssey* |
| Schol. *Il.* or *Od.* | Scholium/scholia (ancient commentaries) on the *Iliad* or *Odyssey* |
| *Vit. Hom.* | *Vita Homeri* [*Life of Homer*], in Allen |

# Illustrations

# Timeline

All premodern dates are *circa* unless otherwise indicated.

BCE

| | |
|---|---|
| 1600–1100 | Late Bronze Age |
| 1200 | Bronze Age systems collapse and the fall of Troy |
| 1200–700 | Iron Age |
| 730–700 | Emergence of the *Iliad* and *Odyssey* |
| 725–720 | Nestor's Cup |
| 700–480 | Archaic period |
| end of 7th c.–early 6th c. | Lyric poets (Stesichorus, Sappho, Alcaeus) |
| 580–523 | *Homeric Hymn to Apollo* |
| 6th c. (?) | Core of the *Contest of Homer and Hesiod* circulates |
| *fl.* 540–510 | Hipponax |
| 570–480 | Xenophanes of Colophon |
| 566–522 | Pisistratus and Hipparchus (the "Pisistratids") introduce and regulate performances of Homer at the Panathenaea festival in Athens |
| *fl.* 500 | Heraclitus of Ephesus |

| | |
|---|---|
| 480–323 | Classical period |
| mid- to late 5th c. | Hellanicus of Lesbos; Protagoras and other Sophists |
| early 4th c. | Alcidamas of Elaea revises the *Contest of Homer and Hesiod* |
| 390–380 | Plato, *Ion* and *Republic* |
| 340–335 | Aristotle, *Poetics* |
| 323 | Death of Alexander the Great |
| 323–31 | Hellenistic period |
| 284 (?) | Founding of the Library of Alexandria and the Museum |
| late 3rd–late 2nd c. | Archelaus of Priene, *Apotheosis of Homer* |
| *fl.* 150 | Aristarchus of Samothrace |
| 29–19 | Vergil, *Aeneid* |

## CE

| | |
|---|---|
| 40 (?) | Longinus, *On the Sublime* |
| 50–250 | Greek "Second Sophistic" (Dio, Lucian, Philostratus) |
| 1180 | Eustathius of Constantinople, *Commentaries on Homer's Iliad and Odyssey* |
| 1353–1354 | Petrarch obtains a Greek manuscript of Homer |
| 1360–1362 | First translations of the *Iliad* and *Odyssey* into Latin by Leontius Pilatus (never published) |
| 1474 and 1497 | First published translations into Latin of the *Iliad*, then the *Odyssey* |
| 1474 (?) | *Battle of Frogs and Mice* printed in Brescia |

| | |
|---|---|
| 1488 | First Greek edition of Homer in the West, published in Florence (*Iliad, Odyssey, Homeric Hymns, Battle of Frogs and Mice*, the Plutarchan and Herodotean *Lives of Homer*) |
| 1561 | Julius Caesar Scaliger, *Poetices libri septem* |
| 1566 | First critical edition of Homer published by Henri Estienne in Geneva |
| 1664–1676 | Abbé d'Aubignac (François Hédelin) composes *Conjectures académiques, ou Dissertation sur l'Iliade* (published anonymously in 1715) |
| 1711 and 1716 | Anne Dacier, translation of the *Iliad* and the *Odyssey* |
| 1715–1720 | Alexander Pope, translation of the *Iliad* |
| 1730 | Giambattista Vico, "The Discovery of the True Homer," in *Scienza nuova*, 2nd ed. |
| 1795 | Friedrich August Wolf, *Prolegomena to Homer* |
| 1827 | Jean-Auguste-Dominique Ingres, *Homer Deified*, or *The Apotheosis of Homer* |
| 1869 | Friedrich Nietzsche, "On the Personality of Homer" (published as "Homer and Classical Philology") |
| 1870–1890 | Heinrich Schliemann excavates Troy |
| 1928 | Milman Parry publishes his theory of oral-formulaic composition |
| 1932–1938 | Carl Blegen re-excavates Troy |
| 1940–1941 | Simone Weil, *L'Iliade, ou le poème de la force* [*The Iliad, or The Poem of Force*] |
| 1941, 1944, 1947 | Max Horkheimer and Theodor W. Adorno, *Dialektik der Aufklärung* [*Dialectic of Enlightenment*] (composed, mimeographed, then expanded and published) |
| 1942 | Erich Auerbach composes "Odysseus' Scar" (published in *Mimesis* in 1946) |

| | |
|---|---|
| 1943 | Rachel Bespaloff, *De l'Iliade* [*On the Iliad*] |
| 1947 | Jorge Luis Borges, "*El inmortal*" ["The Immortal"] (reprinted in *El Aleph*, 1949; "Postscript" added 1950) |
| 1988–2005 | Manfred Korfmann re-excavates Troy |
| 2005–present | Excavations at Troy are ongoing |

# — 1 —
# Why Homer?

The *Iliad* and the *Odyssey* have been required reading in Western culture from its beginnings, despite the mystery surrounding their date and authorship and despite their obvious blemishes—the inconsistencies, repetitions, and anomalies—which have led to their impeachment as products of a single mind. We might as well ask with Gilbert Murray, the future Regius Professor of Greek at Oxford writing in 1907, "Now why is it that the *Iliad* is a good poem when it has so many of the characteristics of a bad one?"[1]

All the uncertainties about Homer and his poems notwithstanding, their place in the Western cultural imagination has been unrivaled. Indeed, as secular texts with no pretensions to revealed truth, and yet conferred with nearly biblical stature already in antiquity, the Homeric poems have enjoyed a status in world literature that is absolutely unique. Not even Vergil, the great poet of the Romans and of later Latin readers, could escape the long shadow cast by his Greek predecessor. Though it was Vergil, the most Christian-friendly of the pagan poets, who escorted Dante most of the way to Paradise, it was Homer, not Vergil, whom Dante called "the sovereign poet" (*Omero poeta sovrano*) without ever having read a word of him.[2]

How can we account for Homer's standing and his enduring attraction? Whatever the answer, approaching the question will involve confronting the monumentality of his two poems, less their quality as great works of literature than their role as cultural icons, as signifiers of value, and as landmarks in the evolving relationship between literature and culture. To look at Homer in this way is to consider his place—the very idea of Homer—in the culture wars of antiquity and modernity. But it is also to recognize that the meaning and value of Homer (provisionally, the poet and the poems that have been attributed to him) are the products of a particular kind of fascination: they have been a compulsive and productive source of culture since antiquity. This achievement is all the more remarkable given the fact that nothing whatsoever is known about Homer. Who he was, when and where he lived and died, what he sang or wrote, whether he was blind, and so on—all this is unknown and, alas, unknowable.

The oddity of the situation cannot be emphasized enough. An absolute *chiffre,* Homer is a peculiar kind of object in the history of culture inasmuch as he enters the cultural record as an object that is lost from the moment it is found. And with each new attempt to "discover" the true Homer again, that primordial loss is repeated as well. The real problem, then, is not just that Homer is an unknown object whose identity is clouded over with endless uncertainties, nor even that Homer may never have existed as an identifiable person, as is widely believed today. It is that Homer is an *impossible* object, an entity who only becomes tangibly real and actual in the very failed effort to grasp him. A Homer like this, about whom nothing is known, cannot help but produce a sense of puzzlement, not simply at the level of his texts but in the very conception of Homer as the author of his poems. "Homer" simultaneously names this predicament of logic and conceals it from view, which has ensured that Homer continues to exist even if the person never did, but also that he is continually enlisted in causes that were never his, like a blank check.

A simpler way of putting the problem is to recognize that Homer's status—his monumentality and his value—was never a self-evident given: it was not bestowed on him from birth. On the contrary, it had to be repeatedly struggled over, argued, established, and reestablished over time, which is to say that the monument of Homer had to be built and rebuilt from one generation to the next. And because it did, Homer has for the most part appeared not only as the oldest poet in the West but also, paradoxically, as the youngest. The usual claims that Homer possesses a value that is innate, inviolable, and everlasting cannot escape the irony that those very same claims are not themselves inviolable and everlasting. Not only have they proved eminently contestable, as will become abundantly clear in this book, but they have also assumed radically different meanings as historical circumstances change. Looking at Homer from this angle, as an object of cultural production rather than as a producer of literature, is an invitation to study the intellectual and cultural history of value, and that is one way in which I would like the following pages to be understood. Homer will in a sense merely be our guide.

A perspective like this can throw a valuable light on the often circuitous logic of culture. Logic or illogic? For leaving aside the nearly self-evident truism that what is finally at stake in the contests over Homer are the identities of the various combatants involved, surely Homer's greatest attraction has to lie not in his greatness, however that comes to be defined, but in his utter mystery and unreachability. Consequently, if there is any value at all to Homer, it has to be sought in the very indeterminateness of his definition and his unrivaled mystique, which have provoked intense reflection and served as an instrument of endless debate, contest, and redefinition. One suspects that in settling on Homer as an object of contention, the ancients and the moderns have made a rather telling choice, one that ceaselessly *authorizes* the imaginative work of culture. Culture is not just an arena of contestation. It is a deviously calculating and self-enabling thing.

But while Homer offers clues to many of the larger processes by which the core values of a culture come to be shaped and revised, he also has a particular story to tell that is all his own. The question of how the idea of Homer came to signify differently in different cultural settings over long stretches of time involves a history that is both rich and at times utterly bizarre. And so this book is meant to expose some of the marvelous strangeness that the problem of Homer has produced over the millennia and continues to produce today.

## Aims of This Study

Given the scope of the problem, my discussion will have to be selective and, inevitably, reductive. A list of the writings that have accumulated around Homer since antiquity would fill dozens of volumes by itself, and it is not my intention to do more than sample this literature. Nor will I be rehearsing the ways in which Homer's poems, understood as literary works, were read, translated, or adapted over the ages, though there is much excellent scholarship on this and much to be learned from it. My study has a narrower compass: it is focused by the person of Homer and the problems that sprang up around him rather than by the poems that were passed down under his name. This is not to say that the poems are irrelevant to the story I want to tell. But it is one thing to read the *Iliad* and quite another to read it as the work of a poet known as "Homer" who lived and sang at a certain time and place and whose presence in his poems is everywhere to be felt but nowhere to be seen. And that is exactly what ancient and modern readers do whenever they look for meaning in the *Iliad* and *Odyssey* or attempt to situate the poems in time and space. With each new understanding, Homer's readers are extrapolating an image of the poems' creator or creators from the poems and then giving these images independent life: they are painting Homer's portrait and producing his "idea." But what is that, exactly?

Here it is helpful to bear in mind the way in which the young Friedrich Nietzsche framed the problem in 1869. In Homer, he asked, "has a person (*Person*) been made out of a concept (*Begriff*), or a concept out of a person?"[3] Nietzsche leaves the question dangling and unanswered, because it is, he believed, unanswerable. But to frame the problem in this way is already to say a good deal about Homer. The upshot of Nietzsche's thesis, as I understand it, is that "Homer" is never the result of some positive act of creation or invention that leaves no residue of doubt. On the contrary, Homer's name has no positive content at all: "The poet [of the *Iliad* and the *Odyssey*]," he continued, "is an empty name, fragile wherever one lays hold of him, nowhere the stable core of an underlying, coherent individual."[4] Featureless and faceless, and so too empty of meaning, "Homer" is only a momentary stopgap for an act of imagining that vacillates uncertainly between the two poles of personhood and idea whenever Homer is put on the table for discussion.

But no sooner is Homer named than the pendular swing of indecision begins all over again. Problematic to the core, Homer disintegrates on contact. He is the ongoing problem of his own identity.

My interest, then, is not in Homer the historical individual who might have lived some time around the end of the eighth century BCE, which is where the current consensus places the first crystallizations of the *Iliad* and the *Odyssey* as we know these two poems, and which it assigns, by metonymy and convention, to "Homer." Nor am I interested in Homer as a poet, which is to say as the supervising architect of either or both of these two epics, or in mining the poems as aesthetic objects. This book is not intended as a work of literary criticism, although on rare occasions targeted readings of the poems will be necessary to illustrate a larger point. Neither is it meant as an introduction to the history and culture of Greece that form the background and context of Homer and his epics, or as a reception history in the sense of a study in Homeric influences. Rather, it is conceived as a cultural history, in abbreviated form, of an idea, a point of concern, a fascination, and an obsession that was born and reborn every time Homer was imagined as the presumed poet of the *Iliad* and the *Odyssey*, and around which entire canons of literature, disciplines, and whole bodies of knowledge came to be built and organized over the millennia, including the study of antiquity itself.

I say "presumed" because there is no way of proving that such a poet ever existed, let alone that a single individual was responsible for the creation of the two great epics that somehow came to be attached to his name after the eighth century BCE. The ancients certainly did not know who Homer was or how his poems emerged, or even his proper name ("Melesigenes" and "Melesagoras" were among the preferred contenders), though they spent a great deal of ingenuity trying to work out answers to each of these questions. Nor have modern scholars, for all their vastly improved resources and techniques, fared any better, though they would be loath to admit this.

The great irony here—it is really something of an embarrassment—is that the two founding documents of Western culture have no birth certificate, no assignable date, no parents, and no clear place of origin. At their center lies an enigma that goes by the name of Homer, their hypothesized origin. An unknown quantity and a question mark with no answer, "Homer" is little more than a way of bridging this lack of information, one that was given a name, a face, a body, a life, a death, and an immortal afterlife—or rather, innumerable different versions of each of these things. Like a wayward mythical creature fabled for eluding capture (Proteus comes to mind), Homer's identity slipped away whenever one tried to lay hold of him. Instead, it multiplied into countless variations on a theme that had no original: each was merely a variation of the rest.[5] Such is the logic of Homer as an idea whenever it is made into a person. Thomas De Quincey, the Victorian writer and part-time crank, nicely caught the gist of this logic in a wry moment of his astute essay from 1841, "Homer and the Homeridae": "Some say, 'there never was such a person as Homer.' 'No such person as Homer! On the contrary,' say others, 'there were scores.'"[6]

De Quincey was, of course, right: antiquity never knew a single Homer. Instead, it produced a long lineup of suspects, one of whom was said to have been born on Ios, another on Samos, another on Chios, another at Colophon, another on Ithaca, and so on, each the result of the effort to lay claim to Homer and his legacy—though with how much sincerity is a fair question to ask. Homer surely could not have been all of these individuals, and he may not have been any one of them. Were the ancients, deep down, suspicious about their own traditions? There is good reason to think that they were, at least to a degree that escapes the still prevalent assumptions about the earliest Greeks' naïveté. Recognizing this possibility drastically changes how the traditions surrounding Homer in antiquity look to us today.

As it happens, a good deal of culture then and since has been produced in the effort to establish a secure understanding of Homer, a process that was only abetted by the elusiveness of the goal. And an equal quantity of culture has been produced by the opposite effort, namely, to knock down attempted understandings of Homer, whether by challenging them or by proving them hollow.

Homer did become a pillar of subsequent culture, not as its secure foundation but as a question around which whole edifices of meaning were successively built, torn down, and rebuilt, through a process of querying, explaining, doubting, affirming, contesting, and revising every aspect of his identity and every prior account of him. One result of this process was not a singular Homer, as De Quincey correctly observes, but a set of uniquely different Homers, not at random but each fashioned for a different end. While of little value in answering the question of Homer, these several Homers are of great diagnostic value for us: they throw light on their own origins.

Nothing, therefore, could be more horrifically misguided than the belief expressed by the philosopher David Hume in his essay "Of the Standard of Taste" (1757) that "the same HOMER who pleased at ATHENS and ROME two thousand years ago, is still admired at PARIS and at LONDON."[7] Homer was never universally admired. On the contrary, he was subjected to heated debate and controversy from the word go, starting from his earliest recorded mentions. At times he was worshipped like a god among poets. At other times he was raked over the coals as an affront to morality and to humanity *tout court*. This battle of opinion continued well into the bitter Quarrel of the Ancients and the Moderns that shook the earlier part of Hume's own century, above all in France, and in its most extreme form led to the denial of Homer's existence altogether. As the battle lines around Homer multiplied and fragmented, so too did Homer, with the result that no two Homers were ever alike. There is simply no way to square the Homer of Vergil with that of Aeschylus, or of either one with that of Euripides, Gladstone, or Derek Walcott, not to mention De Quincey, whose pluriform Homer from 1841 has nothing in common with Hume's uniform and universalized Homer, though it does fairly capture the ancient biographical tradition of Homer that De Quincey is in effect summarizing and that continued to proliferate into his own day. Plainly, it is hard to generalize about Homer. And yet for all his variety, Homer remains what he has always been, a peculiar cipher who may be unique precisely because he has no observable content and no identity, but merely occupies a structural position that cannot be removed without a disastrous change to the structure itself, like a gap in traffic. The boundaries can be perpetually stretched to accommodate new claims (Athens, Ithaca, Alexandria, Babylonia, Rome, Jerusalem, the Balkans, London, St. Lucia . . .). Homer moves with them.

As I hope is clear from the foregoing, "Homer" is a slippery five-letter word for a complicated concept. In order to clear up any potential misunderstandings before proceeding further, I need to clarify what I mean whenever I use the word myself. "Homer" in this book, whether the name appears in quotation marks or not, is first and foremost a shorthand for all that we do not know about this poet (if he ever existed), and then, by extension, for the two epics and other minor works that have historically been attributed to him. Confusions between an author and his or her oeuvre were as common in antiquity as they are today—for example whenever we say, "I am reading Homer." This book is *about* such confusions, which are inevitable in the case of Homer, given the fact that he nowhere identifies himself in his poems by name, nor do we know when the name of "Homer" came to be attached to those poems. One possibility, if not likelihood, is that the name was assigned to the poems after they were created in an effort to nominate their purported originator. In that case, Homer enjoyed at best a circular existence and at worst a belated one: he had no life but only an afterlife.

Nor do Homer's poems have any clearer identity than Homer. Although Homer is a less tangible entity than either the *Iliad* or the *Odyssey*, the problems of identification, origins, dating, and emergence are as insoluble in the case of the epics as they are in the case of their alleged author. Homer and his poems are in this respect entangled by a common fate. And for the same reasons, the so-called Homeric tradition, it needs to be stressed, was never a singular, self-consistent, and harmonious entity. On the contrary, it was a plural, diverse, and unruly ensemble of conflicting and overlapping strands that sought to wrestle with the problem of Homer. With this proviso in mind, the word "tradition," wherever it is used in connection with Homer below, should be understood in this largest sense—as a plurality, one that is an exact reflex of the uncertainties that have surrounded Homer.

## The Homeric Question and the Problem of Homer

The standard way in which modern scholarship treats these looming uncertainties is by placing them under the rubric of the so-called Homeric Question, which is really a collection of questions: Who composed the epics, when, and where? Are they by a single author or the product of a tradition, if not a committee? Could their author read and write? Was he blind or sighted? Did he compose both the *Iliad* and the *Odyssey* or only one of these poems? Was he further responsible for additional works that came down under his name, for instance the *Homeric Hymns* or any other of the minor poems of uncertain provenance or date in the epic tradition, the so-called Epic Cycle, which narrated prequels and sequels to the Homeric poems, not to mention a raft of smaller minor writings in a lighter key, for instance the *Margites*, a mock-epic about a simpleton that even Aristotle credited to Homer, or other titles that gathered around his name: the *Battle of Frogs and Mice*, the *Battle of Cranes*, the *Battle of Spiders*, and other apocrypha, some of these the products of purported theft and plagiarism?[8] The question in these latter cases ultimately comes down to establishing the difference between Homer and Homeric, but this is merely to invite the problem all over again.

While each of these issues, with the exception of the ascription of works, has perennially nagged amateurs and scholars alike and has evaded solution, my interests are not in the questions per se but in the reasons behind their urgency. Why does it matter so much that we are so very concerned with Homer's identity, the time and place in which he may have lived, what he said or saw, and what he knew? Can we even approach the poems without some preconceived notion of who or what their source was? To put the issue in this way is to isolate the Homeric *problem* that lies behind the Homeric *question*. The problem predates the modern approaches to Homer, as does its natural congener, the Homeric Question itself, although neither fact is sufficiently acknowledged today. Assertions to the contrary, the Homeric Question was *not* the invention of the eighteenth century, when scholars began to doubt the credentials and even the existence of Homer and then coined the phrase "the Homeric Question" to mark out an area for research into the problem. Nor was it the invention of the late French and Italian Renaissance, when humanists posed many of the same problems in their own way, as has been recently demonstrated.[9] In fact, the Homeric Question was alive and well already at an early date in antiquity, almost certainly by the end of the sixth century BCE, if not sooner (we lack the evidence)—not, to be sure, in so many words, but with all the features, uncertainties, and urgency of the later versions of the Homeric Question. The *problem* of Homer existed in antiquity, likewise in much the same form as it did in the modern era. And at the bottom of the problem lay a series of grave misgivings and even doubts that gave it its true content.

This is a crucial point. Merely to ask in all innocence who Homer was is to express a doubt *sotto voce* as to his identity. To dwell on the question for more than a moment is to shake one's faith in what can be really known about Homer. And the same is true of the poems: it is natural to marvel at them—they are astonishing works of art—but it is just as natural to wonder how they found their way into the world in the form they did. The two kinds of wonderment come as a pair: they spring from the same source (a fundamental ignorance), and they add to each other's intensity. How the questions finally get answered is another story. Aristotle would appeal to Homer's grandeur and nobility of soul to account for the form of his epics. For Vico, Homer was a projection of the barbarous Greek peoples. For Hegel, he was an expression of their naïve and beautiful spirit. Classicists after the eighteenth century learned to locate and then explain irregularities in the poems by appealing to their layered and centuries-long oral transmission. However the questions get answered, they all arise from a wellspring of urgency, unknowability, and uncertainty. They originate in mystery, but one that lends itself to exploitation for ulterior ends.

That said, the task this book sets itself is not to solve the mystery of who Homer was but to understand how and why the idea of

Homer arose, the various forms it took, and why it has exerted so great a fascination for so many millennia—almost three, to be more precise—a fascination that shows few signs of waning today. What accounts for this persistence? Sifting through the evidence for the problem of Homer is no less daunting a task than conducting a reception history of the Homeric epics. It is simply the road less often taken in studies of Homer's reappearances in literature and culture, and for that reason is worth risking. Even with the framework narrowed down in this way, the ground that needs to be covered remains incalculably vast. Only brief soundings will be possible in what follows.

In sum, my study is limited to a selection of developments in the repeated manufacture of Homer from antiquity to the present day, arranged by themes that are posed as questions—Homeric questions of a kind: Why Homer? (chapter 1); Who was Homer? (chapter 2); Was he a god, a ghost, or a whipping boy? Was he the product of apotheosis or apostasy? (chapter 3); What did he see, if anything at all? (chapter 4); And why do we credit his poems, steeped as they are in the brutal violence of warfare, with so venerable a place at the foot of our cultural traditions? Why war? (chapter 5).

The discussion will be threaded by four recurrent themes:

- the *persistent classicism* of Homer, which is to say the process by which Homer became a canonical classic and never lost this title, despite every tug of pressure in the opposite direction (and the pressures going the other way were great indeed: classical canonicity, it turns out, does not guarantee inviolability, and reverence need not always be unalloyed);
- the elements of *disavowal* that go into the construction and sustaining of Homer's ever-imaginary identity—for Homer exists only as an imagined and reimagined entity, yet he does so under the pretense that he is always tangible and real;
- the sheer *allure* and *inaccessibility* of Homer and, what proves inseparable from these, the sheer fascination of watching how the story of Homer's imagining—his ideation—continually engages those who contribute to its making;

- the *doubts* and *exasperations* that plagued the uncertain identification of Homer, which tended to take one of two forms: either opportunism (wild speculation and free invention) or critique (criticism of the cultural pieties and blatant falsehoods or inconsistencies that collected around Homer's name).

These four threads are mutually reinforcing, and they typically come as a quartet even when one or the other of the threads is not immediately visible. Whenever one lead gives out, failing to deliver on its promises, the others typically step in to compensate for this failing. Thus, if Homer's historical reality becomes frustratingly elusive, the tenuousness of his reality can be redeemed by his very allure; or it can be forgiven owing to his unimpeachable canonical authority; or else it can be impugned owing to the troubling uncertainties that beset Homer's identity. The study of Homer is the study of the repeated interplay of these moves, some of them outright declarations either for or against Homer, others compensatory dodges. Homer emerges from antiquity, both on balance and more frequently than one might like to admit, not as a homogeneous entity, but rather as a heap of contradictions that never fully get sorted out.[10] This, too, is one of the sustaining features of Homer's profile: he survives not owing to any one single factor, but because he can be any number of things to each of his readers and a perennial topic of discussion and debate. Far from detracting from the study of Homer's life and afterlife, these complications make Homer the *interesting problem* that he is.

## The Other Homer

A further conviction that runs through this study is that the idea of Homer is a popular one before it is a learned one, and that popular and scholarly approaches to Homer continually inform each other, for the simple reason that both are driven by the same imperatives. We don't know who Homer's first audiences were, but we do know that from an early date he was regarded as a poet of the people, very like the bards he depicts. The name of Demodocus, the Phaeacian court singer in book 8 of the *Odyssey* who earns Odysseus's praise for the songs he sings about Troy, means "received (*dok-*) by the people (*dēmos*)." Elsewhere in the same poem, bards are called "workers who serve the people" and who are "honored by the people," perhaps meaning those in the audience who would have identified with the world of the Homeric similes that bring the loftier epic action closer to home—the world of nature, of humble farmers, shepherds, goatherds, woodcutters, hunters, and craftspeople. A later document, very likely with roots in the sixth century or earlier, shows Homer and Hesiod testing each other's skill and popularity in song (the *Contest of Homer and Hesiod*). The audience is described as being made up of "all the Greeks," even if the final arbiter of the competition is figured as a king. The king's decision in favor of Hesiod, a surprise, was manifestly unpopular. And the several ancient *Lives of Homer* to which the *Contest* generically belongs show Homer mingling more often with commonfolk than with kings in his travels through Greece. He was of their kind.

In short, singers may have sung for elite audiences, but they also sang for and about the widest reaches of society.[11] This was the true source of the epics' popularity, which down to the end of antiquity showed up in demotic forms, for example in funerary epitaphs in which children are compared to the offspring of Hector and Andromache, and dutiful wives are compared to Penelope, all this in language that is borrowed from Homer, often with a canny sophistication equal to any that can be found in more learned corners of the ancient world.[12] Everywhere we look, the story is the same: Homer's reception owed its success to the diffusion of his name beyond the high canons of literary taste and beyond elite circles; and popular readings tended to be shrewd readings. Early biographical anecdotes suggest as much, as does the *Contest*, which is packed with folkloric motifs. The contamination of Homer with perspectives from below has consequences that ramify through his reception and diffusion among poets, philosophers, and literary critics across antiquity and into modernity.

One of the most notable of these consequences is his capacity for debasement. Though likened to an Olympian god, Homer was never just a highbrow conceit. He was repeatedly taken down from his pedestal and placed in the margins and gutters of culture, where he could be defrocked and dethroned like an interloper or a fraudulent perjurer, as frail and fallible as any other human creature. According to a source from later antiquity, Homer's very name was synonymous with the verb "to lie" (*homērizein*, "to Homerize"). But this was merely the consecration of a long-standing prejudice that Plato, its most famous exponent, inherited. Even Aristotle makes the extraordinary claim that Homer "taught other poets the proper way to tell lies."[13] And these are just the tip of the iceberg. Assaults on Homer's authority could take place at both the upper and the lowest reaches of literary production and at any point in time, which makes one wonder how useful such evaluative hierarchies really are.

Excavating this "other" Homer—the debased and disgraced if not demotic Homer, whose image could be manipulated at will—is essential to understanding the processes by which Homer was continually imagined and reimagined over time. In fact, to neglect this "other" Homer would be to distort the picture of who or what Homer was. If the canonically divine Homer was crowned in the corridors of cultural power and made into a potent symbol of political and cultural authority with popular appeal, the irrepressibly other Homer was the inversion of these forms of authority and a protest against them. The deepest but least appreciated secret of Homer is the fact that his apotheosis and his rude takedowns are two sides of a single coin: both are the product of a manipulation of what is but an image and idea of "Homer." In a word, Homer disturbs his own paradigm.

That said, the disparity between these two Homers—the one unquestioned, the other questionable—is seemingly unique in the history of world literature, which raises a series of further issues that urgently need to be incorporated into the Homeric Question of conventional scholarship: Why *Homer*? Why was it that this one poet, who was exalted like no other ancient poet, could be so consistently and obsessively brought down from his Olympian heights, likewise to a degree experienced by no other ancient poet? Vergil famously had his posthumous detractors, but the charges were mild by comparison.[14] And though Vergil's popularity waxed and waned along with the changing fortunes of Latinity, there never was an explosive "Quarrel over Vergil" comparable to that which took place around Homer in early eighteenth-century France. What features of Homer's profile lent themselves to this bipolar treatment? Only speculations are possible, but the phenomenon cannot be ignored. In order to launch this inquiry, some additional background will first be necessary, starting with the unsolved mystery of Homer's sudden and inexplicable emergence.

## The Arrival of Homer

The two major poems attributed to Homer, the *Iliad* and the *Odyssey*, often reckoned among the finest treasures in the world, are also among the most puzzling and mysterious. Springing full-grown like armed Athena from the head of Zeus, the poems miraculously appear sometime around 700 BCE, each the size of a hefty novel (nearly 16,000 verses for the *Iliad* and 12,000 for the *Odyssey*, and later divided into twenty-four books apiece), each perfectly self-contained and of the greatest narrative sophistication, and neither one overlapping with the other, as if obeying some silent convention or territorial prerogative.

No two works of literature could be more different, yet the *Iliad* and the *Odyssey* complement each other like a pair of gloves. Most remarkable are their shared ties to a background event that gives them their *raison d'être* but that neither poem narrates or describes in any detail: the fall of Troy. Both are in some crucial sense fixated by this catastrophe, but instead of confronting it directly they circle around it, warily and from different sides. The *Iliad* brings us within a few days of the capture of Troy but stops short of the event itself. The *Odyssey* tells of its aftermath. The choice, whether it was made by the tradition or by some poet, is shrewd and effective. Other minor epics after Homer filled in the missing ground, but those poems quickly fell into oblivion, while the two Homeric poems alone were remembered from the mass of songs whose stories they presupposed. To say that the Homeric poems were "remembered" is practically to utter a euphemism, because the poems were in fact subject to considerable puzzlement and intense controversy. It was these latter kinds of response, even more than piety, that helped to ensure the survival of Homer and his legacy.

Homer's debut on the world stage was as sudden as it was baffling. How was it possible for the two great Homeric epics to come into existence, seemingly out of the blue, and on a monumental scale at that? From all we can tell, it would seem that nothing comparable existed before the emergence of the two poems as we know them—and, many would argue, ever since. Not even Vergil's *Aeneid* from the end of the last century BCE compares with Homer. A mere 10,000 verses long and thus a third the size of the *Iliad* and *Odyssey* combined, it compresses into twelve short books an afterimage and counterimage of the two epics in their forty-eight books all told, whether the decision to downsize Homer was made out of diffidence, deference, or in obedience to a wholly different ("slender") aesthetic.

Scholars today believe that the Homeric poems evolved out of a song culture that reached back into the early Iron Age (ca. 1200–750 BCE), if not further back into the Late Bronze Age of the Mycenaeans (1600–1200 BCE), with less direct influences stemming from sources in the Near East (Anatolia and Mesopotamia, first and foremost).[15] But as plausible and even likely as these scenarios are, they cannot be proved. With external evidence lacking, the origins of Homeric poetry can at most be inferred on internal grounds, for instance based on its pervasive formulaic character (the repetition of words, phrases, metrical patterns, verse clusters, and whole scenes), which points to a process of oral composition and performance within a centuries-long tradition out of which the two Homeric epics must have crystallized at some point toward the end of the eighth century, roughly in their current form. Alas, here too certainty is forbidden. For although the oral-formulaic model finds support in comparative evidence from other cultures, the theory of oral Homeric composition remains just that, a theory, and the details of the process that led to the rise of the Homeric poems are almost entirely unknown. Nor does the material record offer anything more than a few telltale hints of this process.

How the early songs came to be organized around the exploits of Achilles abroad at Troy and of Odysseus making his way back home to Ithaca, and how they subsequently emerged as the monumental poems of the *Iliad* and the *Odyssey*, remains a complete mystery to this day. Did a single poet, or two individual poets, combine earlier songs (possibly episodes of different lengths) into coherent epics? If so, how did this happen, and when? Did the epics have to wait for writing to be developed on a significant scale, around the mid- to late eighth century, for this consolidation to occur? Did the poet or poets possibly dictate to a scribe who could record these songs as sung, whether on leather or papyrus? Was the so-called monumental poet, the poet who presumably produced this grand consolidation for the first time, himself literate? Did he edit his own poems during or after their transfer into the medium of writing? And even once the poems were established as written texts, to what degree and for how long did the epics remain fluid, which is to say open to change through improvisational performance or through significant textual intrusions? All this is unknown today, and if the process was ever known in antiquity, that knowledge was quickly forgotten. All that we have to go by is the ignorance that covered over the origins of the poems like a receding wave, and the puzzles that remained. In this respect, we are no better off than the ancients, who themselves had no satisfactory way of accounting for the emergence of the two epics. And though on occasion it was mooted that Homer was not the first poet to sing about the Trojan War, rival claimants were never more than a name, and the suspicions never deepened beyond a vague surmise.

If antiquity could not quite picture literary history before Homer, nevertheless such a prehistory was widely suspected. The legendary poets Orpheus, Musaeus, and Linus, and a string of other less well-known names, all belonged to the mists of time, or rather to myth. Hesiod was on some reckonings thought to predate Homer. But none of these poets sang about Troy, and only Hesiod's poetry was known. Other epics, centered around Thebes and Troy (both belonging to the Epic Cycle) and possibly around the Argonauts and Heracles, may have been familiar to Homer, but the *Iliad* and *Odyssey* eclipsed these as poems, if not as myths. That said, the ancients had an inkling of the haphazard transmission of the Homeric songs prior to their consolidation as texts. The poems were thought to have been literally "stitched together" from the scattered fragments of now lost and imperfectly recovered original wholes. According to one such story, Homer's poems, scattered over time by fire, floods, or earthquakes, resurfaced again in the sixth century BCE, but in random quantities and in need of surgical reconstruction. The poems were eventually stitched back together into wholes and perhaps as written texts under the supervision of Pisistratus, the tyrant of Athens. But in the process the poems accumulated spare and very likely inauthentic parts (so-called plus verses or extra verses), as was only inevitable. Compounding matters, rewards were said to have been paid out by the verse to anyone who could salvage and present bits of Homer. The worry that the poems contained non-OEM parts and were missing others could not be erased.

Other stories or legends suggested that Homer's poems were never originally whole at all, but existed as snatches of verse and songs, sometimes called "rhapsodies" or "lays," that were later made whole either by a particular guild of singers (generally known as "rhapsodes," perhaps meaning "stitchers of songs") who claimed to be Homer's descendants and called themselves "Homeridae" ("Homerids" in English) to indicate their status as the official, but no doubt self-appointed, curators of his legacy, or else by poets or rhapsodes other than the Homerids who were commissioned for the purpose. Some of these latter were portrayed as unscrupulous intruders who "maltreated" Homer and his poetry by interpolating their own verses into it or by forging entire poems under Homer's name. In other cases, they were accused of stealing Homer's poems outright and putting their own names on them, in one instance by transcribing Homer's verses when Homer, naïve and impoverished, dictated them in exchange for food and shelter. Professional rivalry among Homerids and other rhapsodes may be to blame for these recriminations, with each camp exerting a different claim to the Homeric patrimony, though some of the stories may simply reflect the way Homeric rhapsodes sang and improved on Homer's poems through improvisation, a method that would have been unintelligible to readers in the literate era. The story about oral dictation is especially intriguing, as this method is one of the leading theories today about how Homer's poems came to be preserved. Its complement is the theory that epic lays were organized into monumental poems only at the end of a long evolutionary process, though these too had eventually to find their way into writing. A third possibility is that the process had to wait for a literate bard to reach completion.[16]

Though of doubtful accuracy, stories like these are not without value, as they raise hard questions that are not easily answered today, for example, How can one improvise on a canonical text? What *is* a canonical version of a text? When and how does it become this? And how do orally transmitted songs come to be written down? Whatever the case may be, these accounts are precious documents of ancient attitudes to the Homeric heritage that take us far beyond the baseline reflex of unblinking veneration. At the very least, they bring to the fore the obscurity of the poems' origins and the complexity of their transmission, both of which were obviously a problem already in antiquity. At worst, they express lingering worries about the authenticity of the poems and their integrity. Either way, in posing the questions they do, they give us the earliest antecedents of contemporary oral theory.

Notable in most of these parable-like stories is the absence of Homer. Homer stood somewhere at the head of the process; his poems, scattered into bits (and, seemingly, bits of *text*), were all that remained. This outlook may indicate the view of the past as it appeared in the Hellenistic Age. If so, it reflects the activity and the anxiety of the Alexandrian grammarians who assumed the arduous task of reconstructing in a more unified and definitive form the texts of Homer that had been disseminated widely across the Greek-speaking world, accumulating local variants as they did. If anyone was aware of the problems lurking in Homer's texts, it was the Alexandrian professionals, though they were by no means the first or the last to notice the discrepancies—the many contradictions, apparent lapses of memory, the rough joins, and the other anomalies that drew Gilbert Murray's notice in 1907 and that trouble scholars to this day. Hence the Hellenistic nightmares of Homer having been scattered into his *disiecta membra* and then, somehow or other, pieced back together again. But there was more than scribal anxiety circulating around Homer. Politics were also involved.

While the stories that the Pisistratids supervised the first collection and editing of the Homeric texts appear to be legends without historical backing, what does seem certain is that the Homeric poems were first performed in their totality and on a grand scale by rhapsodes at the Panathenaea ("all-Athenian") festival that was instituted under this regime in Athens during the sixth century and held every four years. This would have been a spectacular event. In normal practice, Homer must have been performed piecemeal, which is to say episodically, with this or that scene or sequence of scenes being sung at a time. A full-blown presentation of either poem would have taken around a week to stage, assuming daily performances of three or four hours. The Panathenaea was for this reason alone an absolute rarity. What could have prompted Pisistratus to undertake so lavish and costly an event?

The details are vague, but everything points to an attempt by Athens to claim and control the legacy of Homer and to reap cultural, ideological, and political benefits from this move, which is exactly what happened. In later years, the Athenian text of Homer gained the reputation of being the most reliable and best curated text available. It also bore telltale signs of having passed through Athenian culture: it contained Attic dialectal forms; the texts were transcribed into the alphabet form that was influentially adopted by Athens; Athens enjoyed a conspicuous (if suspicious) presence in the roll call of armies listed in *Iliad* book 2; and both poems contained distinctly Athenian myths and symbols. All of this suggests not merely incidental contact between the epics and Athens or the inevitable influence of Athens as Greece's cultural hegemon in the fifth century and in later memory, but rather a concerted effort on the part of the city-state to write itself into Homer's poetry. The final triumph of the "Athenianization" of Homer is reflected by the mistaken belief, promulgated by the Alexandrian grammarian Aristarchus, that Homer's language was an older and the purest form of the Attic dialect and that Homer was himself an Athenian. Aristarchus is also thought to have regarded the Athenian text of Homer as the standard against which all other versions and variants should be measured.[17]

To be sure, Homer's popularity, and to some extent his canonization, were guaranteed well before any of these changes took place. Athens was responding to Homer's cachet, not creating it, and the same is true of every ancient account of Homer that we have, whether he is imagined as living or as having passed into posterity. And yet at some point toward the end of the sixth century, the balance of power shifted away from the poet's alleged homelands. Homer was patriated from the Ionian coast, where the poems originated, to the mainland's chief cultural centers, Athens first and foremost, but also (according to a competing tradition) Sparta under the legendary lawgiver Lycurgus. Homer was becoming institutionalized and a permanent fixture and even a signature element of Greek culture—its principal brand. He became Panhellenic.

As Greece unified in the coming centuries, so did its cultural legacy. In the last part of the fourth century, Alexander the Great enlarged the scope of Greek political hegemony across the known world, and Homer traveled with him. Alexander was a passionate devotee of the poet. He apocryphally slept with a copy of Homer under his pillow, had dreams of the poet, and fancied himself a second Achilles. After Alexander's death in 323 BCE, Homer found his way to the library of Alexandria in Egypt, a city that Alexander had founded and where the process of stabilizing the texts of Homer continued, thanks to an army of Greek scholars who produced the first rigorous editions and commentaries of Homer's poems. By around 150 BCE, that stabilization was more or less complete. A definitive edition, tamperproof and revered like a sacred relic that had been meticulously restored, was permitted to circulate in copies, sometimes in deluxe editions, for schools and scholars across the Mediterranean, including at Rome. From there Homer's texts were passed on to medieval Byzantium, and eventually they were exported to Europe in the fifteenth century, where they were further edited, studied, and translated, at first in Latin and then in the European vernaculars.

## From Doubt to Controversy

Homer survived, in the form of his texts and, as will be discussed in the next chapter, his iconography, but in both cases as a question mark of meaning and a problem. However one looked at the evidence, Homer's poems were so baffling—so inexplicable, so magnificent, and so manifestly flawed—that their genesis could not be coherently imagined, while their earliest fate was shadowed by suspicion. In any scenario, they remained scarred by the process that brought them into existence. Vulnerable to maltreatment, plagiarism, interpolation, and manipulation, were Homer's poems ever truly his? The question haunted the rest of antiquity, which struggled to establish a narrow corpus of authentically Homeric poetry out of the raft of epics, hymns, sundry occasional verses, epigrams, minor poetry, and other apocrypha that attached to Homer's name. The *Iliad* and *Odyssey* typically formed the core, but other works made their way into the canon as well. In some quarters, attempts were made to remove the *Odyssey* from Homer's list of titles: different in tone and language, it must be by a different poet. And Homer fared little better, as is only to be expected: his person followed the fate of his poems. Behind all the speculation was the nagging question, Who was responsible for their creation?

The question brings us back to our point of departure for this chapter and indeed for the book as a whole, which is among other things an inquiry into the fascination that Homer has exerted on his posterity since the beginnings of his recorded history, and the often strange effects this fascination has had on the way he has been understood. Why this persistence? And why Homer? Surely other relics of antiquity are equally mysterious. In order to understand the attraction of Homer more fully, we need to look at some of the practical mechanisms and contextual factors that not only supported but actually elicited the fascination with Homer. Three immediately come to mind: (i) the resonance of Homer's voice, which echoes suggestively but elusively in his poetry; (ii) Homer's connection to Troy, a place of fascination in its own right; and, at a deeper level still, (iii) the connections that bind both Homer and Troy to a traumatic past, a trauma that was all the more difficult to bear as it could only be felt but never confirmed. Let's take up each of these factors in turn, starting with the beckoning voice of Homer.

## Homer's Voice

Perhaps the single greatest factor that lured audiences into trying to identify Homer was his absolute anonymity. Homer famously never names himself in his poetry. But it is not just this absence that stimulated the desire to identify the epic poems' originating source. Rather, it is the way in which the singer of the *Iliad* and *Odyssey* makes his anonymity felt. He flashes suddenly into view and then just as suddenly retreats, taking refuge behind the screen of an unnamed but audible first person ("*Sing*, goddess," "Tell *me*, Muse") who is also palpable in occasional second-person addresses to characters ("And now, dying, *you* answered him, O rider Patroklos") and is implied wherever a scene is narrated in the third person ("Then the haughty suitors came in"). As if out of a studied refusal, the poems divulge nothing about their author, a fact that readers both ancient and modern lament as often as they find ways to explain it away.[18] The mechanisms that produce this Homer-effect deserve closer scrutiny.

Grammatically, Homer is no more than a pronoun. Linguistically, he is what today is called a "shifter," a deictic marker that points our attention from a *here*—the immediate reality of the poem's experience, wherever "Homer" is imagined to be or to have been and whenever the performance or the act of reading takes place—to a *there*—wherever the Muses happen to be and whatever reality they disclose at the singer's request. Acoustically and imaginatively, Homer is a voice, but one that is, precisely, of the moment, audible only when heard. The distinguishing feature of shifters, according to the French linguist Émile Benveniste, who pioneered the category in the 1950s, is that "they do not refer to a concept or to an individual." Instead, they have only a "momentary reference," one that is indexed by the speaker's utterance and lasts only as long as this utterance can be heard.[19] The same can be said of the status of Homer as a grammatical pronoun and as a voice: the "I" who speaks at any given moment in performance is but a literary device and an artifact of the Homeric oral tradition, while the voice is but an effect of these circumstances, a mere auditory hallucination. If we take Benveniste's suggestion to heart, we will have to say that Homer's voice in itself refers neither to a person nor to an idea. But in its material insistence, it suggests both of these things: it creates the possibility of such a reference. And that is where the problem of Homer first takes root. Listening to Homer's verses, one longs for their source. And the poems, with their abundance of place-names and temporal markers, provide further reasons to look for Homer and to connect him to some distant reality.

The gap created by each of these levels of self-disclosure ("I"/"you," "here"/there") and the impersonal narrating voice were both a hindrance and an enticement to audiences. The greater the gap, the greater the need to surmount it, but also the harder it proved to do so. The sudden eruptions and disappearances of the poetic ego, rare but always strongly marked precisely because of their rarity, only stimulated the urge to name their author or the person behind the voice, even as that urge was frustrated again in turn: all roads ultimately led back to the same unknown starting point. Much of the impetus behind the ancient Homeric Question owed its life to this situation: the words were there for all to hear and see, but they urgently required a source. And the moderns followed suit, reaching results that, however different from those of the ancients, proved no more definitive.

In order to appreciate the problem, we need to imagine the conditions in which it made itself felt. In a world where songs were transmitted from one generation to the next, bards will at least in theory have performed the Homeric poems or their precursors anonymously, deferring all authority to the divine instance of the Muses, appropriating the name of "Homer" once this name became attached to the poems (presumably by the seventh century), but otherwise demurely melting into the background as their audible mouthpiece, which is what the tradition required. Since each bard sang in Homer's name, the effacement was doubled: the bards disappeared into the poems just as their original had done earlier.

It is here, in the gap between poem and performance, that a chasm opened up before the hearer. And wherever the poems were performed, audiences for the rest of antiquity found themselves faced with a twofold pretense: standing before them was a singer who was channeling—ventriloquizing, if not mystically "becoming"—Homer ("Tell *me* now, you Muses"), while at the other end of the line stood the original "Homer," who lived some unknown number of years or centuries after Troy fell and who must in turn channel the Muses to recall what he never saw. Homer amounted to a persona that was produced—literally, *performed*—by professional rhapsodes who assumed his role and identity whenever they sang in his voice and name. The tradition, in other words, required the effacement of Homer for the sake of its own expediency, even as it depended on his name for its prestige and glory. From this perspective, we can see how Homer could truly have been lost as quickly as he was found.

Nor did the chain of transmissions end here, for the singer was, additionally, a speaker who voiced the words of the characters that appeared in the poems, both mortal and divine. The poems were a labyrinth of sounds, voices, and impostures. With the advent of writing, the problem of locating Homer's voice became more urgent, not least because the cues for "voicing" the poems had faded into letters on a page: Homer's original voice could be resuscitated, but only with the assistance of one's own breath. To be sure, rhapsodic performances lived on well after literacy was introduced, but these appear to have involved recitations of an increasingly familiar and fixed text, while rhapsodes remained self-effacing mediums who sang in Homer's name. Either way, to read or listen to Homer was to hear and to imagine the sound of his voice. In sum, Homer's voice did not sound in antiquity: it resounded, whether in the ventriloquistic mouth of a virtuoso impersonator or in the reader's inner ear.

Nor was this all. For to hear or read a verse of Homer was to do more than simply listen to song. It was to be put in touch with a reality that was no longer accessible except through the medium of the poems: it was to see directly through the poet's eyes. This impression was enhanced by the unusual quality of Homeric descriptions of persons, places, and actions, which were felt to be incomparably vivid and even cinematographic. Homeric poetry excelled not only at telling but also at showing what it told. The upshot of this effect, which is much admired even today, is that the poet himself is paradoxically eliminated by the very mechanism that permits us to see into his poetic reality: no longer a voice or a palpable presence, he is the equivalent of a roaming camera lens that unobtrusively takes in the scenery being described. Once again, Homer disappears into his poems. In each of these instances, whether heard, read, or "seen," the Homeric poems conjure up the silhouette of their author. But they leave that silhouette vague and shapeless, a formal outline that is empty of substance. Homer comes to us as a voice that issues from somewhere in the deep past, or else as an all but transparent screen through which the past can be glimpsed. A ghostly figure, he is nonetheless compellingly present in his absence.

There was something improbable about this situation, which led to a combustible mix of astonishment, admiration, doubt, and speculation. The temptation was to extrapolate a person from the pronoun-shifter "I" and to give Homer a life and a death, though all that Homer ever enjoyed was in fact an immortal afterlife. Did he even exist? The thought barely passed the lips of ancient writers, though more often than is suspected today. Early modern writers, less circumspect and more exasperated, were quicker to allow that Homer was a fiction—though fiction of what? Admitting that he never existed did not solve the underlying problems of the origins of the poems and their authorship. Nor does the hypothesis that Homer was an "invention" by later generations who sought to explain the mystery of the poems' original creator bring us any nearer to an understanding of the poems' origins or take us any further along than the ancients' own hypotheses.[20] The ancients were as uneasy about the identification of Homer as modern writers have been. They gave Homer more names than any single individual should ever have ("Meles," "Melesigenes," "Melesagoras," "Melesianax," "Maeonides," "Altes," and "Homer" were all put forward), and there were nearly as many different explanations of those names' origins and meanings as there were accounts of his birth and subsequent life. The surplus of information suggests both an awareness of a problem and a certain skepticism toward any resolution of it. We will come back to the competing accounts of Homer's biography in the next chapter. For now, we need only note that the history of Homer is the history of an uneasiness that is persistently felt even when it is not named—and, appearances notwithstanding, whenever Homer is named. Of greater interest than the question of Homer's invention is the inventiveness of his readers, who found endless ways to skirt the unhealable problem of knowing who Homer really was.

## Homer's Troy and the "Trojan Question"

Now to the second consideration as to what contributed to the ongoing fascination with Homer. For surely one of the greatest allures enjoyed by Homer is the fact that, for all his elusiveness as a voice or a person, he can nevertheless be linked to a place on a map with GPS accuracy. If Homer's birthplace and every other fact about him were subject to dispute from the word go, his ties to a specific geographical place were never doubted: Troy, the site of the Trojan War, was Homer's unimpeachable link to the Real. By "Real" we should understand not some historical reality, but an event that strikes us as real whether or not it ever happened. Indeed, debates about whether the Trojan War was a historical event or an imaginary and mythical one continue to divide scholars today. Whatever the answer, we can see how the Homeric Question is inextricably bound up with what might be called the "Trojan Question." To put this in a sharper form, one that is directly aligned with the aims of this study, we can say that the very idea of Homer is wrapped up with the very idea of Troy: neither one can be imagined in the absence of the other. It is the marriage of these two complexes of problems that has given Homer the particular urgency he has. But because Troy is a place and Homer is unplaceable, a series of strange consequences cascades from this fact.

The first of these is perhaps the hardest to fathom, but let us try to formulate it anyway: it is doubtful that Homer would enjoy the canonical privileges he does if he had not from the first been connected to Troy. *Take away Troy and Homer would not be "Homer."* His allure and his mystique are entirely dependent on the imagined, if contested, historicity of Troy. From this a second consequence follows, though it is in reality a paradox: Homer remains our single best witness to the occurrence of the Trojan War *whether or not that war took place*. Nor is this all, because the Trojan War was not just any war. It was a particularly violent and traumatic event, lasting a decade and leaving grievous wreckage in its wake. Homer's approach to Troy, as will be seen, magnifies this fact by accentuating its horrors from the twin perspectives of an unfolding present moment and an inexorable past. Through Homer we are permitted to experience an overwhelming event of massive proportions that registers itself viscerally in its heroes and its victims—and in us. It burns into us like a wound that cannot be forgotten. And this is true whether you believe that the Trojan War was a historical event, a myth, or some admixture of the two. Both poems are stamped by this traumatic occurrence. The *Iliad* commemorates the event; the *Odyssey* commemorates its aftermath and memory. And both poems do so by parading brutal deaths, mayhem, and destruction for much of their narrative space.

But if Homer owes much to Troy, it is also true that Troy owes much to Homer. Troy's cachet is unique among archaeological sites precisely because of its connections to mythology and to Homer's two poems, which captured the myth of Troy as no other early poetry did. This may be one reason why Homer quickly eclipsed the competition and why this other poetry has come down to us in tatters or through the barest of second- and thirdhand reports.[21] Take away the Homeric poems, and Troy would be just one more Bronze

Age site—impressive in its own right, but devoid of the special mystique that has made it an object of fascination since its destruction at the end of the second millennium. Without Homer, other Neolithic or Bronze Age sites in Anatolia would take precedence, for example Çatalhöyük (7400–5200 BCE), a protocity that is recognized as one of the world's most important Neolithic and Chalcolithic sites, or Hattuşa, the Bronze Age capital of the Hittite empire in whose orbit of power Troy appears to have operated. Both places dwarf Troy physically, but Troy dwarfs them mythically.[22]

This is not to deny the significance of Troy. A fortification that occupied a commanding spot on the Dardanelles, where land and sea routes converged and could be controlled, Troy is thought to have been the capital of the surrounding region known as the Troad and a western outpost of the Hittite empire. By the same token, however, although Troy remained inhabited for more than a millennium following its destruction around 1200 BCE, these later historical layers enjoy no place in the popular imagination. Hellenistic Troy is of no interest to anyone but specialists, and the same is true of its Iron Age antecedents (1190–700 BCE), while Bronze Age Troy, the place enshrined by the Homeric tradition and the place we imagine when we read either epic, is of uncontested value. Not even Ithaca, Odysseus's homeland, commands anything near the attention that Troy enjoys. A rather unglamorous island in a remote region of the western part of Greece, "a place to feed goats," not horses, and "very far from Achaian country" (*Odyssey* 4.606, 13.249), Ithaca is no Troy. Its exact Homeric location is uncertain, nor is it tied to the immediate trauma of the Trojan War. To be sure, this has not stopped some hardier folks from searching for its traces.[23] But the interest in Ithaca is backlit almost entirely by the interest in Troy, a point that confirms the general rule that we have been witnessing.

What all of this goes to show is that the appreciation of ancient Greek civilization, and of Homer in particular, is dominated as much by fantasy as by historical and academic imperatives. The combined power of Homer and Troy, reinforced by three millennia of cultural perceptions, has been overwhelming. Whereas the evidence of the poems can only gesture toward historical reality, archaeology holds out the promise of finally proving Homer right and establishing that the Trojan War actually occurred. Can it succeed in this? As it happens, closing the gap between Troy the place and Troy the site of the Trojan War has proved impossible to do. Though scholars have tried to close this gap, whether through examination of the texts or through soil samples, they have consistently failed. The reason is simple: Homer's "Troy" is not to be found on the ground but only in the history of ideas. And the same holds for Homer.

But there is one more twist to this already intricate plot. The connections running through and across Troy and Homer may be fragile and even phantasmatic, but they are rooted nonetheless in a *possible* materiality, that is, in a historically real place known as Troy and a historically possible Trojan War. Homer contributes to this possibility by making the events on the ground spring as if to life. In a word, the materiality of "Troy" is impregnated with the mystique of Homer, and the ruins of Troy speak only within this enabling framework: they materialize value and embody structures of feeling. And for the same reason, wherever one looks, ideas do not grow spontaneously in the air. They take root in the conception of some possible reality. But they flourish in the imagination.

This predicament, while in some ways peculiar to Homer and to Homer's Troy, is characteristic of the study of classical antiquity in general. Antiquity is a place that is filled with physical objects in addition to being a realm of ideas. The trouble is that objects and ideas are forever joined in one place only: in the imagination. Historically, Homer has been the imaginary place where these two ways of approaching the past come together in an exemplary fashion. He is both a material thing (we have "his" poems) and a material absence (we cannot put our finger on "Homer"), very like the city he helped to make world-famous. The seductiveness of this link is undeniable. But the linkage runs in both directions. The question of what Homer knew about Troy—what he saw or could have seen—is hardwired into the way Homer has been conceived as *himself* possible: it plays directly into the ways in which he has been imagined. For this reason, the fate of Homer and the fate of Troy together form a pair that needs to be treated as a hyphenated entity by us because they were treated this way in the past, with each member potentially standing in for the other in the other's absence (if we can't have Homer we can at least have Troy, and vice versa), but also with each potentially invalidating the other (Did Homer invent Troy? Does Troy falsify Homer?). This tension has shaped the way questions about Homer have been framed throughout history. Given the deep cultural significance this tension has had for antiquity and for us, by exploring it we can elaborate something like a logic of the classical imagination and its cultural efficacy. Considered in this light, Homer turns out to be less a solitary individual than the result of a triangulation that occurs between three entities: the poet called Homer, the place called Troy, and the ideas of both in an ever-shifting present.

## The Trauma of the Past

As we ask what makes Homer so compelling a presence even in his absence, we reach the third and final consideration—namely, the fact that Homer is, and probably always was from the time his name was first recorded, an idea of something that remains permanently lost to culture, be it a Heroic Age, an ideal of inimitable poetic excellence, or some irretrievably vanished past. It was only natural that Homer, the narrator of Troy, should become inseparably linked to the violent destruction of Troy. That destruction was thought to have been complete, and its memory was felt to be traumatic in the ancient world—and, in different ways, it has remained this for the modern world—not in a clinical sense, but in an imaginary sense, one that works through the artifices of cultural memory.

Homer inevitably acquired some of the traits of this trauma, in part by dint of association and in part owing to the force of the imagination. He has from the beginning represented an irreparable loss. Consequently, the mere thought of Homer has always had something traumatic about it too. As it so happens, the place and the person suffered similar fates, which gives us a first clue to their imaginary bond. If this seems far-fetched, consider again the anecdote that describes how Homer's poems were destroyed by fire, floods, or earthquakes, and were then stitched back together like a wounded body that remained scarred for life. To read Homer was to be painfully aware of this history, which was comparable to a natural disaster, but one that, as it happens, was hauntingly similar to the disasters that befell the plain of Troy. For it, too, was destroyed by fire, floods, and earthquakes, an event that is described early in book 12 of the *Iliad* in a way that is unmatched elsewhere in the ancient record apart from Babylonian epic and the Hebrew Bible.[24] (We will come back to this pivotal moment in chapter 4.)

It would appear, then, as if one of epic's key roles was to preserve in the vaults of collective memory not only the great splendor of the vanished past but also the idea of its utter destruction. In any case, the two disappearances—that of Troy and that of Homer's "original" works—were yoked together from the start and have remained so ever since. Both would have to be painstakingly recovered and reconstructed, each resembling an excavation site, real or metaphorical, that revealed different temporal layers of deposits or "strata" (the term appears in both the archaeology of Troy and the philology of Homer). If Homer's loss was traumatic, so was his recovery: the survival of his poems was in ways too good to be true, a thought that led to further doubts and endless complications. But in another sense, Homer was never recovered. Only his poems survived, never quite in their original form, to be sure, while he disappeared into them again as their ghostly prime mover. It was as if the loss of Homer was the price that had to be paid for the restoration of his poetry. Homer became as improbable as his poems.

## Homer: Person or Idea?

The permanent loss of Homer, the loss that he came to stand for and embodied in his own person, was felt more acutely as time went on. Homer would haunt antiquity as no other poet or historical figure ever would, part golem, part revenant. And it is in this same form that he entered modernity, freighted with meaning and imponderability, and surrounded by a nimbus of godlike mystery.

The moderns took their cue from the ancients, though it was the particular achievement of modernity finally to name Homer as the idea he had always been. The modern problem was provocatively summed up by Nietzsche in 1869, as we saw. But it was Giambattista Vico who in his *Scienza nuova seconda* from 1730 first articulated the view that Homer was not a person but an idea (*un'idea*) created and believed in by the Greeks. Vico's denial of Homer's historicity is tied to his rejection of the historicity of the Trojan War ("It never in the world took place"), but this doesn't prevent Homer from being somehow more *real* than Troy. Troy, after all, has vanished, whereas Homer's poems have not. But, Vico muses, this can't be right: the Trojan War is no less "famous [an] epoch in history" for its never having happened. And so, in the last analysis, both Homer and Troy have to be equally real.[25]

Not willing to let go of Homer entirely—unlike some of his French predecessors from the Quarrel of the Ancients and the Moderns, such as François Hédelin, abbé d'Aubignac, who in the late eighteenth century damned Homer to nonexistence, or some of their lesser-known Renaissance predecessors—Vico here is playing out the logic of disavowal that would typify Homer's reception for centuries to come and that runs: "Homer was the best poet ever, but he never existed (and here are the proofs for both claims—his poems)."[26] Denying Homer's existence wasn't unthinkable in antiquity; it was merely unnecessary. Instead, Homer was given a *surplus* of existence—*too many* lives and *too much* reality. And despite casting doubt on the historical reality of the Trojan War, Vico continued to rely on it as a cornerstone in his history of humankind. Here, too, he was carrying over the ambivalence of antiquity, for which the Trojan War was not merely the most talked-about event in history but was also greatly disputed in its details (above all in Homer's account of it); was radically tampered with in revisionary accounts; and was even denied existence altogether, to a far greater extent than classicists have been willing to recognize. A case in point is provided by the ancient allegorists who, from the sixth century BCE on, saw in the epic battles of men and gods a working out of the physical principles of the cosmos, not the capture and destruction of a city. Others, including the Roman Stoic Epictetus, laughed off the Homeric world as figment of the imagination: "Of course, you will tell us all about Helen and Priam and the island of Calypso—things which neither exist nor ever will."[27]

Vico's simpler hypothesis, anticipating by half a century the great modern Homer scholar Friedrich Albert Wolf, is better known, and it was hit upon independently by Robert Wood, a freelance explorer who traveled to Troy, Homer in hand, and then wrote up his findings in 1767 (*A Comparative View of the Antient and Present State of the Troade, To Which is Prefixed An Essay on the Original Genius of Homer*). This was the belief that Homer's poems were the final deposit of a long tradition of oral composition and compilation. Vico drew from this premise a consequence that Wood did not, which was that Homer, not being distinguishable from the tradition that produced him, was in essence a synonym for this process itself: "The Greek people were themselves Homer."[28] Vico was in turn anticipated not only by such ancient writers as Josephus, Cicero, and Aelian (he cites all three), in addition to the legends about the Pisistratean and the Lycurgan recensions (he knew at least the former), but also by some Renaissance and early modern humanists, many of them exceptionally well read in the ancient sources, who have since fallen into the shadows.[29] But the world would have to wait for Wolf to put all of these findings on an academic footing and to establish them with philologically rigorous arguments in his great *Prolegomena to Homer* of 1795. In doing so, he gave birth to classical philology in its modern form. Wolf's arguments were startlingly revisionist. He tore down the widespread assumption that Homer was a poetic genius in the Romantic mold and the sole author of the two great poems that were handed down under his name. This so-called monumental Homer was a mere hypothesis, he showed, and it had no foundation in reality. In fact, Wolf was merely saying out loud what most contemporaries had refused to say to themselves.

Not only did Wolf establish that the "Homer" transmitted by antiquity was a fiction, but he also brought this demolition to bear on the Homeric texts themselves. Teasing apart the various layers of composition and editing that had produced the poems in their current form, he concluded, was an impossible task. Consequently, locating the original form of the poems was out of the question: "The Homer that we hold in our hands now is not the one who flourished in the mouths of the Greeks of his own day, but one variously altered, interpolated, corrected, and emended."[30] The "original" Homer was lost forever, and not even the details of the poems' transformations could be fully recovered. The best that one could do was to accept defeat and marvel at the mysterious historical process that stood between us and Homer.

Even so, Wolf did manage to smuggle something of an original Homer back into his own reconstruction of this loss: he needed the ghost—the idea—of an original form to make his case. (This is acknowledged in the Latin subtitle to Wolf's study: "Or Concerning the Original and Genuine Form of the Homeric Poems.") Paradoxically, what kept the prospect of this original form afloat was the evidence that we no longer have it. Wolf was convinced that he could detect differences between the poem's original form in those parts of the *Iliad* that were "by Homer, that is, by the man responsible for the larger part and the order of the earlier books," and those parts that were later additions by another hand or hands. That earliest form was genuine, even if (Wolf equivocated) it "could [n]ever be laid out save in our minds, and even there only in rough outlines"—another silhouette, in other words.[31]

And yet, despite the *succès de scandale* that he enjoyed, Wolf had been scooped. He later apologized for having been unaware of Vico's findings. His mentor at Göttingen, Christian Gottlob Heyne, knew enough to anticipate Wolf's conclusions in 1789.[32] And both German scholars were influenced in crucial ways by writers from the French and Italian sixteenth and seventeenth centuries who likewise wrestled in vain with the Homeric Question. Wolf's argument was thus the meticulous expression of a frustration that had been brewing for a much longer period of time.

The myth of Homer died hard. Goethe, Schiller, and others from the Weimar circle were scandalized by Wolf's findings, which they protested. Homer must exist, and his poems must be his. They took solace in a sliver of hope, namely, the possibility that Wolf, who could not show what was true, might still be wrong. Wolf's argument did not, in fact, amount to a proof: it was at best an argument for what could not be proved. Even Wolf protested his own findings: Wolfian philology was not simply a philology grounded in skeptical doubt; it was a self-doubting philology. His edition did not eliminate the existence of an original poet Homer so much as it ruled out in a definitive fashion the possibility of his recovery. His eventual edition of Homer, published in 1804, bore the equivocal title *Poems of Homer: Works and Remains of Homer and the Homeridae*. And the frontispiece to this edition showed a bust of Homer that was no less equivocal. Thanks to the framing of the portrait and the dramatic use of light and shading, Homer as he appears in this image is both lifelike and not: he is at once a recognizable individual and a copy of a well-known Roman marble head of Homer from the Farnese collection in Naples (Fig. 1.1).[33] In vacillating between denying and accepting the fact of an original poet called Homer, Wolf was reenacting the sinuous, uncertain logic that Vico had earlier put into motion. Both are following the logic of a MacGuffin—an impossible, nonexistent, and empty object whose effects are nonetheless real.[34] Such is the position of most readers of Homer today.

Milman Parry (1902–1935), the brilliant classicist who in 1928 culminated the modern study of Homer with a theory of oral-formulaic compositional technique, produced the still reigning paradigm for understanding the earliest phases of the Homeric tradition. Yet not even he could entirely banish the ghost of Homer, not least because he merely displaced Homer's unity onto that of the oral tradition that Homer embodied. Parry's notion of Homer is ultimately Platonic: Homer is for him both the expression of an Idea and an ideal of consummate artistry that the oral tradition realized in the two Homeric poems.[35] But that is not all. As he was conducting research into the living oral traditions of Yugoslavia, not only did Parry believe that he could draw conclusions about Homeric oral poetry, but he was also seduced into imagining that he could hear Homer's *voice* in the living Serbian bards, as through a distant echo: "When one hears the Southern Slavs sing their tales *he has the overwhelming feeling that, in some way, he is hearing*

FIGURE 1.1. Bust of Homer. Frontispiece to F. A. Wolf's 1804 edition of the *Iliad*.

*Homer*." Astonished by his own confession, Parry then steps back and qualifies what he has just let slip: "When the hearer"—meaning himself—"should seem to be hearing Homer, he finds precise reasons: he is ever hearing the *same ideas* that Homer expresses, . . . in phrases which are rhythmically the same, and which are grouped in the same order."[36] Parry is not listening to Homer. He is listening to his idea.

## Is Homer Dead?

Before proceeding any further, we might want to pause to consider whether Homer hasn't outlived his usefulness to culture. Have we reached the end of the line? Is it true, as a small but vocal minority have suggested, that although he was once a burning issue, Homer is now "dead," having been killed first by the professional study of classics itself and then by the waves of trendy theory, multiculturalism, and cultural nihilism that gradually swept over the field and turned Homer, the onetime fountain of value, meaning, and classically centered knowledge, into a meaningless bibliographical citation?[37]

It is a bit hard to make out just who Homer is in this account, because much of the time Homer seems to stand for nothing less than the sanctity of the classical tradition itself and its transmitted ideals. But to fulfill this role and then to be proclaimed "dead," Homer and his two monumental poems have to be imagined the way they appeared on the day they were born at some point in the late eighth century BCE, and then were delivered, pristine and intact, to posterity. And that is pure fantasy. The assumption seems to be that Homer and the classical tradition exist prior to the debates about both, and that each of these entities somehow persists through the din of debate to emerge victoriously alive—until recently.

One problem with this complaint is that it imagines, wrongly, that either Homer or the ancient tradition was ever a stable entity from which a sure base of culture and learning could flow. This is nothing but an idealization and blurring of the past. The so-called classical tradition (if one wishes to insist on this somewhat unhelpful notion) is not a stable entity.[38] Rather, it is the sum of its diverse and unruly parts, which include fierce debates and critiques from within—a virtual war zone if there ever was one. The tradition was as vibrant as it was, and as exciting as it is for us today, because it was constantly posing difficult challenges to itself, as the case of Homer shows in spades. It was never a coherent whole, much less a harmonious symphony of diverse parts. Plato, one of the greatest philosophers from antiquity, rudely banished Homer from his model republic. As shocking as this still is, in point of fact Plato was merely continuing a line of thought that originated centuries before him. Homer has continually been the controversial flash point of culture wars past and present. Simply to declare Homer "dead" is to bring him back to life again, and in a form that was itself well rehearsed from antiquity to the early modern era. Only the trappings are different, but not the substance of the argument.

The purists notwithstanding, classical studies have been constitutionally in crisis from their inception, however we chose to date this event. Plausible candidates include the age of the early Greek philosophers from the late sixth to the late fifth century, the age of the sophists at the end of the fifth century, the age of the Alexandrian Library from the fourth to first century BCE, and the modern period, from the Renaissance to the age of Enlightenment to the second half of the nineteenth century to the present. Each of these moments is marked by a sense of intellectual unrest and ferment. And, not coincidentally, each is bound up with a crisis of meaning that gathers around Homer himself, who often merely encapsulates these larger worries. Indeed, it is no exaggeration to say that Homer died repeated deaths in antiquity alone. Just as remarkable as this history of Homer's repeated demise is the fact of Homer's repeated resurrection. Homer has proved easy to declare irrelevant but difficult to kill off.

Although Homer today is often little more than the modern idea of what is ancient about classical antiquity, it would nevertheless be wrong to take the problem of Homer as an artifact of modern anxieties that has been banished to irrelevance today. Quite the contrary. The problem has flourished from antiquity into the present, more or less without interruption, though at all times inflected by particular historical and cultural concerns. Better yet, we should say that Homer provided cultures with one of the more fruitful avenues around which these concerns could be voiced and tested. He was a convenient reference point and an empty silhouette whose features needed to be filled in before he could become a discussable entity. By appealing to Homer, a Homer shaped differently to match each occasion, philosophers could argue about virtue and vice, about the ethics of war, and about the nature of the cosmos. Poets could generate new forms of poetry. Artists could reimagine art. Historians could debate problems of historical time and its severance from myth. And philologists and archaeologists could advance their own sciences, even if neither one succeeded in coming any closer to unveiling the secrets of Homer or Troy. In a word, "Homer," the problem and the puzzle, has been good to think with.

Neither does the interest in Homer show any signs of abating. For proof one need only glance at Christopher Logue's powerful adaptation in free verse of the *Iliad* (*War Music,* 1959–2005), Cy Twombly's disturbing series of ten canvases scrawled with Greek names and blood-red, smoky blue-gray, and pitch black blotches (*Fifty Days at Iliam,* 1978), Derek Walcott's remake of both epics in an Afro-Caribbean setting (*Omeros,* 1990), Isaac Julien's tribute to Walcott's Homer in his film installation across three screens (*Paradise Omeros,* 2002), Alice Oswald's stark epitaphic rendering of the *Iliad* (*Memorial: An Excavation of the Iliad,* 2011) and her later reinterpretation of the *Odyssey* as a "shoal of sea voices" (*Nobody,* 2019), Kate Tempest's idiomatic updating of the epic rhapsode as an urban rap artist (*Brand New Ancients,* 2013), Ocean Vuong's recasting of the Trojan War and its aftermath from the jarring perspective of a Vietnamese refugee (*Night Sky with Exit Wounds,* 2016), Paul Chan's lithe and suggestive kinetic sculptures (*Odysseus and the Bathers,* 2018), Anne Carson's performance piece and mind meld of Marilyn Monroe and Helen (*Norma Jean Baker of Troy,* 2019), A. E. Stallings's illustrated translation, in children's book format, of the whimsical mock-epic attributed to Homer in antiquity (*The Battle between the Frogs and the Mice: A Tiny Epic,* 2019), and dozens of published translations of both the *Iliad* and the *Odyssey* into English alone since the year 2000, never mind the countless translations, adaptations, reworkings, and live performances of Homer across the globe over the past century, from the US to the UK and Europe to South Africa, Egypt, Albania, Argentina, and Asia.[39] With each new intervention, Homer becomes richer, more complex, and more provocative. Homer is here to stay. It only remains to continue asking, Why?

# — 2 —
# Who Was Homer?

> "Where can I find the dear fellow?" someone asked me not long ago about Homer. "Why has he remained *incognito* for so long? À *propos*, do you happen to know where I can get a silhouette of the man?"
>
> —Andreas Heinrich Schott, *Ueber das Studium des Homers* (1783)

In an essay entitled "The Life of Homer" and published in 1711 by Anne Dacier, the leading champion of Homer in the Quarrel of the Ancients and the Moderns and his most recent translator into French at the time, we read the following:

> Nothing is more natural than the desire to know the life and adventures of a great poet like Homer, who has bestowed so much honor on mankind by the sublimity and reach of his mind. Everyone wants to know the person whom one cannot help but admire. Alas, this is a curiosity that will never be satisfied. The most famous of men will forever remain the least known.[1]

There is more than a trace of regret in her remark, which sums up the sentiment of several millennia of reflections on Homer's life and circumstances. Strategically placing the essay at the head of her prose translation of the *Iliad*, Dacier is in fact sounding a refrain that was already common in antiquity.[2] A *Life of Homer* falsely attributed to Plutarch makes the identical point at the start of its own presentation: "It may perhaps seem to some people superfluous to bother about Homer's parentage and place of origin, seeing that he himself did not see fit to speak of his personal details but was so reserved as not even to mention his name."[3] Dacier and Plutarch share the same resignation. But they also share the same desire to plunge ahead and tote up the accumulated facts or legends about the poet nevertheless, whether out of obstinacy or obligation to some unstated higher duty. This divided awareness is what characterizes so many of the inquiries, both ancient and modern, into the more general Homeric Question that was discussed in the previous chapter and that began and exhausted itself in the initial question, Who was Homer? To answer the question of who Homer was, one had to picture him in one's mind, in effect by asking what he looked like. As it turns out, the desire to bring Homer into view in whatever form could outweigh any reservations one might have about the prospect of succeeding in doing so. This chapter will examine some of the forms that this imagining took in the search for Homer and the problems that were associated with the effort.

## Biofeedback: Visualizing Homer

First, we need to take a step back. As we saw in chapter 1, the hunt for Homer is a perennial quest that takes place on different fronts. Philologists, critics, and readers seek clues to the identity of Homer in his verses. Here, the intimate experience of reading creates the illusion either that the poet has left biographical traces in his creations that can be used to ferret out the details of his life or else, in the words of a contemporary classicist, that the poems "bring us close to the thought processes of the poet Homer himself; we feel that we are looking over his shoulder."[4]

The Renaissance humanist Petrarch, writing in 1360, had a similar sensation. Upon reading Homer for the first time in Latin translation (the only access he had to the Greek poet), he saw "flash" before him "the face of the friend whom I had been longing to behold, a momentary glimpse, dim through the distance, or, rather, the sight of his streaming hair, as he vanished from my view"—a glimpse that he quickly recognized was no more than a powerful imagining: "For a long while I have been talking to you just as if you were present; but now the strong illusion fades away, and I realize how far you are from me."[5]

Tourists, antiquarians, and archaeologists have long sought out clues among the ruins of Homeric palaces and other locales—

whether at Troy, Mycenae, Pylos, or Ithaca and sometimes, more fancifully, in Sicily or on the Baltic—hoping to stand on the very spot where Homer stood as he surveyed the ground, sea, or sky before him. This is the physical counterpart to the sense of intimacy afforded by the shared spaces in literature, and it is just as imaginary too.

Art historians and antiquarians have looked for Homer in his ancient portraits, of which there are many—too many, in fact, for any of them to capture the poet's original features, despite their promise to do just that. This third way of reaching out to Homer merely marks a natural progression from the first two: the assumption is that if we squint hard enough as we gaze at a bust of Homer we can see the poet standing before our very eyes, just as we can hear him in his verses or see what he saw on the ground. All three approaches were tested by the ancients long before the modern age. In fact, our modern approaches to Homer are merely extensions of the ancient attempts to do the same. But the visualizations of Homer are undoubtedly the most appealing, because they are the most intuitive way of making or confirming an identification of his person, just as images promise to do today.

Nowadays, whenever we wish to match a name with a face, we simply turn to the internet and begin hunting for images. In the millennia before Google, Facebook, and Instagram there was a more direct way of performing this kind of research: one only had to look for sculptures, paintings, coins, or gems, and there he or she was. The more famous the person, the more opportunities there were to consult an image: replicas of historical figures were scattered across the Greek and Roman worlds, where their quantity functioned as the ancient equivalent of Facebook "likes."[6] The sheer abundance of these images demonstrates how natural the urge to identify historically significant individuals was in antiquity. As the Roman polymath Pliny the Elder (23–79 CE) writes in a chapter on portraiture from his *Natural History*, "There is no greater proof of success than that everyone for all time should desire to know what kind of a man a person was" by seeking out images of the person (35.10; trans. Rackham, modified). And, as Pliny goes on to say, nowhere was that desire greater or more easily fulfilled than in the portraiture of Homer, whose images filled every corner of the ancient Mediterranean in the form of full-length sculptures, busts, paintings, and coins.

The desire to know what Homer looked like never abated, and, if anything, the demand for images of the poet increased over time. But while these images in one way set out to satisfy the desire to "see" Homer in the flesh, in another they did nothing of the kind. Instead of representing Homer, they represented "Homer" as he belonged to the genre and tradition of visual depictions of the poet that stretched back into early antiquity. In fact, it was impossible not to refer to this tradition if one wished to depict Homer, be it in paint, marble, metal, or any other plastic medium: the tradition was the only point of reference available and the only means by which Homer would have been recognizable to a beholder. Depicted in these visualizations was not Homer but his idea.

One of the most widely reproduced modern representations of Homer is a perfect case in point: *Homer Deified,* more commonly known as *The Apotheosis of Homer* (fig. 2.1), by the French neoclassical painter Jean-Auguste-Dominique Ingres (1780–1867). Originally commissioned as a ceiling painting for the inauguration of the Musée Charles X in the Louvre in 1827, the work was later removed from the ceiling for display as an easel painting at the Universal Exposition in 1855, Paris's version of the World's Fair, before being returned to the Louvre, where it remains to this day. Ingres was being touted as the successor to Jacques-Louis David (1748–1825), the great neoclassical painter of the previous generation who was known for his large-scale heroic themes, so he was given a room all his own for a grand retrospective of his paintings in the 1855 exhibit, the centerpiece of which was *The Apotheosis of Homer*. Spanning seventeen feet across and standing thirteen and a half feet tall, this was the artist's most famous work, showing Homer as a godlike presence surrounded by his posterity. But as celebrated as the event was, neither the painter nor his painting could escape criticism. Some observers found the work painfully morbid, lifeless, and "embalmed." "How is it surprising that we should think of death," wrote one detractor, a certain Théodore Laborieu, "when we stand before

FIGURE 2.1. Jean-Auguste-Dominique Ingres, *Homère déifié,* or *L'Apothéose d'Homère/Homer Deified,* or, *The Apotheosis of Homer* (1827). Louvre. Inv. no. 5417. Photo © RMN-Grand Palais / Art Resource, NY. Thierry Le Mage, photographer.

M[onsieur] Ingres, the enemy of life—M[onsieur] Ingres, the artist-gravedigger." Defenders came to the rescue and insisted that if Ingres was not a painter of life, it was because he was a painter of the afterlife and eternity: "No," the taste-maker and critic Théophile Gautier put it tartly, "he is not of his time—he is eternal."[7]

This is probably not a dispute that can be amicably settled, but perhaps both sides have a point. Looking at the painting, one has to ask whether Homer is being shown alive or dead. Crowned by Nike, the goddess of Victory, Homer is seated regally on a golden throne like Zeus as he appears in ancient images and like Ingres's own Zeus from an earlier work, *Jupiter and Thetis* (1811). At once placid and inert, more monument than human form, Homer occupies the space before a temple that bears an inscription in Greek. The inscription is partially obscured by a crown that hovers over the poet's head, poised to rest there—suspended—for all time. Enough of the writing on the stone overhead is visible to make out what it says: "To Homer, (a) god." At Homer's feet sit his two poems, both personified as feminine and captioned with their Greek titles on the face of the marble riser on which they are seated, ensuring their identification. The *Iliad* is cloaked in a blood-red robe, with a short stabbing sword, sheathed and festooned with a red ribbon and resting against the stone to her side. The *Odyssey* is wrapped in verdant green, a broken oar leaning at an angle on her thighs. The two epics are either brooding (like Achilles) or pensive (like Odysseus), possibly bored with the prospect of eternity. Surrounding this ensemble stand other figures, from Pindar and Phidias to Dante and Raphael to more recent European cultural eminences down to the end of the eighteenth century, making offerings of their works or gestural homages to the central figure of Homer, who holds a staff in one hand and a papyrus roll in the other as he stares vacantly off into the distance, toward the future and us.

The pedestal below Homer is adorned with an inscription in Greek lettering: "marshaller [or "adorner"] of heroes." Further epigraphs fill out the remainder of the stone's face in chronologically descending steps: two verses from a poem in the *Greek Anthology*, likewise quoted in Greek ("If Homer is a god, let him be revered as one of the immortals; but if he is not a god, let him be believed to be one"), a quotation in Latin from Quintilian warning readers to approve of great literature even if they fail to understand it (evidently, we are meant in turn to approve Quintilian whether or not we understand his Latin), and a quotation in Greek from Longinus recommending the emulation of great writers from the past as a path to sublimity: "that is the goal we should always keep before our eyes" (a goal we are tricked into realizing just by reading what it says).[8] The last two inscriptions are tagged with footnote-like annotations listing author, title, and page in case anyone wishes to do further homework.

The scene makes for a peculiar tableau. Bookish and theatrical, it allegorizes rather than depicts Homer's deification, not least by compressing into a single moment and along two dimensions the full sweep of historical time down to the recent present. The present day is, however, not depicted in the painting. Rather, it stands outside the painting, in the form of the beholder whenever she contemplates the painting and in this way completes it, virtually proving the painting's thesis. For the painting *is* a thesis. Rather than staging an epiphany of the god Homer, the painting constructs an argument about him: "Homer is forever."

And yet for all the pomp and circumstance, there is something dead or deadening about the scene. The image as a whole is stiff and unreal, static rather than dramatic, posed rather than natural, more flat than deep. Perspectival effects create a general recession into the background, but they clash with the painting's surface, which takes on a peculiar kind of agency of its own, as if to remind us that we are looking at a painting that makes few pretenses to illusionism. The figures might as well have been pasted onto the backdrop of the temple, which oddly is more realistically painted than the scene that unfolds before it, even as the temple, washed out in pale tones, fades off into a misty pallor beneath the architrave. The supporting columns hint at a vanishing point that is significantly *blocked* by Homer, while the crowd of figures repeats the triangular shape of the pediment behind them, forming a human temple in their own right. (Ingres fondly referred to these figures as his "Homeridae," Homer's "children" or "offspring," after the guild of rhapsodes who claimed descent from Homer and jealously guarded his memory.[9])

It turns out that the figures *have* been pasted into the painting. The image of Poussin, sternly glaring at us on the left while directing a pedantic finger at Homer, has been lifted from his self-portrait in the Louvre, while the waxen head of Corneille behind him was familiar from French banknotes (themselves copied from Charles Le Brun's celebrated portrait from life), and so on down the line. The ancient figures are likewise borrowed, this time from Ingres's personal library, which contained countless reproductions of Classical art. As one art historian puts it, "*The Apotheosis of Homer* is first and foremost an immense accumulation of copies"; Ingres's contribution "consisted in arranging the many borrowed faces."[10] To look upon this work is not to look at a painting. It is to flip through a museum catalogue.

Homer is of course Exhibit A. As the centerpiece of the painting, the poet embodies the clash between the competing forces of art and

FIGURE 2.2. The Louvre Homer (Herm). 2nd century CE copy of a Hellenistic sculpture. Inv. no. MR 530 (MA 440). Photo © RMN-Grand Palais / Art Resource, NY. Hervé Lewandowski, photographer.

reality in his own person. The head, a quotation of the Hellenistic bust of Homer that Ingres knew from the Louvre (fig. 2.2), has been attached to an aging body and virtually photoshopped into place, while the posture of the body has been lifted from earlier portraits of Homer, most notably the heavily allegorical and learned relief sculpture by Archelaus of Priene from the Hellenistic period and known by its modern title as *The Apotheosis of Homer* (here, Ingres could draw on several seventeenth-century engravings of this ancient monument, which he both owned and annotated; see fig. 3.1).[11] A further source are the innumerable images of Zeus on which these various Homers were typically calqued, whence the similarities with Ingres's own *Jupiter and Thetis* from sixteen years earlier. Ingres takes no pains to disguise these references, and if anything he advertises them. His painting quotes Archelaus's Homer by rotating the figure into a frontal view, and, of course, by borrowing the title from that earlier work. The feminine-personified epics are likewise a quotation from Archelaus's sculpture, though not the sword and the rudder or oar. That iconography is attested elsewhere, for instance in a Pompeian wall painting of Homer depicting a scene from the *Contest of Homer and Hesiod* (fig. 3.2) and on a Roman silver cup from Herculaneum (another *Apotheosis*).[12]

Ingres was in effect combining two kinds of representation that had gathered around Homer since antiquity: on the one hand, the image of Homer as a living poet en route to being canonized, and on the other, the image of Homer as a long-dead but by now securely elevated poet. Rembrandt's two portraits of Homer, set apart by a decade in the middle of the seventeenth century, take each of these tendencies to new extremes. The later painting, *Homer Dictating His Verses* (1663), shows the blind poet caught in the act of reciting, gesticulating with his raised right hand, brows knitted, eyes round but dark and vacant, and mouth ajar as he dictates his verses to a scribbling young pupil or scribe who has been all but cropped out of the lower right-hand corner. Homer here resembles a biblical prophet more than a pagan poet, as a comparison with other works by Rembrandt confirms.[13] Rembrandt's earlier portrait, *Aristotle with a Bust of Homer* (1653), is perhaps the best-known modern image of Homer before Ingres's. There we witness the philosopher, dressed as a wealthy Dutch burgher or merchant, pondering a life-size bust of Homer set before him on a table, his hand gently cupping the top of Homer's pallid marble head. Homer's eyes and features are lost in shadows, and his shoulders are cut off at the arms, proclaiming the bust's identity as a relic of antiquity. Based on a plaster cast that Rembrandt owned, the bust is a close relative of the Louvre Homer that served as Ingres's point of reference.[14] But in contrast to the breathing, reciting, and lifelike Homer from a decade later, the bust is safely zoned off in a region of the deep past, virtually a cult object rather than a person, blind and deaf to Aristotle's searching inquiry—unless Aristotle is in fact a Dutch contemporary, in which case the gap between the artifact and the present of the painting is that much greater.

Ingres departs from the tradition in the way he conflates these two strands by affixing the marble bust, now enfleshed but visibly borrowed, to Homer's living body. A closer but ultimately partial approximation to Ingres's painting is the engraving of Homer that accompanied F. A. Wolf's edition of Homer's works as its frontispiece in 1804, likewise modeled after a Hellenistic bust of the blind Homer (see fig. 1.1 above). There, Homer is shown in three-quarter view. The light and shadows that are cast on Homer almost deceive the eye into taking him for a living, breathing creature. The cropping of the shoulders within a decorative lunette artfully suggests the torso of a body, which in reality was squared off and bolted to a short pedestal (both the bust and the pedestal were modern additions).[15] Wolf's Homer is no more than a stylized replica of a sculpted "original," that of the Farnese Homer in Naples, which would have nicely adorned a table in the library of a Roman patrician, just as Wolf's edition would do in modern libraries across Europe.[16] All the *trompe l'oeil* effects of Wolf's frontispiece notwithstanding, Homer's features remain true to their original sculptural form. He is more stony than alive.[17]

Not so in the case of the painting by Ingres, who takes what is manifestly an inherited ambivalence one step further by affixing a well-known statue's head onto a living body. As grotesque as this procedure may seem to us, it *is* how Ingres conceived the image in his mind, as his drawings for the final work—some of these preliminary, others produced later on—establish beyond a shadow of a doubt. One of his preliminary sketches methodically traces the Louvre bust (fig. 2.3). Another sketch shows the insertion point for

FIGURE 2.3. Jean-Auguste-Dominique Ingres, Sketch of the Louvre Homer placed beside the original. Graphite pencil on paper. Musée Ingres, Montauban. Inv. no. MIC.31.3A. Photo © Montauban, musée Ingres Bourdelle. Marc Jeanneteau, photographer.

the missing head (fig. 2.4), and a third fills in the blank with a faceless outline (fig. 2.5).[18]

No longer a human figure, Homer is statuesque. And that is how he appears in the final version of the *Apotheosis*. Only his left big toe, jutting into the foreground, seems to resist embalmment,[19] while the rest of his body clings stiffly to a single dimension, the flat surface of the canvas. But even here we find a clash: the lively toe is poised above what is in fact a tombstone, Homer's own, which is mentioned in the closing two lines of the ancient biographical work the *Contest of Homer and Hesiod*, as is Homer's burial epitaph (allegedly composed by the poet for himself), which Ingres reproduces in reduced and slightly altered form on the face of the marble slab that serves as both pedestal and tombstone, thereby repurposing the epitaph as a dedication: "To the marshaller [or "adorner"] (*kosmētori*) of warrior heroes." The epitaph's original wording, rearranged by Ingres and distributed between the pedestal underfoot and the lintel of the temple above and behind, is repeated in most of the

FIGURE 2.4. Jean-Auguste-Dominique Ingres, Sketch of Homer with head removed. Pierre noire on paper. Musée Ingres, Montauban. Inv. no. MI 867.887. Photo © Montauban, musée Ingres Bourdelle. Marc Jeanneteau, photographer.

ancient biographies of Homer, including that attributed to Plutarch, who may be Ingres's most immediate source (more on this in a moment). Ingres has captured the original but shuffled its parts—in keeping with his *modus operandi* in the rest of the *Apotheosis*, and, apparently, in his other dealings with ancient imagery as well.[20]

There is something ghostly, even ghastly, about the painting, which presents less a moment frozen in time than time as itself frozen. There is an imbalance to the work that keeps it teetering on

FIGURE 2.5. Jean-Auguste-Dominique Ingres, Sketch of Homer captioned with "Plutarque." Graphite pencil on paper. Musée Ingres, Montauban. Inv. no. MI 867.1455. Photo © Montauban, musée Ingres Bourdelle. Marc Jeanneteau, photographer.

the brink of life and of death: Where should we place the accent? Homer hasn't yet been crowned by Victory, though his presence before us tells us that he already has. He is not yet dead, yet he somehow is. If he is still alive, then he is only precariously alive. If he is already dead, then he doesn't yet know that he is. It seems that we are being confronted not with the immortality of a poet but with some of the difficulties that come with its conception. The trouble with immortality is that in order to achieve it you have to give up something precious—animation itself. Monumentality demands it.

What ought to be a joyous occasion—Homer's canonization by

eternity—is instead bleached of all joy. The moment is fateful, indeed. The stagey chill of the atmosphere spreads to the faces in the crowd of Homer's historical admirers, nearly fifty all told, ranging from the Archaic poets Hesiod, Sappho, and Pindar to Pisistratus, Homer's legendary first redactor, to Aristarchus of Samothrace, who completed the job of editing Homer's texts at the Library of Alexandria in the Hellenistic period, and from there to modern tributaries in art and music, including the likes of Camões, Shakespeare, Gluck, and Mozart. Their faces are for the most part expressionless. Some are more finished than others, and in a few cases they are not finished at all. Orpheus, standing to Homer's left behind him with his mouth ajar, barely shows any modeling, as though he were either perpetually young or else so ancient as to lack any ascertainable features, a mythic blank (which he in fact always was).[21] Is Homer, having been touched by Orpheus's spirit, dead or alive? Or is he simply flatlining? Ingres seems to waver indecisively, unwilling to remove Homer from life and unwilling to give up his claims to eternal life. His *Apotheosis* enacts, down to the level of the medium, the paradox of monumental fame that it both wants for itself and resists. Ingres's critics picked up on only the deadening qualities of the painting, not its programmatic ambivalence.

A study for the painting from the same year makes all of this explicit. It is known as *Homer Deified: Bust of Homer and Orpheus*, but it might just as well be known as Ingres's "Cyborgian Homer" (fig. 2.6). This extraordinary sketch in oil on canvas, housed today at the Ingres Museum in his home town of Montauban in the South of France, virtually gives away the problematic of the finished painting, which is to say its genesis, its anxieties, and its indecision.[22] Looking at this image, one is led to ask, Is Homer a mortal poet who is becoming a god, or is he an immortal figure who is being rendered human again? The modeling of the arms, hands, and torso is perfectly realized in pink flesh tones—they are a thing of nature. The marble statue of the head, set off in stony yellow tints, is ghastly in itself. Is Homer becoming his own idea, or is the idea of Homer, passed on by antiquity to us in the present moment, becoming palpably human?[23] The transformation, in whichever direction

FIGURE 2.6. Jean-Auguste-Dominique Ingres, *Homère déifié: Buste d'Homère et Orphée/Homer Deified: Bust of Homer and Orpheus* (1827). Oil on canvas. Musée Ingres, Montauban. Inv. no. MI.16.1.1. Photo © Montauban, musée Ingres Bourdelle. Marc Jeanneteau, photographer.

it is moving, is jarringly demarcated by a razor-sharp line across the beard. Orpheus, meanwhile, is no more than a spectral wraith in the background, as befits this mythical prototype of all song. He is himself statuesque and yet barely emerging as a human form as he hums wordless nothings into Homer's ear, while a white halo of gauze surrounding both figures shades off into a hazy blur at Homer's left shoulder, where a chiton garment will eventually materialize.[24]

Homer has been left in a half-materialized state, or rather in a hypermaterialized state. The realism of his human musculature outdoes that of the head, while the marble head, though less realistically modeled, bids fair to be a truer or at least more authentic representation of Homer than the enfleshed avatar imagined for us in the monumental painting by Ingres—if only we knew what Homer looked like. On the other hand, it is doubtful that the Roman copyist of the second-century Hellenistic bust borrowed by Ingres for his image had any better idea of Homer's features than Ingres, let alone ourselves.

In order to appreciate this fact, we need to understand that Homer is and always has been a faceless poet. Ancient busts, reliefs, and engravings of him exist, with the earliest dating from the mid-fifth century BCE, but none of these can be considered a likeness. Instead, they are all fanciful imaginings, drawn from a tradition of replicas that imitate one another but no one in particular. The series constitutes one of those strange but not uncommon artifacts in the history of art, especially in ancient portraiture: a series of copies that lacks any original. Not only is it highly improbable that a portrait of Homer could have survived from before the fifth century and then been transmitted faithfully to later generations, but it is also clear from the wide disparity in the surviving portraits of Homer that they lack a single origin. Artists had to "invent" Homer's likeness in order to depict it.[25] The more forbidding problem haunting all visualizations of Homer is the question whether Homer ever existed as a unique historical individual who could in theory have lent his traits to later portraiture of him. The answer is unknowable, but also irrelevant to the serialization of Homer in visual form. What these portraits represent is not a person but an idea—the idea of Homer.

## Portraits of Homer in Antiquity

The earliest known image of Homer comes to us in the form of a Roman imperial copy of a head, now in Munich, that once belonged to a standing life-size statue dedicated at the Temple of Zeus

Olympia in 460 BCE.[26] Later examples of original portraiture, each engendering families of sibling copies, run from the High Classical period (430 BCE) to the Hellenistic and Roman periods and then on into later antiquity. As we know from ancient travelers and other writers, considerably more visual representations of Homer once existed in sundry media, sizes, and poses, but these were lost over time. In most of the surviving images, Homer is shown as old and blind, listening quietly within to whatever divine voice moves him. In some he is sighted and, not infrequently, shown silently reading. His hair can be either elegantly coiffed or disheveled, sometimes with a bald forehead (as in the Louvre bust), but not in every case. The disparity is considerable. At a minimum, the variances serve as a confession of ignorance, which in turn reminds us that the mystery of Homer was as great and as insoluble in antiquity as it is today.

Pliny is frank about the difficulties of lighting upon the "true" Homer, visually speaking, given the plethora of Homers in circulation in antiquity. The mere proliferation of these portraits betokens an underlying need and its inevitable frustration:

> We must not pass over a novelty that has also been invented, since likenesses, if not of gold or silver, then at all events of bronze, are set up in libraries in honor of those whose immortal spirits speak to us in those same places. Not only that, but those whose likenesses we no longer have are modeled *ex nihilo,* and *a sense of loss gives birth to countenances that have not been handed down to us, as in the case of Homer.*
>
> (Pliny, *Natural History* 35.9; trans. Rackham, modified; emphasis added)

Pliny knew very well that representations of Homer were imaginary projections and nothing more, all of them driven by a powerful desire to put a face on a name. Nor was Pliny's insight exceptional among the ancients. Whenever they were faced with a claim about Homer or his likeness, they too had to struggle with competing impulses, which typically took the form of the admission "I know very well that the evidence of Homer before me is the result of illegitimate imaginary construction, a mere stab in the dark, but I will treat it as if it were authentic, valid, and probative just the same." Such is the logic of fetishistic illusion, which overcomes the oddity of the experience that Pliny so perceptively puts his finger on: For how can you feel a sense of loss for something that you never possessed to begin with? One obviously can, which does not yet give us much information about the nature of the loss; it merely confirms its effects. The effects of this kind of thinking were confirmed in practice: Homer may have been lost forever, but his cultural value and cachet were inextinguishable.

Identifying Homer was a perpetual problem but also a risky venture that promised unlimited rewards. Suppose you wanted to write a poem in praise of Homer. Where did you look for inspiration? Lucian, the Syrian Greek satirist from the second century CE (or else some clever writer pretending to be Lucian), gives one answer. A poet named Thersagoras woke up early one morning. It happened to be "Homer's birthday" (surely a flippant joke), a fine occasion to break out the writing tablets and to ask for divine inspiration to celebrate this esteemed poetic ancestor.[27] Thersagoras quickly found himself frustrated, and he compares his difficulties to those of anyone seeking to praise a historical figure such as Demosthenes. The latter have it easier. With Demosthenes, the material for praising the person behind the works is abundant. With Homer, there is no place to begin:

> I have no firm foundation on which to build my praises except his actual poetry. All else about Homer is uncertain—his country, his family, the time when he lived. If at least any of these were certain, "mankind would be free from disputatious strife" [Euripides, *Phoenician Women* 500], for they give him for country Ios or Colophon or Cyme or Chios or Smyrna or Egyptian Thebes or countless other cities, while they say his father was Maeon, the Lydian, or a river, for at any rate they even prefer the name Melesigenes [offspring of the river Meles in Smyrna] to his familiar one, and his mother was the daughter of Melanopus, or, for want of human parentage, a Water

> Nymph, and that his time was the age of the heroes or the Ionian period and they admit they do not even know for sure how he compared for age with Hesiod. They say his lot was one of poverty or that he was blind. But perhaps it would be better to leave these matters shrouded in obscurity. My eulogy, you can see, is limited to a very narrow field; I must praise his poetry as distinct from his life and collect an impression of his wisdom inferred from his hexameters alone.
>
> (*In Praise of Demosthenes* 9; trans. MacLeod, slightly modified)

So complains Thersagoras, at the same moment that he and his interlocutor are standing beside a statue of Homer, the sight of which baits the eye but reveals nothing to the would-be encomiast: "You know," explains the narrator of the dialogue to the reader who may be wondering which statue is meant, "the one to the right of the temple of the Ptolemies"—possibly the Ptolemaion library in Athens built in the late first century BCE, or perhaps another temple at Rhodes—"with the flowing locks" (2).

Evidently, the mystery of Homer could chafe and attract in equal measures, and at one and the same time. The more one sought to pin down facts about Homer's physical appearance and his life, the harder it proved to do so. As the urge grew greater, so did the corresponding anxiety. After antiquity, attempts to capture Homer's likeness in a visual medium continued to rely almost exclusively on citations and re-elaborations of the ancient tradition's own guesswork: they constituted a continuation of the ancient series. Ingres was inserting himself into this venerable tradition, which he both extended and implicitly commented on. The ancients had already turned Homer into an idea. Ingres, with his *Apotheosis of Homer*, was documenting the birth of that idea. In doing so, he was pointing to an event that could no more be located in space or time than Homer's actual birthday.

Ancient portraiture solved the problem of representing Homer by skirting it. Artists produced images that declared their generic character with an iconography that in effect said, "This is (a representation of) Homer." Then they added details that gave their images an effect of the real and the illusion of authenticity: a twist of hair here, a crease of flesh there, extra contouring on the cloak, a certain heaviness in the eyelids, and so on. Where the particulars failed to convince, the typological character of the portrait stepped in to assure the beholder's gaze that it was at least trained on an identifiable subject: portrayed in any given instance was, if not the reality, then at least the idea—someone's idea, or antiquity's collective idea—of Homer. Just so, the original sculptural rendering in the Louvre that served Ingres as his model (fig. 2.2) is divided in its allegiances: it is both a type and a token, a universal masquerading as an individual. True, the Louvre Homer bears the marks of old age—sagging eyes, slackening facial musculature, receding hair (in an archaizing style), flowing beard—while the figure as a whole reposes in quiet and expressionless grandeur. But the apparent realism is a ruse, the more so as several different sculptural types of Homer existed in antiquity, each with its own distinct set of features and lineage.[28] Looking at this scatter of images, one would literally have to shut one's eyes to be able to say that they were depictions of the selfsame figure.

Given this array of possibilities, identifications of Homer are often difficult to make with any certainty, and they are more or less taken on faith, except when an inscriptional tagline labels the subject and clinches the identification. In several cases, the alleged portraits border on being all-purpose and generic—plausibly representing a god (usually Zeus), a tragic poet, a sage, or royalty—and hence of disputed identity. Thus, for example, the contemporary art historian Paul Zanker notes how Ionian coins from the fourth century BCE that boast portraits of Homer barely make a pretense to representing a likeness of the poet. They are transparent calques:

> The die cutter probably did in fact simply use a Zeus type with which he was already familiar. We see from this how early Homer was turned into a mythical figure, and how the assimilation of his image to that of Zeus derived from an earlier notion of Homer's unique significance. The figure of the singer is assimilated to that of the gods and heroes of whom he sang.[29]

All that remains to add is that this mythical typecasting began already in Homeric poetry itself, owing to the singer's self-declared proximity to the Muses ("Tell me now, you Muses") and to the closely guarded anonymity of the singer (the speaking "I" within the poems is nowhere named). Homer was thus a myth not only from his first mentions, whenever those occurred, but before them as well, because he was already a mythical figure in his own poetry.

The ancient visualizations of Homer are thus governed by the underlying paradoxical logic of a type/token dilemma: the token is itself a type; what each token depicts is not Homer but "Homer," an instantiation of the idea of Homer. Ingres's *Apotheosis* is itself a calque of its own, much like the ancient Homers discussed by Zanker, as a glance at his *Jupiter and Thetis* painting from 1811 and his still earlier *Napoleon I on His Imperial Throne* painting from 1806 will confirm: all three subjects, enthroned, sceptered, aloof, and expressionless as they face the spectator, are virtually interchangeable instances of a single type. But even more to the point, Ingres's large-scale *Apotheosis* captures the type/token dilemma more explicitly than the ancient depictions ever could, in part because of the way it juxtaposes the two media of painting and sculpture, and in part because of the way it objectifies the passage of time: Homer here is both a type (pointing to "Homer" as celebrated across the millennia into the present) and a token of that type (pointing to the flesh-and-blood Homer as imagined by Ingres). The artist's sketch from the same year spectrally materializes the dilemma and puts it on full view for the beholder. In both works, the technical problems of painting give way to referential uncertainty. And as they do, Homer the poet recedes from reality by becoming not hyper-real but hypo-real: spectral, ghostly, and ghastly.

Ingres knew full well that any depiction of Homer would have to be a complete invention. "Nothing," he wrote down, or rather quoted, in one of his notebooks, "[is] more famous than his [Homer's] works, and nothing more obscure than his person. Homer, the father of poetry, is for us a cipher (*inconnu*). For all the tales he had to tell, he never once speaks about himself."[30] This entry, a quotation, in fact, of a quotation, is from one of the some 3,000 notes on Homer that Ingres jotted down from secondary sources over the full length of his career, from his student years to his last days, with the fever of an obsessive philologist.[31] He was, in fact, an untrained amateur with no knowledge of Greek or Latin and so all the more dependent on derivatives of the tradition. But then, in the world of Homeric studies, so is everyone.

In this case, Ingres is quoting a contemporary authority, though both are merely stating what was a commonplace long before Ingres conceived his *Apotheosis*. It was known to Anne Dacier in 1711, as we saw at the start of this chapter, and it was also known to Wolf's teacher Christian Gottlob Heyne in 1801, when he collaborated with the painter Johann Heinrich Wilhelm Tischbein in a study of the visual portraits of Homer that were handed down from antiquity:

> Because we know nothing definite about Homer, and because his life was set in a time before portraiture was even conceivable, it goes without saying that the bust of Homer [here, the Farnese Homer] is no more than an idealized image of the head (*ein blosser Idealkopf*), albeit a great and noble one, a masterpiece of a creative genius.[32]

So far, Heyne is largely purveying commonplaces (an identical judgment is found in Dacier's *Life of Homer*). He then goes on to detail the process by which this superb ideal of Homer came about. The account is jarring, not least because it is phrased in an unexpectedly Lucretian idiom. Lucretius, the Roman atomist from the last century BCE, insisted that all myths and divinities are literal thought-constructs that issue from the human mind in the form of simulacral images and then confront the mind as if they were self-originating:

> If we strip down our current notion (*Vorstellung*) of Homer and his person to its constituent parts, we arrive at the following: there were the ancient poems, there was a name, the two were put together, and the result was a Homer, understood as their author. An idea (*Begriff*) of him was conceived in the light of the poems, and his image

> (*Bild*) was modeled after this idea. Both image and idea were elevated into an ideal, which was passed on by posterity to us. . . . *cadit persona, manet res* ["the mask (or "the person") falls away, the true reality remains." (Lucretius, *On the Nature of Things* 3.55–58)][33]

In other words, once you take away the person and his life, all that remains is an idealized afterlife—a splendid yet falsified mask of a hypothesized individual. Ingres's portrait of Homer did not simply reflect a truth that by 1827 was a secret to no one. It was a portrait *of* this truth. And his unfinished sketch from that year spells out, as it were, the underlying truth of that truth, like a disturbing X-ray image that unmasks the "true reality" of the persona of Homer as he appears in Ingres's *Apotheosis*.

## The Too Many Lives of Homer

To speak about "the life of Homer" was and still is to say something about nothing: the phrase is a contradiction in terms. Homer could not be identified, and he may never have lived. And yet the complete ignorance about Homer in antiquity triggered the opposite reaction. The least known and greatest of early poets gave rise to an unappeasable biographical itch. As with nature, so too with Homer: literary history abhors a vacuum. Faced with so much uncertainty surrounding the author of the *Iliad* and the *Odyssey*, the ancients rushed to fill in the gaps, in essence producing a biography of the poet who, it was assumed, must have lived at some point in the past like any historical individual, and whose exploits and experiences, both good and bad, could be traced in narrative stories about him. Homer had to be equipped with a genealogy, a pedigree, a place of origin, a *curriculum vitae*, a list of titles, a knowable death, and a place of burial. Out of this necessity sprang an entire genre of writings about the life of Homer, known as the Homeric *Lives*, that flourished throughout antiquity and spread into early modernity, as with Dacier's *Life of Homer*. Homer was not alone in having been awarded a series of *Lives*; other poets enjoyed this fate too. He simply stood out as having spawned the greatest number and the most elaborate and most discrepant of these, and from an early date at that—at least from the end of the sixth century, and very likely earlier.[34]

The result was a large mass of speculations, much of it late (Hellenistic to Byzantine), at least in the form that has come down to us, but very likely with antecedents in early oral legends and lore dating to the time when Homer's name first came to be attached to the two monumental poems, at some point after 700 BCE. Accounts like these are records not of Homer's biography but of attempts to wrestle with an insoluble and increasingly unwieldy tradition or lineage of traditions that sprang up around Homer. The *Lives* and their spin-offs are in fact collective hallucinations, crowd-sourced documents that have been multiply overwritten. And because of the way they continued to grow and change over time, they often seem to have had more life to them than Homer ever had himself. Partly owing to the nature of the genre and partly owing to its sprawling existence across long stretches of space and time, the limits on this kind of fantastical guesswork were few, and the stories that were told varied wildly within and across each compilation of *Lives* and their derivatives that accumulated over the centuries.

Their tone varied as well. At times, the stories were entertained in all earnestness. At other times, they were indulged in for the sake of the exercise or simply for high jinks. Although the *Lives of Homer* were in some sense hagiographic, they were not always this, and given their compulsively conservative bent (they tended to hoover up every conceivable fact that was ever told about Homer's person) and given the amount of scurrilous detail that attached to Homer, as the next chapter will discuss, no representative *Life* could ever really be a bona fide hagiography. Many of the speculations that were put up for sale were created not as serious claims but to expose the ignorance of others, while the truthfulness of any claims about Homer immediately fell under the suspicion of being unverifiable. What ultimately came to be exposed in the harsh light of day was the fact that the frameworks by which Homer was capable of being imagined and received were exceptionally malleable. Nor was Homer's life confined to the *Lives.* It could be retold, disputed, revised, and remade across a range of literary and paraliterary writings that fell outside the confines of the official genre of the Homeric *Lives.* No one owned Homer, because Homer belonged to everyone. To narrate a detail about Homer's life was to enter into a literary Wild West.

The starting point for everyone—the only secure foothold anyone had—was the poems themselves (as the would-be encomiast Thersagoras complained above), which were mined for clues to Homer's life and circumstances. Places and dialects could be used to indicate the extent of Homer's travels. Poetic characters were roped into his *curriculum vitae* and made to embody teachers, mentors, relatives, lovers, or thinly disguised self-portraits (Helen's tapestry from *Iliad* book 3 is called "a striking emblem of Homer's own poetry"; Demodocus, the blind Phaeacian singer from the *Odyssey*, is said to be a "self-portrait" by Homer; Odysseus's penchant for tall tales and downright lies and his polymathy are frequently assimilated to Homer's qualities as a poet or sage).[35] Out of this same speculative urge arose a further subgenre of literary phantasms that imagined poets not only as once living and eventually dead, but also as ghostly revenants who rose from the dead and made themselves available for visions and conversations in their afterlife. Homer took pride of place here too. Finally, there was another line of speculation that sought to understand who Homer was based on what he said in his poems—namely, the tendency to imagine different racial and ethnic identities for him, all of this depending on the time, place, and mood of the interested party. In such cases, Homer's credentials as an ethnic Greek were stretched to an uncomfortable limit.

The lore that accumulated around Homer was prolific. No other poet had so many lives, or *Lives.* (Some ten or so of these have survived, depending on how they are counted. Many more must have existed.) Homer was born of a river god and a nymph. He had up to six different fathers, one of whom was Odysseus's son, Telemachus, another being "a teacher named Phemius" (Odysseus's court bard), who, it was said, hailed from Smyrna and took on the role of a stepfather. He had as many mothers as he had fathers, one candidate being Polycaste, the daughter of Nestor (the Greek warrior and elder statesman who figures prominently in both epics). He was born in at least seven places (this was the official number; the number grew as the traditions did) and was imagined to have lived either at the time of the Trojan War or as many as four centuries afterward. According to one later source, he fell madly in love with Penelope, moved to Ithaca, and gave her a starring role that rivaled that of her husband. According to another, Homer was the younger cousin of his own sometime rival, Hesiod. When all other evidence gave out, there was always Homer's name (*Homēros*), which could serve as a clue to his identity and fate: *homēros* (a noun) was variously understood to mean "hostage," "bondsman," "guide," "fellow traveler," "blind person," or "the one-who-does-not-see" (*ho mē horōn*), depending on the dialect and the claimants.[36] One source uniquely suggests that "Homer" derives from his father's name, "Omyres." (The name occurs nowhere else and has no obvious sense.) Modern and contemporary philologists have come up with speculations of their own that are no less inventive or fanciful, for example deriving "Homer" from the verb *homērein,* "he who fits [sounds/voices/verses/songs] together in unison" or "in tune."[37]

In any event, "Homer" was no more than a nickname given to him by others and an afterthought. His original name was said to be "Meles," "Melesigenes," "Melesagoras," or "Melesianax," usually in honor of his father, the river god Meles in Smyrna, near the coast of Asia Minor, but otherwise, in a minority of cases, as a remembrance of his place of birth "by the river Meles"—a far less illustrious pedigree, as it deprived him of divine ancestry. Either way, the tradition knew that something was afoot here. *Homer's name was clearly not his own.*

The reasons for the name change were mired in controversy and in even greater obscurity. Behind the shuffle from myth to wearisome rationalization without consensus was a fact that needed to be explained. Settling on one or another of Homer's names as his "actual" name, or arguing for the meaning of any individual name, misses the point and distracts from the nub of the issue, which is contained in the mere fact of the name change itself.[38] Inexplicable in its own terms, what the change tells us is that Homer had no proper name, indeed no proper identity, and the tradition knew this to be the case. Not even *Homer* knew who he was.

That he did not emerges vividly from the *Contest of Homer and Hesiod*, an early instance of a *Life* that playfully reflects on the gaps and dissensions within the biographical tradition of Homer, not least by parading a long list of Homer's possible names and their several explanations but without pronouncing a final verdict on the matter. As if on cue and in response to these uncertainties, Homer journeys to Delphi to consult the oracle about his origins. The answer is cryptic, as oracles tend to be, and is cast as forbidden knowledge; he is warned not to seek out the answer lest it prove fatal to him, and above all to avoid the island of Ios ("your mother's home") and "the young boys' riddle." Perplexed and resigned to uncertainty, Homer goes on with his life, first by taking part in a poetic competition that he loses to his rival Hesiod (whence the title of the work; the contest is largely based on linguistic traps and riddles that Homer negotiates with ease). Disgraced, he wanders about Greece for years. Toward the end of his life, having long forgotten the oracle's warning, he makes for Ios, where he is outwitted by fisher boys who stump him with a one-line hexameter riddle (the meter of epic). Homer, the icon of poetic memory and champion of riddle-solving, suddenly recalls the oracle and grasps its meaning. Embarrassed and dejected, and having lost his final "contest," he retreats from the seashore, and then, in a magnificently inglorious decrescendo, slips in the mud, falls on his side, and dies three days later. A tomb and an epitaph (the one quoted by Ingres in his *Apotheosis*) mark Homer's final resting place on Ios. So ends the *Contest*, which leaves the question of Homer's origins as unresolved as his name. The upshot is clear: solving the riddle of Homer's origins is a structurally impossible task. Homer can try to unravel the clues only at the cost of undoing himself, much like the unfortunate Oedipus. And the same is true of all those who would solve Homer's riddle for him. They, too, are doomed to fail.

The worries about Homer's identity must have enjoyed considerable antiquity. Aristotle seems to have known the fairy tale about

Homer's divine origins, though it is hard to credit him with any belief in the story. Similar stories were known a century or two before Aristotle.[39] We don't know when the anecdote about the Delphic oracle first arose, but it conceivably existed in the sixth century in an early version of the *Contest*. And the worries only deepened as the centuries wore on. By the time we come to scholarship from the last half century, statements like the following are common: "'Homer' was not the name of a historical poet, but a fictitious or constructed name," possibly a back-formation invented by the rhapsodic guild called the Homeridae (the "descendants of Homer"), who needed an eponymous ancestor to validate their status as custodians of the epic traditions. Perhaps, then, they are to be blamed, or thanked, for having invented the name of Homer and then for having equipped Homer with his first biographical stories in order to flesh out the contours of their namesake.[40]

As tempting as this account is, it begs more questions than it answers, not least about the change in Homer's name. Did the Homeridae invent that story too? If so, why? Or is it a telltale sign, like a clue to a crime scene, of their forced entry into an already existing lore about an epic poet previously known under some other name or anonymous and now baptized, out of convenience, as "Homer"? We simply do not know. However it happened, there was something suspect about this whole affair: Homer was once not "Homer," and the stain of uncertainty could not be washed out of the tradition. And once Homer's name was assigned to the *Iliad* and *Odyssey*, he became a permanent fixture of the landscape—or rather, a permanent *mystery*, around which subsequent generations built entire edifices of meaning in an effort to comprehend him, as much by seeking to explain who he was as by challenging prior understandings of this same question.

All doubts and disagreements notwithstanding, every bet in the ancient guessing game had to be hedged: the impulse in the *Lives* was to gather, not edit out, all facts that might conceivably pertain to Homer, on the grounds that they might contain some kernel of truth about his hallowed figure, much the way manuscripts of his poems moved through time like a glacier, accumulating and preserving debris even when certain forms, verses, or entire scenes were suspected of inauthenticity. As a result, Homer's biographical details tended to dilate beyond all reasonable expectations, while the sum total of this data grew not more probable but only increasingly improbable as time went on.[41] Conservatism and indiscriminate wildness went hand in hand.

By the time we reach the pseudo-Plutarchan *Life of Homer* (perhaps in the second or third century CE), all bets are off, and we can read a passage like the following, which contains a farrago of disparate claims about Homer's birthplace, many of which we encountered a few pages ago in the Lucianic dialogue *In Praise of Demosthenes*:

> Pindar names both Chios and Smyrna as his home, and Simonides names Chios alone. Antimachus and Nicander say he was from Colophon, Aristotle the philosopher, Ios, and Ephorus the historian, Cyme. Some have not hesitated to call him a Salaminian from Cyprus, others an Argive. Aristarchus and Dionysius Thrax say he was an Athenian. Some say he was the son of Maion and Critheis, but others make his father the river Meles [in Smyrna].
>
> ([Plutarch], *On Homer* 2.2; trans. Keaney and Lamberton)

And as the geographical boundaries of Greece and Greek culture spread across the Mediterranean after Alexander's conquests, so too did Homer become a diasporic figure who was assimilated to these new cultural environments: he became an Egyptian, a Babylonian, a Syrian, and a Roman. Some of this information found its way into the *Lives*, but much of the time it was developed independently as a kind of para- and counter-*Lives* tradition.

With Homer's ethnicity pushed into the margins of Hellenism, it was only natural to ask whether his name was even Greek, which is exactly what the great wit from the Roman imperial period, Lucian of Samosata, did. Venturing into the Underworld, Lucian chanced upon Homer and decided to use the opportunity to quell the debates that had been raging for some eight centuries now. Instead, he ended up adding more fuel to the fire:

> Hardly two or three days had passed before I went up to Homer the poet when we were both at leisure, and questioned him about everything. "Above all," said I, "where do you come from? This point in particular is being investigated even yet at home." "I am not unaware," said he, "that some think me a Chian, some a Smyrnian, and many a Colophonian. As a matter of fact, I am a Babylonian, and among my fellow-countrymen my name was not Homer but Tigranes. Later on, when I was a hostage (*homēros*) among the Greeks, I changed my name."
>
> (*A True Story* 2.20; trans. Harmon, slightly modified)

Flipping the script, the Syrian-born Lucian shows how Homer had indeed been taken "hostage" by the Greeks, though his birthright was to be a barbarian. But all that Lucian is in fact doing is exploiting the uncertainties that loomed over every aspect of Homer's identity, in the guise of solving them all. Nor did this tendency come to a halt in modernity. As time passed and as new cultural needs arose, more identities were added to the list of Homer's ethnicities. He was fancied to have been an Eastern Asiatic, a Trojan, a "Semite," a Jew, an Assyrian, and a pure-blooded Aryan.[42] Not all of these labels were benign. The sheer elasticity of Homer's identity was in itself nothing new. Only the applications and labels were.

Homer's identity was at once plagued and kept aloft by doubts. As we saw, as many as a good dozen and a half cities across the Mediterranean laid claim to Homer's birthplace, effectively ridding him of any.[43] Wearied by the debates and in exasperation (or affecting this), Antipater of Sidon, a Hellenistic epigrammatist, drew the obvious conclusion and declared that *no* place on earth gave birth to Homer. After running through the usual suspects ("Some say that your nurse was Colophon, others lovely Smyrna, some Chios, others declare happy Salamis, some Thessaly. . . . Some this land, others that . . ."), he dismissed them all with a sweeping gesture: "The great heavens are your fatherland; no mortal gave you birth, but Calliope"—the epic Muse—"was your mother."[44] Born of the heavens, did Homer have any earthly existence at all? Handbooks by classicists today insist that Homer's reality, like that of Troy, was never questioned until late seventeenth-century France, but this is not quite true. *Sotto voce* doubts were prevalent throughout antiquity, and at rare moments these doubts bubble up to the surface and become audible to us. Antipater's poem seems to be one such backhanded instance.[45]

Another comes from Philostratus the Elder, a successor of Lucian's and a fellow sophistic wit, who has one of his characters in a dialogue called the *Heroicus* resume Antipater's line of thinking all the way to its logical conclusion: "Homer's poetry is divine, beyond human powers. . . . So when some people say that Apollo wrote it and *merely put Homer's name on it*, it seems to me to have some force; it would take a god to know all this, not a mere man" (43.2–5; trans. Rusten; emphasis added). The risk in deifying Homer's poetry was that Homer could be defined out of existence altogether. A second speaker aims to reassure the first, but his reassurance comes out the wrong way (he protests a bit too much), and in the process entrenches the doubts it would allay: "Obviously Homer's *poems* are divine, but that does not mean that Apollo himself or the Muses actually wrote them. *No, there was a poet named Homer, there really was*, and he sang, as some say, twenty-four years after the Trojan War. . . . So then, *there really was a Homer*, and these poems were written by *a man*" (43.6–10; trans. Rusten, modified; emphasis added).[46] We can be relatively certain that Philostratus, who engineered this exchange from behind the scenes and whose work is unabashedly anti-Homeric, was content to see it dissolve in a mutual stalemate and to return Homer to the fold of humankind, with all the shortcomings that come with that greatly diminished status.

## God or Ghost?

The real problem with Homer was not the question whether he existed but the fact that he had *too much existence*. Though he was never conceded to be a fiction, Homer was in fact treated as both real and fictional at the same time: his historicity was etched around the borders with transcendental hues. Consequently, Homer became more than real—he became surreal. His name continued to sprout more life than any individual could bear. It took on a strange afterlife, spectrally insisting, in its very overdetermination, that Homer was less an immortal poet than he was an undead poet, one who exhibited an uncanny "inability to die."[47] Homer could never finally be put to rest once the machinery of Homer—the mass of speculations that grew up about him in almost every reach of intellectual life—was set in motion. Eric Santner speaks of the phenomenon of undeadening as a "disturbing" yet generative "surplus animation, not unlike the king's 'second body'" posited by the medieval historian Ernst Kantorowicz in *The King's Two Bodies*.[48] In medieval law, the king never dies: his earthly body passes away, but his office—his "sublime body," which is inhabited with a "mysterious materiality" of its own—never does. "*Le roi ne meurt jamais.*"[49] In the case of Homer, this mysterious vitality is grounded in the pulsation of life that takes place around an empty locus. Living a life without origin, Homer enjoyed *only* an everlasting afterlife, which is to say a disturbing surplus of life. Consequently, Homer haunted antiquity as no other poet or historical figure ever did.

Two factors may be speculated as the cause. The first I have just named: Homer was unlocatable from the beginning, yet he was seemingly everywhere to be found. He enjoyed an unaccountable omnipresence in the Greco-Roman world from an early date—in fact, from any date since literature was first recorded: there simply is no time when Homer did not exist in the written record of antiquity. Prior to that, all we have are archaeological remains, most notably those of Troy. But it is precisely at that point, once we pass from verbal texts to mute relics in a backward search in time, that the clues connecting Homer to reality run out. The second factor is the intrusion into his poems of a traumatic past, one that occurs with such power and vividness that it renders hearing or reading his poems at any given moment in the present a descent into Hades (a *katabasis*) and a communion with the dead, much like the infernal ordeal that Odysseus is made to undergo in book 11 of the *Odyssey*.

The scene, involving necromancy and known in antiquity as the *Nekuia (Visitation of the Dead)*, is one of Homer's most famous. In it, Odysseus tells how he made blood sacrifices and prayers to the

Underworld shades, who then swarmed around him "from every direction / with inhuman clamor" as "green fear took hold of me" (11.42–43). The list of visitors includes a pageant of mythical heroes and heroines that runs from Antiope (daughter of the Boeotian river god Asopus) to Epicaste (Oedipus's mother in the pre-Sophoclean story) to Leda, but also includes Agamemnon, Ajax, Achilles, and Patroclus. The impact on Odysseus's immediate audience, the members of the Phaeacian court, could not be greater: "So he spoke, and all of them stayed stricken to silence, / held in thrall by the story all through the shadowy chambers" (11.333–34). The lesson is plain: to hear or listen to Homer, Odysseus's alter ego so to speak, is to be escorted into an Underworld and an afterlife of heroes. The *Iliad* itself might as well have begun, "This time sing to me, O Muse, of the battle *of the shades* of the heroes." According to Lucian (*A True Story* 2.24), this was the opening verse of a poem given to him by Homer when he visited the poet in the Underworld. The poem's subject was an Underworld battle involving Greek epic heroes that recalls both the Trojan War and the Titanomachy (the war between the Olympian gods and the Giants), albeit in a farcical tone, and it would inspire similar scenes in later works, for instance in Jonathan Swift's *Gulliver's Travels* and *The Battle of the Books*. Lucian's creation is a sly reminder that the Homeric heroes are already dead whenever we lay eyes on them, but also that Homer, being a conduit to the literary Underworld, inevitably takes on the contours of the heroic dead himself: he speaks their language.

Of course, the flip side of this kind of communication is that in it the dead typically appear to be more lifelike than the living: they become undead. Homer accomplishes this magic act by making the dead past come to life in the present moment, a feature of his poetry that was celebrated as his unparalleled capacity for vivid description (*enargeia*), which gives the scenes he describes an illusion of immediacy and reality: one feels as if one were "present" to the action, much like Homer himself. (Dante, one of the great poets of the afterlife, would later repeat this technique in his *Inferno*.[50]) The hidden cost of this vivification of the heroic past, however, is the bleaching out of Homer himself. As the past obtrudes into the foreground, Homer fades away into the background. He is reduced to a viewfinder and a barely audible voice ("Sing, goddess"), more a ghost than a god.

If we return to Ingres's *Apotheosis*, we can see how he produces a parallel effect by means of a contrasting color scheme. By daubing the moderns in somber black and brown hues and the ancients in light hues and bright colors, he makes the ancients, who crowd around Homer and represent the bulk of the population on the canvas, seem livelier to the eye than the darkened moderns, who occupy the immediate foreground. Nor are the moderns permitted to lay foot on the stairway that leads up to the temple where Homer sits on his throne. Homer, meanwhile, is caught in a state of suspended animation, existing somewhere between life and immortal afterlife.

Ingres's preliminary sketch of Homer's bust makes the same argument on the body of the poet. Homer's torso, arms, hands, and his lower beard are rendered as colorful and alive, while his head and the figure of Orpheus behind him are rendered as lifeless marble: both are monochromatically ashen and ochre in hue. Homer is at once live and dead; he has, in effect, incorporated the "two body" syndrome that is described by Kantorowicz. All that remains is to decide which of these two bodies represents the immortal, ever-living Homer and which represents his dead, mortal frame. As it turns out, the question is impossible to answer, and Homer's identity is aligned with this problematic point of indecision. That indecision was hardwired into the ancient traditions of Homer, which recognized that Homer was at once real and unreal, a mortal who had to die in order to be reborn as an eternal being—a poet who, in other words, was endowed not with a life but only with an afterlife.

One of the Homeric *Lives* describes Homer's fate in the form of an oracle that is delivered to an uncomprehending Homer. Homer will grasp its truth only when it is too late to act on it:

Blessed and ill-starred one—

. . . . . . . . . . . . . . . . . . . . . . . .

For you have two allotted lives: one that is dimmed

for your twin suns [viz., "eyes"], the other matching the immortals'—
one for life, one for death; and in death you shall not age.
([Plutarch], *On Homer* 1.4; trans. West)

Such are the two lives of Homer, one of which is real and the other symbolic. By the same token, being incapable of undergoing a second, symbolic death, Homer in his second life persists as a ghost in the machine of the tradition, an ineradicable presence that can never be dislodged or marginalized in some final way, despite every effort to diminish him—of which there are surprisingly many, as we will see in the next chapter. It is this second, uncanny Homer that gives his image an authority that only a cyborgian portrait such as that by Ingres could ever fully materialize.

The *Lives of Homer* are one of the places where Homer's irrevocable afterlife is perpetuated. In these, Homer is repeatedly born, dies, and is monumentalized for eternity, under roughly similar but never fully identical circumstances. Read as a genre, they present a rather perverse appearance. How many deaths can a single poet undergo? The name of this genre is accurate in the precise sense that they are not conventional biographies: they are collections of life stories that in their sheer proliferation and mutual contradiction index the surplus vitality of their subject—a surplus that signifies its own failure to narrate a life and to search for its origins. Here, we can say without exaggeration that the process of searching itself *produces* the object that causes the search.[51]

Another related literary tradition is less a genre than a device. It consists in the long trail of epiphanies of an undead Homer who visits readers, poets, and critics in the form of a dream or fantasy, or by wandering into strange souls through transmigration. These spectral parades are functionally linked to the *Lives*. Typically, the visitees try to obtain from Homer answers to the questions that the *Lives* leave unresolved and that wracked the consciences of scholars and antiquarians throughout antiquity and continue to haunt Homer's readers today—not only where and when Homer was born or lived but also such questions as these: Were the lines of his poems that Alexandrian editors bracketed as doubtful indeed his?

Why did he begin the *Iliad* with the word "wrath"? Did he write the *Odyssey* before the *Iliad*?

The list of visitations by Homer's shade is a long and illustrious one, and it is more or less coextensive with the reception of Homer himself. Stesichorus (*fl.* 600 BCE) was said to have given Homer's soul "a second home."[52] The story has an apocryphal air, but as a metaphor for poetic creation it is accurate. Stesichorus, after all, did revise Homer's tale about Troy, which earned him the rare title of "most Homeric" from Longinus. Evidently, the fact that Stesichorus radically upended Homer's version of events (he claimed that Helen never went to Troy; it was only her phantom image or "shade"—her *eidōlon*—that appeared there) did nothing to diminish the former's bona fide Homeric credentials. Nor was Stesichorus alone. The early Roman poet Ennius, of whom only meager fragments survive, claimed to have been visited by Homer in a dream. Homer informed him that his soul had migrated into Ennius's own body, after first turning into a peacock (an emblem of Pythagorean palingenesis; Pythagoras himself reportedly claimed to be an incarnation of a Trojan warrior mentioned in the *Iliad*, Euphorbus from Phrygia). The story was later retold by Lucretius, the Roman Epicurean poet, who added that Homer's shade revealed to Ennius "the nature of things," and thereby associated himself with this hallowed lineage. (He omitted the detail of the peacock.)[53]

Scholars got in on the act too. Apion (*fl.* early to mid-first century CE), the Homer-obsessed grammarian and noisy celebrity derided as "the world's cymbal" in some quarters and as "the Drudge" in others, had a gift for magic and poisons and for raising the dead through necromancy. The first person on record to have actively summoned up Homer's shade, he did so, Pliny says, in order to "ask Homer where he was born and who his parents were." The scholar coyly refused to reveal what Homer told him, and Josephus, the first-century Jewish historian, polemically used this as evidence that the alleged Jew-hater Apion was fabricating.[54] (In the tradition, asking and feigning not to reveal something is a well-worn gesture, as we already saw in the case of Lucian.[55]) What Apion *did* choose to divulge, Seneca records, is something else that he learned from the encounter—namely, that after completing both epics, Homer added a preamble to the *Iliad* in order to "copyright" his works: "He deliberately put two letters in his first line indicating the number of books that his poems contained," meaning the first two letters of the first word of the *Iliad*, *mēnis* (wrath). For in Greek, the letters mu and eta are used to signify "48," which corresponds to the total number of books that make up the two poems.[56] At a stroke, two long-standing Homeric questions could at last be solved: Did Homer really compose both the *Iliad* and the *Odyssey*? and, Why did he begin the *Iliad* with the odious word "wrath"? Plainly, Homer's text was not only sacred. It was a secret code that only the best-informed readers knew how to decipher.

From there, the tradition of Homer *redivivus* carries on to Longinus, who advises writers aspiring to sublimity to imagine Homer as their audience and judge combined. The word for "imagine" involves the term *eidōlon* again (*eidōlopoiein*), for what is really meant is a trafficking in great writers from the past via their animated shades (*On the Sublime* 14.1–2). And Lucian carried the tradition forward with his interview with Homer's ghost in the Elysian Fields, where he pressed him about his origins and about the truth of his poems. But visitations by Homer hardly ended there. They were a fixture of the tradition, and they accompanied it into the modern era, where they continued to be either harrowing or hilarious.

Petrarch in his never-finished epic poem *Africa* (ca. 1338–1343) retells Ennius's dream:

Then, in the depth of night—behold, I saw
an aged man draw near, his body wrapped
in fragments of a toga, with a beard
unkempt, his grizzled hair with strands of white.
His sockets had no eyes. That spectral face,
hollowed and gaunt, bore a crude majesty,
yet moved my heart to horror. I lay frozen.[57]

No wonder Petrarch was both fascinated and terrified. He had long dreamt of reading Homer, though he knew no Greek. Homer was for him a complete mystery. He eventually brought the manuscript of the Homeric poems to Europe in 1353 and commissioned their first translation into Latin. After Petrarch, the experience of ghostly visitation repeats itself in different forms, from Chapman (1609) to La Motte (1714) and Marivaux (1716), to Swift (1726), who in his *Gulliver's Travels* riffs hilariously on Lucian's dialogue with the dead and has the shades of Homer and Aristotle appear amid the swarm of their equally ghostly "commentators" (in this, Swift is anticipating Nietzsche, who in 1875 took Homer's bloodless shades to be future classicists!), to the Greek poet Solomos, whose poem "The Shade of Homer" (1818–1824), presented as a "fragment," is a virtual translation of Petrarch, to the Irish writer Patrick Kavanagh, whose fourteen-verse poem "Epic" (1938) features Homer's ghost "whispering to my mind" and frowning on epic pretension, and finally culminating in Borges, whose short story "The Immortal" (1947) rehearses the tradition in all of its bizarre, Escher-like complexity, offering up a Homer who forgets who he is, and then remembers this detail, only to prove to be the sum total of every version of himself that was ever imagined in words, pictures, or thought—and a handful of other instances that only Borges could have dreamt up.[58]

Yet for all his brilliance Borges has nothing on the tradition that he is encapsulating. In the *Contest of Homer and Hesiod*, for example, Homer is made to ask the Delphic oracle about the mystery of his *own* identity, as though he were a symptom of the tradition that sought to find him, which he of course is.[59] Each new appearance of Homer in the world is an incarnation of his idea, now transmigrated into another soul. If it is true that "Classics became a ghost-written tradition," as Edmund Richardson suggests for the Victorian period, it only remains to add that it was always this from the start.[60] Homer is the dark matter of the classical tradition, visible—if at all—only by negation, in the form of his silhouette.

## Reanimating the Past

Ingres's *Apotheosis of Homer* from 1827 and his preliminary sketch from the same year reincarnate this tradition, as they only could.

However, by embodying the tradition in the way they do, both paintings appear to be at once lifeless repetitions of the familiar and attempts to bring to life what the tradition tells us is permanently lost. We might say that Ingres's paintings of Homer from this year pay homage not so much to Homer as to their own innumerable predecessors in the visual tradition that sought to picture Homer. Both paintings, but the *Apotheosis* in particular, are made up of countless footnote-like allusions that create a thick impasto effect on the canvas. The most obvious of these is of course to the Hellenistic relief sculpture by Archelaus of Priene, *The Apotheosis of Homer*, but Ingres's sketchbooks reveal further details about the canvas.

In the preliminary drawing of the faceless bard mentioned earlier (fig. 2.5), Plutarch's name, written at an oblique angle next to the bare outline of the poet's head ("Plutarque"), functions like a caption, as if to say, "This image is drawn from a *Life,* not from life" (in this case, the pseudo-Plutarchan *Life*), and as if to explain why Homer's features are missing. Were one to fill these in, the result would at best be an *Idealkopf,* an idealized head of the poet. There was no way around it: even the ancient artists relied on the only sources of information that were available to anyone after 700 BCE, namely, second- and thirdhand reports of the poet's personality and circumstances. Only the furious industry of ancient compilation and imaginative recreation over the centuries, to which pseudo-Plutarch's biographical writings belonged, kept the images of Homer alive in antiquity—and in modernity too. Ingres's own faithful transcription and annotation of these materials in his massively sprawling notebooks perpetuates these traditions without reaching behind them to some lost original. Far from having been effaced from the final painting, the traces of Ingres's textual and pictorial borrowings are in fact its formal substance, which points not to the epiphany of a godlike poet but to his eerie construction from antiquity into the present. Ingres is fully conscious of this fact, and nowhere more so than in his *Apotheosis* painting.

The first hint of this piecing together of Homer from the scintillae of his remains is found in the figure of Pisistratus, Homer's earliest redactor and resurrector—for it was he who apocryphally assembled the *disiecta membra* of Homer's fragmentary texts. Standing off to the left and nearly cropped out of the picture, he is clutching his copy of Homer (a papyrus scroll) with both hands. The effect is disorienting, for which copy of Homer is *Homer* holding in his own right hand, clutching as it does a second papyrus scroll? To the far right stand Boileau and Longinus. Involved in a dance of gazes, the two form a triangle of desire with Homer. As Longinus looks up and back over his shoulder toward Homer, scribbling down his pages on the poet from his great critical essay, *On the Sublime*, Boileau looks on anxiously—not at Longinus, and not even at Homer, but at Longinus's *text*, with his quill and his own considerably smaller notebook in hand, preparing to inaugurate the most successful translation of Longinus in modern Europe (1674), a work that did much to nourish the modern cult of Homer.[61]

Given the way Ingres's painting stages its own artifice, with no pretense to realism or chronology (the work collapses time beyond the point of radical anachronicity, achieving neither timelessness nor its illusion), it seems that the question the work poses is not whether Homer is a mortal or a god, and not even whether he is alive or dead, but whether he is a person who was made into an idea or an idea that has been made into a person. This is the real puzzle that haunts the Homeric Question throughout history, long before it came to be formulated in this form by Vico and then Nietzsche, as we saw in chapter 1. One *could* say that the *Apotheosis* celebrates the uncontested sublimity of Homer and so too the harmony of the tradition with itself,[62] as if its object were no longer Homer but rather the tradition that made him possible. But all such harmoniousness comes at a great cost, Homer being its greatest victim. For once Homer is identified with the tradition something drastic takes place: he disappears back into the tradition from which he emerged, a faceless and featureless entity.

It is undeniable that Ingres made this same leap. This could be inferred from the finished painting alone, but Ingres's train of thought is again attested in his sketchbooks. One of his preliminary sketches for the *Apotheosis* replaces the figure of Homer with his barest outline, a mere silhouette. Its title reads *Antiquity on a Pedestal* (fig. 2.7).

FIGURE 2.7. Jean-Auguste-Dominique Ingres, *L'Antiquité sur un piédestal/Antiquity on a Pedestal*. Pen on paper. Musée Ingres, Montauban. Inv. no. MI 867.2789. Photo © Montauban, musée Ingres Bourdelle. Marc Jeanneteau, photographer.

Homer here has become a figure for the tradition, and an empty one at that. The sequence of sketches of Homer is now complete: Homer is progressively emptied out and universalized. As we run through the sequence, we pass from Homer to his outline to his interchangeable identity with antiquity as a whole, itself a bare outline. The tradition's contours now match Homer's own, and neither entity can be imagined in the other's absence: each has become the other's idea.

This powerful integration of Homer and antiquity is in fact historically accurate. At some early point before the High Classical period, Homer became synonymous with its own ideal of itself: he marked the quintessence of antiquity and all that was good or great about that past. And once that idea formed, the two notions became inseparable. Efforts were made at various points to detach these entities and free antiquity from the tyrannical grip of Homer. During the Peloponnesian War, Pericles declared Athens a Homer-free zone: "We have no need of a Homer to sing our praises" (Thucydides, *Peloponnesian War* 2.41.4). In the centuries following, Vergil would later attempt to create a Roman epic that could vie with and even surpass Homer. And Jews and Christians would claim to have a culture that predated and exceeded the fame of Homer. But with each of these efforts, Homer's authority was strengthened, not weakened, as was his symbolic power to represent the past.

In casting the tradition as Homer's empty silhouette, Ingres gave pictorial expression to the contradictions that make up that tradition. Ingres's versions of Homer may give us an apotheosis, but they do not give us an ascension. There is no final transcendence in Ingres, only a fretful indecision and a heavily mediated presencing of Homer, which is in even greater evidence in the final *Apotheosis* than in the earlier sketches. In fact, the finished painting, we can say, is merely a fleshed-out version of this last sketch: it too represents Homer as a figure of the tradition and nothing more. What both works demonstrate is the fact that the tradition that stems from Homer cannot finally be reduced to Homer or abstracted away from him. Homer is unthinkable apart from the tradition that sustains his afterlife, just as that tradition cannot be conceived without him, so closely bound together are the two sides of this equation. The result is that Homer is not allowed to occupy the ideal vanishing point of eternity; his very presence stands in the way—quite literally so in Ingres's painting—with the stubborn obstinacy of a materiality that remains spectral, a haunting trace of what it can no longer be and what may never have been at all.

# — 3 —
# Apotheosis or Apostasy?

> Homer is a god, not a man.
>
> —Greek grammar school exercise (third century CE)

> I [Homer] am but a mortal, one of the most unfortunate ever!
>
> —André Chénier, *L'aveugle* (1787)

Homer suffered a fate that was unique among the poets from antiquity and very likely from any other time or place. Though he could be worshipped like a god, he was just as often treated like a social outcast. Over the centuries, he was dragged through the mud, made a fool of by children, defeated unfairly in competition, accused of immorality, gluttony, and cultural primitivism, ostracized, labeled a plagiarist and a liar (indeed, his name was made into a *synonym* for lying), and generally attacked, satirized, plagiarized, corrected, rewritten, and divested of his titles. Deracinated at birth, he was rendered homeless and destitute, accused of serving the whims of his own protagonists (whether out of infatuation or as their dupe), and finally made to die covered in shame. Such was the fate of Homer, who had to suffer all this and more at the hands of his ancient readers, never mind what lay ahead for him in modernity.

Some of these incidents come from the *Contest of Homer and Hesiod*, a short and raucous work of unknown date but one that, much like the Homeric *Lives*, was a living document that was compiled, adapted, altered, and recompiled over the centuries, probably long before the sophist and rhetorician Alcidamas of Elaea put his name to it around 390 BCE, and long after that as well, at least down to the time of Hadrian in the late first to early second century CE. The work reads like a never-ending rap sheet. The rest of the catalogue of wrongs mentioned above appear in the farrago of biographical literature and other writings in prose and verse that attached themselves to Homer, whose poetry and person spawned not only the origins of ancient literary criticism from as early as the sixth century BCE but also the origins of ancient critique, rebuff, parody, subversion, and revision that kept his image alive down through the centuries, albeit in mangled and barely recognizable form.

Dio Chrysostom, Lucian, and Philostratus—all three from the so-called Second Sophistic, when Greece flourished under Rome—are only the best-known later practitioners of Homeric revisionism.[1] In fact, an entire genre of writing was devoted to unraveling the mystery of Homer, or rather to venturing guesses as to the identity of the poet, an activity that turns out to have been one of antiquity's favorite parlor games. But guessing meant filling in blanks, and each new guess entailed a reimagining and a revision of Homer that could aim either high or low. In this class of literature, two instances stand out at opposite ends of the spectrum: the many competing biographical accounts or *Lives of Homer* (these were at least outwardly hagiographic), and a remarkable clutch of verses from Hermesianax of Colophon's poem *Leontion* (early third century BCE) that show Homer falling in love with Penelope, moving to "meager" Ithaca, and then writing her into his poetry, all for the sake of his passion. But the lines were easily crossed, which makes the tonalities difficult to parse. The *Lives* can be as scandalous as any other accounts, while Hermesianax insists that Homer is peerless as a poet and akin to the gods.

"The divine Homer" (as his tomb marker in the final line of the *Contest* reads and as the poet was widely called at least from the time of Aristophanes) was simultaneously the most revered and the most reviled poet of antiquity. Though considered the foundation of so many if not all branches of learning, from philology and literary criticism to rhetoric, philosophy, and geography, Homer was also the most maligned and interfered with of ancient poets. Consequently, Homer lived on not only as the archetypal poet—in Greek and in Latin, "the Poet" (*ho poiētēs* or *poeta*) sufficed to conjure up his memory and his glory[2]—but also as the archetypal whipping boy who was subject to all manner of criticism. In other words, he lived on both in the gutter and at the top tier of the literary and cultural traditions of Greco-Roman antiquity.

And while the veneration of Homer seems to have had no limit in time or in pretension (Ingres is a case in point, and Homer is widely considered a paragon of literary greatness even today), we should not imagine that the tradition of maligning Homer came to a halt with the end of antiquity. On the contrary, it continued well into the modern age, the two most colorful instances being the French controversialist François Hédelin, abbé d'Aubignac, who in the late seventeenth century shocked the Parisian world by declaring that "Homer was not a good poet, and what is more he never even existed," and then Samuel Butler, the Victorian prankster and classicist *manqué*, who in the last decade of the nineteenth century set out to prove that the *Odyssey* was in fact written not by Homer but by a woman who was vehemently opposed to him and that Troy never fell, a fact that Homer, the conniving author of the *Iliad*, knew "perfectly well" but chose to conceal.[3]

How can we account for the absolute disparity of responses to Homer's standing and his stature in a cultural imaginary that has shown itself so willing to elevate and debase its own values, seemingly uniquely in the case of Homer? No answer is likely to satisfy, but the aim of this chapter is not to unravel this larger mystery. Instead, it has a more limited goal: to take a rapid overview of the evidence for this divided reception of Homer and to remind ourselves that a good part of ancient and modern culture was generated as much in opposition to Homer as it was in kneeling before his altar. But in order to appreciate the reach of this phenomenon, we will first need to go back to Homer's earliest recorded appearances. Then we can follow the progression as it develops over time.

## Earliest Attestations of Homer and of Homeric Criticism

Astonishing though it may seem to us today, the first secure attestations of Homer are without exception harshly critical and even derisive of the poet. The earliest of these originate among the Greek philosophers from the sixth century. Only fragments remain of their writings, but the most scandalous were preserved for a reason.

Xenophanes (570–480 BCE) is the earliest known writer in any genre to mention Homer by name, and he is not a kindly witness:

> Homer and Hesiod have attributed to the gods everything
> that is a shame and reproach among men,
> stealing and committing adultery and deceiving each other.
>
> (fr. 11 DK = fr. 166 Kirk, Raven, and Schofield)

With this rebuke, Xenophanes inaugurates one of the strongest lines of criticism that would plague Homer over the millennia to come, from Plato to the early Christian writers and well beyond: Homer's poetry was blasphemous, morally flawed, and full of scandalous fictions (*plasmata*), as he puts it in another fragment (fr. 1.22 DK).

Close on Xenophanes's heels, Heraclitus (*fl.* 500 BCE) declared that "Homer deserves to be expelled from the competitions and beaten with a staff (*rhapizesthai*)—and Archilochus too!" (fr. 42 DK; trans. Kahn). *Rhapizesthai* may be an allusion to the staff (*rhabdos*) traditionally borne by Homer's most conspicuous emissaries, the rhapsodes (*rhapsōidoi* or *rhabdōidoi*, "song-stitchers" or "staff-bearing singers"), whether to mark their own authority as keepers of the Homeric legacy or as a way to keep time. Heraclitus is not speaking literally about beating Homer and expelling him from poetic competitions. Rather, he is conflating Homer with his verses and their performance by others, and then by extension with their meaning or value, just as we do today whenever we use the phrase "Homer says." (A generation later, Pindar, with his usual panache, will turn the *rhabdos* into a metonymy for Homer's poetry *tout court*: "his wand [*rhabdon*] of wondrous verses."[4]) We are not told what Homer's faults were, but the implication is that Homer peddled false knowledge to the Greeks, who credulously took him to be the wisest of their race, a point that Heraclitus makes in a second fragment, as we will see in a moment. The association with Archilochus, the unseemly blame poet from the seventh century, only adds insult to injury.

Plainly, the suggestion that Homer should be expelled from the rhapsodic competitions, where his poems were being recited and spread abroad by professional rhapsodes, has a purely symbolic force, one that Plato would repeat more than a century later when he banished Homer from his ideal philosophical city. Heraclitus is tearing down the façade of Homer's cultural authority, which looks to have solidified by the late sixth century but was equally vulnerable to challenges by this time too. In directing his criticisms against the person of Homer, a Homer who could be physically beaten with the symbol of his own authority, Heraclitus is personifying and vilifying the idea of Homer that had taken root in the minds of others and, evidently, in his own mind as well. Finally, we should note that Heraclitus is writing in the present tense long after Homer was no more than a memory being kept alive in the same kind of performance settings as Heraclitus is naming. Homer was manifestly present even in his absence, and in more ways than one.

It is no small irony that Xenophanes presents his teachings in the meter and language of epic poetry and was even said by Aristotle to have striven for first honors against Homer, no doubt because Xenophanes presented his verses in oral performances like a rhapsode (fr. 21.1 Gigon; Diogenes Laertius 9.18). Heraclitus wrote in prose, not meter, but his language was shaped by earlier poetry, and he was later admired for this quality. Equally striking is the way both Xenophanes and Heraclitus single out Homer as a symbol of human wisdom. Neither philosopher could completely cast off Homer's shadow, and both paid silent tribute to his style, if not his thought, in their own expressions of dissent. And while it remains true that criticism in these quarters bespeaks veneration elsewhere in Greek culture—"From the beginning everyone learned from Homer," Xenophanes acknowledges in another fragment (fr. 10 DK)—it is symptomatic of the tradition that Homer in his first certifiable appearances is at once a canonical and a contested entity. Neither Xenophanes nor Heraclitus can imagine a beginning that does *not* start with Homer. Or at least they find it convenient to make it seem so, in order to launch their own critiques of the foundations of Greek culture and knowledge. Homer is little more than a convenient scapegoat.

In another fragment, Heraclitus echoes Xenophanes by proclaiming Homer the "wisest" of the Greeks, only to refute this attribute in the same breath by qualifying it as meaningless:

> Men are deceived in the recognition of what is obvious, like Homer who was the wisest of all the Greeks. For he was deceived by boys killing lice, who said: "what we see and catch we leave behind; what we neither see nor catch, we carry away."
>
> (fr. 56 DK; trans. Kahn)

We have to wait for Alcidamas's rendition of the same riddle in his *Contest* to understand its context and its fullest implications. There we are told how Homer, toward the end of his life, was sitting by the sea on the island of Ios when he noticed some boys who were on their way back from fishing. "O huntsmen from Arcadia, have we caught anything?" Homer asked them in a perfect hexameter. Homer's question was more of a taunt than a greeting: there were no sea fishers in landlocked Arcadia, and the boys were not men. Provoked, they responded with a word game of their own, likewise in perfect hexameter verse form and in a nearly verbatim echo of Heraclitus: "The ones we caught we left behind, while the ones we missed we are carrying with us." Baffled, Homer asked them what they meant. The boys explained "that they had caught nothing on their fishing expedition, but they had cleaned themselves of lice. The lice they had caught they had left behind, but the ones they failed to catch they were still carrying in their clothes." It was at this point that Homer remembered and now understood the Delphic oracle that had warned him to beware the young boys' riddle on Ios, where his mother was born and where death would receive him. Dashed and humiliated, Homer stumbled in the mud, fell on his side, and died three days later.[5]

The riddle of the lice appears tailor-made to mock the limits of what Homer could see and know, a problem that would preoccupy his later biographers and critics to no end. It does so by playing on the invisibility of the tiny lice. If the boys could not see the lice, how could poor old Homer see them? Did the lice even exist? Or were they simply a pretext for pulling a quick one on Homer? However we view the story, in the version told by Alcidamas we have a joke that is being made at the expense of a hapless, destitute, and elderly Homer who was both mentally and physically blind. Heraclitus gave the riddle a philosophical spin, as one might only expect. From the context (the fragment is preserved by the Christian writer Hippolytus) we know that his version was meant to indict Homer for being hopelessly blind to the reality of appearances. But on any telling of the riddle, the divine Homer is being peremptorily brought down to the level of the all-too-human. Ignorant and easily duped, Homer proves that his own powers of perception are no keener than those of the rest of humankind.

Where Heraclitus got this embarrassing piece of information is another story. The likelihood is that the riddle of the lice as we know it from Alcidamas was already a staple of the popular traditions about Homer, in which case the fragment is further evidence that Homer's reputation was in a precarious state before Heraclitus arrived on the scene, a fact that is confirmed by earlier literature, as we will see in a moment. What is certain, however, is that by the sixth century Homer was completely identified with the whole of knowledge, so much so that to challenge traditional ways of knowing the world was to challenge Homer. The early Greek philosophers, the epistemological revolutionaries that they were, had no choice but to take aim at Homer. But neither did Homer come by his place of privilege without a struggle. In the first fragment by Heraclitus mentioned above, in which he recommends that Homer be beaten with his staff, Homer emerges in a context of literal contestation: poets competed for bragging rights, and Homer was no exception, nor did he always emerge victorious, as the *Contest of Homer and Hesiod* painfully brings to mind.

Looking further back, it seems evident that Homer's existence was assumed as a given at least by the middle of the seventh century if not already from the eighth. The traces are sparse and no doubt already contaminated with retrojected fantasy and in some cases projective ambition, but they are suggestive nonetheless. The earliest on record is an alleged reference by the mid-seventh-century poet Callinus, according to whom Homer was the author of an epic about Thebes called the *Thebaid*. Were the report more than secondhand (Pausanias is the source) and the attribution less suspect, this would constitute the first secure mention of Homer. Less specific and only slightly more reliable is an allusion contained in the *Homeric Hymn to Apollo,* which may have circulated under Homer's name from the first part of the sixth century. The poem mentions as its apparent author "a blind man [who] lives in rocky Chios [whose] poems will be the best forever" (172–73). Thucydides and others took this to refer to Homer, while later tradition saw this as an intrusion by a Homeric rhapsode from Chios named Cynaethus, who sought (it was claimed) to father the hymn on Homer by impersonating the poet. Nothing points to Homer as the author of this *Hymn,* let alone any of the thirty-two other so-called *Homeric Hymns* that have survived, despite their epic flavor. One final candidate for a first attestation of Homer is an approving reference to "the man of Chios," backed up by a pair of verses familiar from the *Iliad* (they come just shy of a quotation) that appear in a lyric poem of disputed authorship: it may be by Semonides (seventh century) or by Simonides (late sixth to early fifth century). While of dubious evidentiary value and thus of little help in pinpointing Homer before his first explicit and verifiable mention by Xenophanes, these traces do suggest that Homer was a celebrity from an early date and that poets, unlike philosophers, were keen to associate themselves with his name or aura, and so to attract some of his glory.

Homer had undeniable cachet. But with cachet comes envy, challenges to authority, rivalry, and even hostility. According to some traditions, Homer was exposed to such challenges in his own lifetime. In his lost dialogue *On Poets,* Aristotle recorded that Homer's authority was contested by an obscure contemporary, Syagrus. The grounds for the alleged dispute are not known, though elsewhere

Syagrus is said to have been the first to sing about the Trojan War, and so claims over originality if not plagiarism are as good a guess as any. But the quarrel can only have been as bitter as that between Xenophanes and Homer: "Syagrus quarreled with Homer while he was alive, and Xenophanes of Colophon quarreled with him after he had died." Another poet who is even less well attested than Syagrus, a certain Corinnus from Ilium (Troy), was said in some quarters to have been the first to produce an *Iliad*, which Homer subsequently lifted from him and smuggled into his own poetry.[6] Other figures, equally legendary and little more than names today (Cynaethus, Creophylus, Thestorides, Stasinus), illegitimately gathered together Homer's works and appropriated them in various ways, or so we are told.[7] Whether or not any of these stories are true (all of them sound suspiciously apocryphal), the simple fact that they could be imagined as true is what counts.

There is no question that Homer was from the first a celebrated *nonpareil*. This notwithstanding, the myth of Homer was a fragile one, and his grip on an uncontested legacy was anything but a foregone conclusion. In later times, the tendency to look for precursors and above all reputedly genuine eyewitnesses to the Trojan War flowered, especially in the Roman period between the first and third centuries CE. Three such eyewitness accounts stand out: *On the Destruction of Troy* attributed to the Phrygian (Trojan) fighter Dares, *Journal of the Trojan War* attributed to the Cretan Greek fighter Dictys, and the account by the epic hero Protesilaus as told by Philostratus in his *Heroicus*. While patently fictional documents, each of these works featured a participant in the Trojan War whose testimony was used to discredit and embarrass Homer. Protesilaus was a particularly strained but brilliantly exploited case. The first Greek to die at Troy, as he was setting foot on the Trojan shore, and mentioned only in passing in the *Iliad*, he can hardly have been an eyewitness to the war. And yet that is exactly how Philostratus represents him—as a character who exacts his revenge on Homer for having given him such short shrift (he figures in a paltry five verses in the Catalogue of Ships) and who later achieves quasi-divine status as a lingering ghost who knew more about the Trojan War than

Homer ever did. In contrast, Homer is portrayed as a mere mortal and, worse, as a dubious fictionalizer of what he never saw: Protesilaus pegs Homer's lifetime to the conventional date of 160 years after the war, while he himself can at least boast to have been its contemporary and, as a ghost endowed with supernatural powers that the mortal poet Homer lacked, a credible witness to the events at Troy.

These were not the only firsthand witnesses to be put forward in later periods as a way of impugning Homer's credentials and his testimony, though at stake was perhaps less Homer's credibility than the tremendous leap of faith that any reader had to make to believe any account of the epic past. And if any account was as reliable or unreliable as any other, why limit oneself to Homer? Either way, Homer's standing took a hit. In the Middle Ages, when Homer's texts had not yet reappeared in the West, the works by Dictys and Dares replaced Homer altogether. Fabulously popular and accessible in Latin, they gave new impetus to a counter-Homeric tradition in the vein of romance, of which Shakespeare's *Troilus and Cressida* is only the most famous example.

So much for the earliest overt or seemingly direct mentions of Homer. Prior to this, we find allusions to Homer even when we lack a name. But here too the results are mixed. The unhinged, ribald, and abusive iambographers or "blame poets"—Archilochus and Hipponax—and the great lyric poets from the seventh and sixth centuries—Stesichorus, Sappho, and Alcaeus—likewise challenged, reformed, and sometimes deformed Homeric motifs and values, whether openly, on the sly, or through formal experiments, not least by downsizing Homer. Simply to revisit an epic theme in a few slender lines was to make a statement about Homer, reducing his poetry to a mere thought—an idea—and then turning it this way or that. Casting their writing in a minor form allowed poets to sidestep the heroic posture of the *Iliad* and to discover an alternative first-person human voice to the impersonal divine voice of Homer, that unapproachable monument who was everywhere to be heard but nowhere to be seen. Achieving this kind of distinctiveness involved the creation of new contexts for poetic performance, typically on a more intimate scale, such as private drinking parties for male elites or, as in Sappho's case, a close-knit circle of female companions called a *thiasos*. But it also involved teasing out of epic some of its less than epic-seeming traits and, at a deeper level, some of its internal contradictions. Revision here meant reading Homer from a particular angle and viewing him in an altered light rather than aggressively rewriting his poems.

If Sappho put the value system and aesthetics of epic poetry in their place by subtly relativizing them ("Some men say an army of horse and some men say an army on foot / and some men say an army of ships is the most beautiful thing / on the black earth. *But I say it is what you love*"),[8] the abusive blame poets regularly featured overt debasements of Homeric values, the seeds of which were already sown in Homer. One such instance of a seemingly un-Homeric character in Homer is the upstart warrior Thersites, "the ugliest of the Achaeans," who is harshly beaten for his cheeky behavior by Odysseus in book 2 of the *Iliad*. Another is the figure of Odysseus himself, who appears in disguise as a beggar and a brawler in the *Odyssey*, while a third is the lame, limping, and banausic Hephaestus, who occasions gales of laughter among the gods in both poems. Odysseus in particular afforded a rich seam of unheroic conduct that was brilliantly suited to epic takedowns in later eras. The earliest known of these contrarians is Archilochus of Paros, a mid-seventh-century poet-soldier who boasted that he jettisoned his shield behind a bush in order to save his skin during a battle. He is followed by Hipponax, a contemporary of Heraclitus and a fellow Ephesian, whose fragments indicate an intense involvement with the underbelly of the epic poems.

A slight, ugly, and overall unappealing figure, at least in the eyes of his later readers, Hipponax appears to have made a career of assimilating the less flattering sides of Odysseus to his own poetic persona.[9] Of equal interest, he had a penchant for scenes that involved being beaten (*rhapizesthai*) by a stick or wand (*rhabdos*).[10] The resonances with Heraclitus can hardly be coincidental, though the language of both is derived from Homer's own in the *Odyssey* (Circe strikes Odysseus with her *rhabdos* in an attempt to transform him into a kept animal; Odysseus at one point flagellates himself in order to achieve the appearance of a beggar) and then is perversely made to undermine the dignity of epic. The proximity of Hipponax to Heraclitus is suggestive, to say the least.

Each of these early poets challenges the grandeur of Homer and his epics through implication and innuendo. Not so the lyric poet Stesichorus, who is the first openly revisionist poet in this counter-tradition and arguably its most outrageous instance. A close contemporary of Sappho's, the Italian-born Stesichorus (active from around the end of the seventh century into the mid-sixth century) was widely remembered for a poem possibly in two books and titled either *Helen* or *The Palinode*, in which he made the shocking assertion that Helen never went to Troy but instead sat out the war in Egypt while her phantom image took her place at Troy. Consequently, the war was waged for naught, and Homer, who may or may not have been directly named by Stesichorus but was certainly implied, was either ignorant of the truth or a liar. The key verses are quoted by Plato:

There's no truth to that story:
You never sailed that lovely ship,
You never reached the tower of Troy.[11]

But this is only half the story, because Stesichorus is correcting not only Homer but also himself. The details are sketchy, but if we put together a string of clues we can arrive at the following sequence. After repeating the accepted version of events about Helen's abduction to Troy ("that story" being the version told by Homer), Stesichorus states that Helen visited him in a dream to reveal his blasphemy against her and to punish him with blindness for his sin. Upon awakening, possibly with a theatrical flourish as he bolts up from his seat, the now-blind Stesichorus realizes his mistake and recants his earlier tale through a second song, called a "palinode," that begins more or less the way Plato reports it. Instantly, his eyesight is restored. Unfortunately for Homer, however, Stesichorus's disavowal of his own earlier account means disavowing Homer as well, who is left in the state he had always been: blind, ignorant of the truth, and unable to atone for his sins against Helen (as Plato says, "Homer did not know it, but Stesichorus did"). If this is correct, then Stesichorus will have produced—literally *staged*—a brilliant critique of Homer by enacting his own apostasy from Homer and invoking Helen's blessing in the bargain. Helen is now Stesichorus's Muse, and Stesichorus is the new anti-Homer. It is Homer who is blind, not Stesichorus. And it is Stesichorus who now "sees" and proclaims the divinely sanctioned truth.

Stesichorus's poem, composed some two to three generations before Xenophanes and Heraclitus, is surprisingly brazen for so early a date, and it had a devastating and durable impact on the credibility of Homer. Henceforth, the radical revision of Homer gained a kind of legitimacy and even came into vogue, though admittedly such malleability was written into the DNA of mythical narrative. No stories were so sacrosanct that they could not be retold from a new angle. No doubt the Homeric epics were themselves one such instance: we simply lack the background that would allow us to form a judgment. But why stop here? The earliest apparent comment on Homer is roughly as old as Homer's poems themselves in their monumental form, and it is one of the oldest preserved examples of Greek literacy at that: "Nestor's Cup," found in a necropolis on Ischia and dated to around the end of the eighth century. The cup proclaims its ownership in a verse inscription carved on the face of its bowl: "I am the cup of Nestor, a cup good to drink from. / Whoever drinks from this cup / the desire of fair-crowned Aphrodite will seize immediately."[12] Is the object alluding to Nestor's cup in *Iliad* 11, as most scholars believe, or is it pointing to a myth that Homer would also have known?

Either way, a contrast is intended. The cup is modest and diminutive, remarkable for its lightness of weight and delicacy of construction. The hero's cup of the *Iliad* was golden, ornate, and baroque (it was fitted out with marvelous dove wings for handles), and legendary for its enormous size and heft: "only that great hero [Nestor] could lift it with ease" to his waiting lips "when it was full," while others struggled just to lift it off the table (*Iliad* 11.632–36).

The cup from Ischia, made of humble earthenware but finely manufactured and carefully incised with calligraphic lettering, is inviting, not resisting; it is "good" to drink from (*eupoton*) and may even be "easy" to lift and obtain pleasure from, if that is one of the connotations of the Greek. A diminutive alter ego of a famous epic object, with its three skinny verses that start off in lowly trimeters and are completed by epic hexameters, the cup from Ischia stands at the foot of a long tradition that cuts Homer down to size: it is already a piece of revisionism. The object knowingly places itself at the margins of the still (or newly) nascent Homeric tradition.

Whether the Italian object is the incarnation of a joke (not everyone agrees, but the skeptics are in the minority),[13] it is at least lighthearted and playful, and it activates a cascade of incongruities—of scale and luxury (a larger-than-life cup is being compared to a small, everyday object), of time frames (the mythical past is being brought rudely into the domestic present), and of genre (martial epic intrudes into the world of erotic and sympotic poetry). To be sure, the cup is in a sense simply reverse engineering the mechanisms of epic, which made similar importations of its own. Nestor, after all, drinks festively on the battlefield with this very sort of cup, and Homeric stories about gods and heroes from the misty Bronze Age past were sung in convivial settings for the pleasure of mere mortals in the less enchanted Iron Age present, a fact that ought to be taken into account whenever we wonder about the dissonances of Homer's poems: here, we can see that a cognitive dissonance is hardwired into the experience of those poems at the moment of their performance. It remains to be seen how Homer exploits that dissonance in his descriptions of warfare, a question to which we will return in the concluding chapter of this study.

Over the centuries, the incongruities of Homer's version of Nestor's cup generated increasing disquiet among readers: it became a classic "Homeric problem" in its own right. What were its dimensions? How much did it weigh? What did it look like? Did its golden dove-wing handles represent a cosmic allegory of some kind? In the fifth and fourth centuries, a series of distinguished names (Stesimbrotus, Glaucon, Antisthenes, and Aristotle) are known to have probed and prodded this textual object. They were followed by the Alexandrian and post-Alexandrian grammatical spin-offs (no major philologist failed to address it), all of which made Nestor's cup one of the most talked-about puzzles in Homer. But all this was mere academic speculation. If you really wanted to know the truth about Nestor's cup in Homer, you simply had to go to Capua in Campania in Italy, where you could see the original cup on display in the temple of Artemis, or so it was said.[14] And yet, as puzzling as the cup of Nestor was, no puzzle was greater or more insoluble than that of Homer himself.

## Cults and Cultivation

The main question that dogged Homer's identity was unanswerable by definition: Was Homer a god, godlike, an ordinary mortal, or—worse—a godless poet whose poems were full of impieties, errors, inconsistencies, and incredible nonsense? As we have begun to see, opinions were divided. They existed in that form from Homer's earliest mentions, and they remained so for the rest of time. The official line was that Homer was indeed divine, or at least godlike, given that he was a privileged conduit of the holy Muses. From Aristophanes to elementary classrooms in later antiquity, the official watchword drummed into the minds of all Greeks was the affirmation that "Homer is a god, not a man." This last sentence appears in a set of Greek writing exercises on a clay shard from third-century CE Egypt (Karanis). A nearly identical statement is found on a wax tablet that was used in a Greek schoolroom from the Roman period, and we can be certain that the practice was repeated throughout the Greco-Roman world from an early date.[15] Homer's divinity was also the theme of countless epigrams, for example the anonymous poem from the *Greek Anthology* that Ingres inscribed on his monument to Homer in 1827: "If Homer is a god, let him be revered as one of the immortals; but if he is not a god, let him be believed to be one."[16]

These venerable sentiments found concrete expression in the numerous cults and shrines to Homer that were scattered across the ancient world. Though other poets enjoyed such posthumous honors, Homer nevertheless stood out. He was frequently likened to an Olympian god, and in places he was actually worshipped as one—for instance in Argos, where a bronze statue of "the godly Homer" was said to have been erected with sacrifices made to him "daily, monthly, and yearly," while every fifth year a sacrifice was sent from Argos to Chios, Homer's putative birthplace.[17] Shrines and sanctuaries devoted to Homer and built around a cult statue of the poet existed in at least five other cities, from Hellenistic Smyrna to Alexandria. Whether cult activity occurred in these settings and, if so, what form it took is unclear. The distinction between religious cult and literary cultivation was in any case thin. At Delos, Homer's texts, inscribed on white wooden boards, were deposited in the shrine like the sacred relics they were.[18]

The most famous of the visual representations of Homer today is the Hellenistic relief sculpture by Archelaus of Priene, known as the *Apotheosis of Homer,* which, as we have already seen, formed the basis of Ingres's nineteenth-century painting of the same title. The original is now kept in the British Museum. Its surface is worn, and the engraving by Giovanni Battista Galestruzzi, made at the time of its discovery in 1658 some ten miles south of Rome, preserves a level of detail that is no longer visible in the sculpture (fig. 3.1). Galestruzzi's engraving was one of several used by Ingres as he went about designing his own *Apotheosis*. The conception underlying Archelaus's and Ingres's *Apotheosis* is identical: both artists show Homer being canonized for all time on the threshold of divinity. But the way each executes that idea separates them by a chasm. In both works, Homer is seated on a throne, a book roll resting on his lap and his customary staff (*rhabdos*), with which Heraclitus would have him beaten, now assuming the appearance of a massive kingly scepter. But here the similarities end. Where Ingres's painting presents a historical pageant, frozen in time like a *tableau vivant* that nevertheless makes visual contact with the present, the ancient relief sculpture is self-absorbed in the ritualistic and ceremonial drama that unfolds on its surface, even as the real drama lies in the elaborate exchange between persons and ideas that controls the

FIGURE 3.1. Giovanni Battista Galestruzzi, *The Apotheosis of Homer* (1658). After Archelaus of Priene, *The Apotheosis of Homer* (late third to early second century BCE). Engraving. Thorvaldsens Museum. Inv. no. E1479.

work's visual rhythms: the work gives us an allegory that is at once concrete and abstract. A bull is being led forth to an altar as a sacrificial offering. Facing the poet are his several worshippers, hands raised in a salute, each a personification of the literary genres that he inspired (Myth, History, Poetry, Tragedy, and Comedy), and a series of other allegorical figures besides, including worldly Time (*Chronos*) and Space (*Oikoumenē*), who crown and anoint Homer from behind. These last two figures are identifiable, for those in the know, as portraits of the royal king and queen, Ptolemy IV (Philopator) and Arsinoë III, who together ruled Egypt from 222 to 204 BCE. Indeed, the whole of the monument's design resembles a universal code for the learned.

Kneeling by Homer's side are his two epic poems, likewise personified and captioned with their titles, as in Ingres's painting. Apollo and the nine Muses stand in the second and third registers, representing poetic song. Zeus and Memory (the mother of the Muses) occupy the apex of the sculpture, representing divine inspiration and authority. At Homer's feet, two mice are nibbling on either end of a papyrus scroll, which is sometimes thought to represent the *Battle of Frogs and Mice*, a lighthearted mock-epic poem that continued to be listed among Homer's canonical titles in the Roman period (the title accurately conveys its gist). A lowly work, it would rightfully occupy the bottom rung of the sculpture. If the scroll does not allude to this work, then the nibbling mice can only represent the potential for mortal decay or some other depredation such as criticism or neglect, threats to which not even the deified Homer was ever completely immune.[19] But this is not the only potential complication that bears on the meaning of the monument. Homer's placement in the design and the very pyramidal form of the sculpture also need to be taken into account. Doing so will permit us to ask whether Homer here is in fact being made into a god. The answer is less obvious than it might at first appear.

Despite the relief's modern title, which is at best a guess, the scenario depicts not so much an apotheosis as an induction into literary immortality and a coronation for Homer. Homer may represent the pinnacle of human literary achievement, but he does not occupy the pinnacle of the monument. Rather, he is situated at the ground level of the image a full two and a half registers beneath Zeus and Memory, who hold court atop the pyramid that resembles a mountain (Mount Olympus? Helicon, the Mountain of the Muses? Or the sacred shrine to the Muses, the Ptolemaic Museum, figuratively perched above the Library of Alexandria represented by the literary genres below?). The two gods trade fond glances with each other but are completely oblivious to the goings-on beneath them, the coronation of Homer included. For all his cultic attributes, Homer in the end seems to belong firmly to this lower world and its inhabitants and not to some celestial realm above. Crowned by this-worldly space and time, he lives on in those elements. And yet in that form he was treated as a god.[20] Perhaps what really is being portrayed in this allegorical work, bursting as it is with personified abstractions, is not the deification of Homer but his "idea-ification," his coronation as an idea. It is a celebration of the idea of Homer.

Dated to sometime between the late third to late second century BCE, the relief is at once extravagant and bookish.[21] As such, it celebrates the monumental status of Homer as he appeared to the Hellenistic world under Alexander's dynastic heirs, the Ptolemies—namely, as the fountain of Greek literature and indeed of all Greek culture. But it does so from the perspective of the learning that surrounded Homer on a grand institutional scale, most famously at Alexandria in Egypt, the new political and cultural capital of the Greco-Roman Mediterranean. Alexandria was the seat of the famed library of Greek literature and of the research center attached to it, the Museum, so named because it was originally conceived as a shrine to the Muses and never lost its formal cultic functions. Both institutions were literally built on Homeric foundations: Alexandria was the official repository of the texts of Homer, and it was on the basis of Homeric studies that the ancient methods of editing, reading, and commenting on texts in all genres evolved (principally those named on Archelaus's sculptural relief). As the relief so well illustrates, scholarship and religious worship were united as one in their veneration of Homer. To annotate Homer was to cultivate his image. It was to sing the praises of the Muses in the medium of academic prose.

That, at least, is the Alexandrian perspective. Outside their cloistered world, things could have a very different look. Timon of Phlius, a satirist with skeptical leanings from the third century BCE, mocked "the many tribes of well-fed bookworms incessantly wrangling in the bird-cage of the Muses," meaning the mostly foreign-born scholars who enjoyed tax-exempt tenure, meals, and dyspeptic quarrels at the Library. Timon further added that if you wanted a good text of Homer you had better find a pristine copy, one that had not yet been corrected—that is, ruined—by scholars. Later on, the notion that the Alexandrian scholars had blackened the margins of inferior lines of Homer with their restless reed pens became a joke and a cliché among the Romans.[22] Critiques of the institution that had enshrined Homer naturally devolved into critiques of the cult figure of Homer himself. According to Aelian, the painter Galaton once depicted Homer sick and vomiting up gobbets of his own poetry, while other poets, stationed around him and representing different genres, eagerly drew upon his vomit for themselves. Complicating matters, the painting was said to have been located in the fabled but vanished temple to Homer, built by none other than Ptolemy IV, at the heart of the Library of Alexandria around the same time as Archelaus produced his *Apotheosis of Homer*. At the center of this shrine stood a statue of the poet encircled by all the cities that had ever laid claim to him (probably seven, the canonical number). While the temple was real (it may even be alluded to in the Archelaus relief), the story about Galaton may well be apocryphal, a spoof on the much-repeated trope that Homer was the sublime Ocean from which all other lesser poetic rivers and rivulets flowed.[23]

Whatever the case, the image seems to have stuck. In one of his writings, Lucian shows a seasick Homer vomiting up his verses while being ferried by Charon to the Underworld. Charon, that unofficial god of posterity, gathers up these remainders like a latter-day Pisistratus, and then claims to salvage them, in effect with his memory but in reality by some other, less savory means.[24] A later Greek commentator can barely control his outrage: "Get a load of the way this buffoon touches to the quick what is holiest to the Greeks with his raillery."[25] In both Lucian and Aelian, the clash of competing registers is striking: Homer is simultaneously being shown to be elevated (godlike and revered) and debased (godforsaken and mortal), unable to contain his own Ocean of poetry.

These are two striking examples of the way Homer could simultaneously appear as the highest and the lowest of ancient cultural commodities imaginable, though neither example outbids the account of Homer's final moments on earth as told in the *Contest of Homer and Hesiod*. There, recall, Homer embarrasses himself with the children's riddle of the lice, slips ignominiously in the mud, and then in a last desperate act seeks to shore up his reputation by composing his own tomb inscription, literally writing himself into literary history the way he wishes to be remembered, as a hero among poets: "Here the earth covered over that sacred head, / marshaller of warrior heroes, divine Homer." Ingres's *Apotheosis* is happy to foreground Homer's epitaph, which is, to be sure, heroic and glorious sounding (perhaps a bit less so, given that Homer wrote it for himself). But his painting leaves out all the sordid details that made this epitaph possible and indeed made the final scene of the *Contest* one of the most memorable and quotable, but also the most hotly debated, elements of the legends surrounding Homer in antiquity.

The riddle of the lice and the oracle warning Homer of its dangers were nearly as famous as Homer himself. Both were repeated or mentioned in a vast quantity of learned poems and prose writings, including the *Lives,* and they found their way into visual media too: the oracle was engraved on a statue of Homer at Delphi (Pausanias saw it), and the riddle appears on a Pompeian wall painting, a fresco, that captures the scene's climax (fig. 3.2), with Homer holding court on a throne, a pensive finger pressed against his lips as he ponders an answer and glares fiercely at the two rascals standing before him, one of whom is uttering the riddle, his mouth open and his right arm gesticulating gamely. The riddle itself appears below the painting like a caption. The Pompeian image has all the trappings

FIGURE 3.2. *Homer and the Fisher Boys*. Pompeian wall painting from the House of Epigrams, as drawn by Carl Dilthey (1876b). From *Monumenti inediti pubblicati dell'Instituto di corrispondenza archeologica/Monuments inédits publiés par l'Institut de correspondance archéologique* 10 (1874–1878), Tav. XXXV.2. Credit: Deutsches Archäologisches Institut, Rom.

of an *Apotheosis*. The identical allegorical accoutrements that figure in the painting—the throne, the pedestal, the column behind, the sword, and the oar or rudder—also appear on a Roman silver cup from the same period. All these insignia are familiar from the *Apotheosis* by Archelaus (where a prow ornament takes the place of the oar/rudder), and all make up the key insignia of Ingres's painting as well. But in reality, the Pompeian fresco depicts an *anti*-apotheosis scene if there ever was one: it subverts that genre entirely.

If the canonization of this final episode of Homer's life seems puzzling and even disturbing to us today, we are not alone. It was a source of controversy in antiquity too, an irritant that produced a good deal of head-scratching and an equal amount of creative speculation. Exactly why did Homer die when and as he did? The question was put by scholars and poets, and they outbid one another in an effort to propose a winning solution. Homer was obviously aged, weak, and possibly sick, some said. He died from grief and shame, others insisted. In one extreme case, he was said to have blinded himself out of embarrassment and then, utterly depressed, proceeded to take his own life—a neat if somewhat sensational solution to the question of Homer's final demise, as it bundled up a few different Homeric problems in one convenient package. But it was no more or less credible than any of the other explanations that had been put up for sale.[26]

The closing scene from the *Contest* compressed into a single baffling snapshot the lowest and highest points of Homer's career as this came to be imagined in antiquity. At stake was not only the biographical problem of reconciling Homer's status as an immortal poet with his origins as a flesh-and-blood individual, a puzzle that was on full display here at his life's miserable terminus. The final episode makes palpable another perplexing question that is of equal importance to grasping the problem of Homer. The Homer of the *Contest* stands on the cusp of orality and literacy: he sings and he writes, and in his final act he seems, inexplicably, to do both things at once—his voice becomes an inscribed epitaph (an *epigramma*), though how this happens is left undisclosed. The scene is symbolic, above all in its failure to spell out the details that would illuminate this process of transcription. At some point, Homer's poems became fixed texts. How and when they did was and still is a riddle of its own. (Dictation, the poet's own literacy, and posthumous collecting and editing were among the ancient rival explanations, and they remain this today.) But once the poems became texts, an odd reversal took place: Homer's godlike audible voice was lost the moment it was immortalized in a written form, while his words, once they appeared in a material medium, became subject to every kind of scrutiny and alteration imaginable. Immortality had its costs, and Homer paid for it dearly.

## Homer in Prose

As Homer left behind the world of *epos* and entered the world of literary history, he underwent what the twentieth-century Russian literary critic Mikhail Bakhtin calls a radical "novelization."[27] The point is not that the Homeric poems were transformed into novels, though eventually they were, but rather that they became available to a new and different kind of renewal: they came into direct contact with temporal change and history. Following a somewhat dated and Romantic view of literary evolution, Bakhtin insists that Homer's poems originally appeared as if they had been frozen in time, "walled off absolutely" from all subsequent epochs in an unreachably remote and hallowed past. As such, they could be observed and admired but not touched or manipulated, while Homer was correspondingly both exalted and felt to be strangely alien. Starting with Plato's dialogues, the epics were forcibly brought into communication with the present and with the radically fluctuating stream of time itself. As appurtenances of the living moment, and not only as tokens of the bygone past, Homer's poems could be brought out of the sanctuary and into a "zone of contact" where they could be scrutinized from up close, taken apart, criticized, manipulated, travestied, parodied, and incorporated into the unfinished business of the present and the *prose du monde*. In a word, the epics of the glorious past became *modern*. Much of the story of Homer's afterlife is precisely a story of this contamination by the present.

Bakhtin's theory is too simplistic, but it contains a useful core that can be directed back at Homer and then forward again in the literature he spawned. Epic poetry was never absolutely sacrosanct; it was always subject to the forces of "novelization." Novelty and revision from one performance setting to another were the expectation *du jour,* and no two performances even by the same poet can ever have been identical. We have this on the authority of Telemachus, who in the first book of the *Odyssey* notes how audiences "always give more applause to that song / which is the latest to circulate among the listeners" (1.351–52). The *Odyssey* seems to be one such song itself, and Telemachus's remark merely serves to underwrite the poem's own claims to novelty. From a distance of several millennia the epics may give the impression of monumental immobility, but this is to confuse the realities they projected (the heroic world viewed as it were *sub specie aeternitatis*) with the ways in which they did so (those same worlds brought to life for immediate consumption and from the perspective of audiences in the here and now). Canonicity is not the same as inviolability.[28]

The sanctity of epic is further belied by its lighter and self-questioning elements, some of which were noted in passing above in connection with the later blame poets, and which can only have contributed to the appeal and durability of the epic poems. The poems survived not because they lacked polyphony—or, as one influential view would have it, because in Homer "men say the same things about the same things, and so the world to them . . . is one"—but because they were complex and deeply self-reflexive works of art that interacted with other genres of discourse whose traces have all but disappeared.[29] It is unlikely, for instance, that poetry of abuse ("blame poetry") was born in the seventh century (the scabrous antihero Thersites in the *Iliad* hints at the availability of the genre in Homer's day, as do other aspects of both poems). Lyric and other kinds of poetry in different registers (hymns, prayers, parables, threnodies and laments), as well as popular, folkloric forms (proverbs, gnomic utterances, riddles, the miraculous and the fantastic), must have existed prior to epic as well, likewise leaving deposits in Homer's verses.[30] Consequently, novelization in Bakhtin's sense is best seen as part of an internal dialectic that operates within and not just on epic poetry. If this interanimation of literary and other forms of expression is partly concealed from view today, we can thank the chance survival of Homer and the loss of contemporary and earlier literature in another key as the causes. Later authors working in a "novelistic" vein saw and exploited these potentials in the Homeric poems, whether it was to undermine those poems or simply to amplify the tensions that made them as interesting as they were.

If we ask when Homer first came to be "novelized" in Bakhtin's terms, the answer has to include the blame poets like Archilochus or Hipponax but also the philosophical critiques of Homer, at first in poetry (Xenophanes) and then in prose (Heraclitus and his successors). The philosophers performed the same kind of work as the blame poets: they interfered with Homer. The "prosification" of Homer in the narrower sense blossomed in the fifth century, once prose became the default medium of communication. This was the time when sophists from Protagoras in the mid-fifth century to Zoilus in the next began to question the coherence and defensibility of Homer's poems in maximally intrusive ways.

Examined from up close, Homer's texts revealed a minefield of problems, starting at the surface level. The poetry was littered with words that were no longer current and whose meanings were now obscure or opaque: they had to be either "glossed" (translated into current Greek) or else dismissed as insoluble. Once more, we find a double-edged paradox at work: the same features that lent Homer an aura of indefeasible grandeur could have the opposite effect, rendering him alien- and primitive-sounding, not to say barbaric. Drilling down, there were contradictions in Homer's tellings that had become glaringly apparent. Why, for instance, does Homer say of the division of the universe among the three principal Olympian gods, Zeus, Poseidon, and Hades, "All was divided . . . three ways" (*Iliad* 15.189), when a few lines later he says, "But earth and high Olympos are common to all three"? Stesimbrotus, little more than a shadow today, introduced the problem. Later writers clashed over the answer. Why, Aristotle asks (reporting an anonymous question), did Homer call Ganymede a "wine-pourer" for the gods, when the gods drink nectar, not wine?

These were the easy targets. But Homer's fifth- and fourth-century critics were not content to unearth real or apparent problems that lay on or just below the surface of the texts. Instead, they went out of their way to manufacture specious (non-)problems for the sake of throwing up objections to Homer, usually en route to other ends. Protagoras famously censured Homer for having blundered in the opening verse of the *Iliad*: the poet "thinks he is beginning with a prayer" when he beseeches the Muse with a polite request, but he is unwittingly commanding her when he says, "*Sing*, goddess, the wrath."[31] A confusion at the level of grammar, the mistake hints at a deeper impiety. It is doubtful that Protagoras really believed that Homer was blaspheming divinity any more than Stesichorus did earlier when he accused himself and, by implication, Homer of this charge. On the contrary, Homer was no more than a convenient foil, in Protagoras's case for making a novel linguistic argument about the existence of different classes of utterance (assertions, questions, commands, and wishes—"speech acts," as these are called today) that until then had been used but never named as such. Dragging Homer into the discussion made Protagoras's discovery that much more memorable. It is the reason we know about it at all today.

Protagoras was followed by Zoilus of Amphipolis, a Cynic and contemporary of Plato, who earned the nickname *Homeromastix* or "Scourge of Homer" (a *mastix* is a whip), although he had more in common with Heraclitus, one of Homer's earliest thrashers, than he did with Protagoras. Zoilus's writings included a treatise, possibly in nine books, called *Against the Poetry of Homer* and another called *Censure of Homer*. He had a knack for locating not so much embarrassing difficulties or contradictions as actual absurdities in Homer. At one point, he poked fun at the opening of book 5 of the *Iliad*, where Athena magnifies the terrifying appearance of the Greek warrior Diomedes by causing flames to shoot from his helmet and shield. Zoilus found all this "quite ridiculous," for the hero could have caught fire! When Zeus placed the two fates in his golden scales to determine the outcome of the final combat between Achilles and Hector in *Iliad* 22, Zoilus wondered aloud, "And how did the fates look? Were they sitting or standing?" The list of Homer's offenses goes on, but let's conclude with one final example. Zoilus called Odysseus's crew, "kept as pigs in Circe's palace" in book 10 of the *Odyssey* and bemoaning unheroically their unheroic lot, "whining porkers." Remarkably, it is Longinus, the great champion of the "sublime" Homer, who preserves this comment by Zoilus, and he approves of it too.[32]

Plainly, contending over and with Homer was a productive source of cultural change and renewal. Not only was it possible for the present to change; as it did, the look of the past changed as well. Once these and other similar objections to Homer entered the tradition, they became the catalysts of entire new genres of inquiry into Homer's texts that went by such titles as "Homeric Problems" or "Questions and Solutions." (These are to be distinguished from the Homeric Question, which touched Homer's person, his titles, and the origins of both, not the philological puzzles presented by his texts when read.) The academic versions of these inquiries into Homer could be just as captious as the more hilarious and carping kind. They simply had a different end goal—appeasing the grammatical and literary-critical conscience rather than provoking peals of laughter. Nevertheless, both kinds of observation fall neatly under Bakhtin's category of "novelization." In both cases, Homer's poetry was being made into an object of close, critical viewing and prodding, mere grist for the mill of academic and pseudo-academic prose. Simply to draw Homer near and move him into the present was enough to trouble the automatic reflex of treating the poet as remote, inaccessible, and sacrosanct among those readers whom Protagoras and Zoilus set out to shock.

But how automatic was this reflex, in point of fact? As it happens, the two responses of approval and criticism could coexist side by side, not infrequently in the same author and even in the same work. Aristotle in his *Poetics* recognized that Homer teaches poets how to "lie as they should," but this does not detract one iota from his preeminence as the prince of poets.[33] Longinus adored Homer, but he nevertheless seconded Zoilus's opinion about the *Odyssey* and used it to illustrate "how easy it is for great genius to be perverted in decline into nonsense," as Homer had done in his dotage when he composed what Longinus and others deemed to be his—at times senile—*Spätwerk* (9.14).[34] Dio Chrysostom wrote two tracts about Homer, one praising him to the skies (*On Homer*), the other damning him for all eternity (*Trojan Oration*). The *Lives* could be hagiographic, but they also gave some of the most humanizing accounts of Homer known to antiquity. Think back to the contrasts at the close of the *Contest*, how within the space of a few short lines Homer is shown to be a mortal fool and then a godly poet ("the divine Homer" of his epitaph), while all the events in his life leading up to this diminuendo-crescendo are equally uneven: Homer is made to wander aimlessly, ignorant of his own identity, destitute, dependent on the kindness of strangers for bed and board, but also shown to be the greatest of poets and accorded the highest of honors (statues, dedications, and other trappings typically reserved for gods and heroes). Then of course there is Plato, who claims to admire Homer as much as any Greek did, though he could find no place for him in his model republic, Callipolis. He could not decide whether Homer was divinely inspired, a victim of madness, or just deluded.

We also have Plato to thank for the first prose translation of Homer, an accomplishment for which he has yet to be given credit. In a pioneering discussion of Homer's narrative styles and his manipulation of the speaker's voice, Socrates notes how Homer "conceals himself" behind a veil of mimesis for much of his poems by impersonating the voices of his own characters like a dramatist, a procedure that Socrates condemns as morally harmful: it is a form of deception and an evasion of personal responsibility. Third-person narration in the poet's own voice ("if the poet never concealed himself" and spoke not as his characters "but as Homer") would have been preferable, though hardly exculpatory. To prove the point,

Socrates volunteers a rendition in prose of a portion of *Iliad* 1. The result is a literal revision—a rewriting and abridgment—of Homer:

> It would have gone something like this—I'll do it without metre, for I'm no poet. "The priest came and prayed that the gods might grant them to capture Troy and return home safely. . . . Most of them respected his words and were ready to agree, but Agamemnon was angry, telling him to go away and never come back. . . . Hearing this, Chryses was frightened and went silently away, but when he had left the camp he prayed long to Apollo . . . to avenge his tears on the Greeks with his arrows."
>
> (*Republic* 3.393d–394a; trans. Russell)

In this effort to chase the poet out of hiding, Plato effectively eliminates his *raison d'être* as a poet. In the process, all the signal features of Homer's poetry are cast to the winds—inspiration, possession, song, and rhythm ("for I'm no poet," Socrates apologizes)—leaving a page of compressed plot summary written in the dullest possible prose.

This is novelization done by the book. A few centuries on, this kind of rewriting would become a recognizable genre unto itself: the *hypothesis*, or plot summary, produced in prose by editors from Alexandria and then later by schoolteachers and appended to the beginning of literary texts (Homer's included), telling readers what they should expect from the work they were about to read, and in principle replacing the work they preface. Many plot summaries eventually did just that when their bigger sibling, the epitome, became a popular way to absorb classical knowledge. Why trudge through all 15,600-some verses of the *Iliad* or all 12,000-some verses of the *Odyssey* when you can read the CliffsNotes versions in a fraction of the time? Whimsy is not to be excluded from some of these paraliterary gestures any more than it is from Plato: both knowingly subvert what they advertise, bringing themselves and Homer down to the ground floor of cultural experience, not unlike the productions of the Reduced Shakespeare Company today.

Whittling Homer down to size was, as we saw, the hallmark of earlier Greek lyric revisions of Homer. But perhaps no reduction was greater than the tour de force compression of the entire plot of the *Iliad* into a few spare lines of prose and a single image that Metrodorus of Lampsacus seems to have produced at the end of the fifth century. A pupil of the natural philosopher Anaxagoras, who was known for his physicalist reductions of the universe, Metrodorus stated that the *Iliad* was little more than a vehicle for representing the physical universe: Agamemnon is the aether, Achilles the sun, Helen the earth, Alexander the air, Hector the moon, and so on. With these equivalencies in place, we can visualize a compact image that contains the whole of the poem's plot: Helen (earth), occupying the center, is embraced by Alexander (air), while the planets circle around them both, with Achilles, his armor "shining like the sun," pursuing and eclipsing Hector (the moon), as Agamemnon (divine aether) pervades and governs the totality of the action, giving it its purpose.[35] Usually understood as an experiment in allegory and an attack on literal meaning, Metrodorus's account reads more like a lighthearted subversion of Homer's expansive grandeur, undertaken more as a proof of concept than as a serious contribution to philosophy, which it clearly is not.

From the foregoing discussion, we can see how the canonical figure of Homer spawned a literature in both poetry and prose that was often minor, marginal, and paraliterary, whether this took the form of highbrow technical disquisitions (glosses, commentaries, problems and solutions, historical inquiries, and the like) or lowerbrow knockoffs, which is to say pseudo-versions of these academic studies. An early example after the fourth century was mentioned earlier, Hermesianax of Colophon's poem *Leontion*, which pretends to explain why Homer made Penelope the central figure of the *Odyssey*: he fell in love with her and moved to Ithaca; the rest is history. Hermesianax was competing with the tradition of the *Lives*, which could propose alternative facts that were just as questionable or scandalous, for instance the assertion that Homer introduced the Ithacan named Mentor into the *Odyssey* as a sign of gratitude for having nursed him when his eyesight began to fail as he was conducting research on Odysseus, or that Homer's parents were Telemachus and Polycaste, a daughter of Nestor's, which made Homer Odysseus's grandson and a kinsman of Nestor.

Much of this later "prosification" involved attacking Homer indirectly by taking aim at Homeric scholarship. Chief among these minor works written seemingly from the margins are the *Battle of Frogs and Mice,* the hilarious yet learned mock-heroic send-up in Homeric hexameters from the late Hellenistic or Augustan period (even its title in Greek is an absurd and unpronounceable collision of three nouns: *Batrachomyomachia,* "Frogmousebattle"); Ptolemy Chennus's *Paradoxical History*; Dio Chrysostom's *Trojan Oration*; Lucian's *A True Story*; and Philostratus's *Heroicus.* All of these works (apart from the *Battle of Frogs and Mice*) are in prose, date from the Roman imperial period (first to third century CE), and turn Homer on his head.[36] Later imperial epic poets such as Quintus of Smyrna, Nonnus, and Christodorus, writing in the third to fifth century, actually claimed Homer as their "father." But while they may have been extending Homer's lineage and legacy, they often did so in a deviant fashion, for instance by constructing lipogrammatic versions of both epics by omitting the letter alpha in book 1 ("book alpha"), the letter beta in book 2 ("book beta"), and so on. (Conveniently, each epic contains as many books as the Greek alphabet has letters.) These may have been Homer's children, but they were also his disobedient progeny.[37]

The paraliterary and parodic treatments of Homer are difficult to evaluate. Are they a sign of esteem or perhaps even awe, however awkwardly expressed or disguised, or are they a sign of ridicule and disdain? It seems clear enough that the majority of these works are directed not at Homer but at Homer's readers and the cultural fetishism that grew up around him, be this in grammar schools, among professional grammarians, or among greedy book collectors and Homer-obsessed antiquarians—that is, whenever Homer wasn't being made to stand in for poetry *tout court,* as he was among the ancient moralizers, from Xenophanes to Plato and

Plutarch. In other words, the butt of these critiques is not Homer but something much larger and of even greater cultural significance: his idea.

## Transition to Modernity

As should be evident by now, Homer enjoyed a divided afterlife: his reception—by which we should understand his repeated reimagining—was truly bipolar, from the first preserved mentions of his name to the end of antiquity and from there into modernity, once the manuscripts of the *Iliad* and *Odyssey* resurfaced in Renaissance Europe. This ended the hiatus of the Latin Middle Ages, when direct knowledge of Homer and the Greek language had been all but extinguished. One of the key turning points was the decision by Petrarch, the Italian poet and scholar, to read Homer. Despite being unable to read Greek, he obtained manuscript copies of the Greek texts in 1353–1354 and soon afterward commissioned a Latin translation of both poems from Leontius Pilatus, a Greek-speaking Italian. Pilatus's crabbed prose translations, completed in 1362, were replaced by more competent Latin translations in 1474 and 1497 and by printed scholarly editions of the Greek originals in 1488, 1504, and 1517. The first critical edition followed in 1566. Homer was now reborn in the West—not as a pristine poet but freighted with inherited baggage. With the transmission of Homer came the transmission of the paraliterature on Homer. Renaissance poets and scholars built on these ancient precedents and put them to new uses. It did not take long for the recriminations to begin again, proving the well-established rule of thumb that with veneration comes envy, suspicion, and hostility.

In 1527, Marcus Girolamo Vida published a didactic poem, *De arte poetica* (*On the Art of Poetry*), in which he unceremoniously pushed Homer aside to make a space for neo-Latin writing modeled after Vergil, now in a Christianizing spirit. He was outdone by the Renaissance humanist scholar Julius Caesar Scaliger, who in his own *Poetics* from 1561 mercilessly skewered Homer, preferring the urbane and polished Vergil to his vulgar and immoral Greek predecessor. Although there was never a time when the otherwise divine Homer was deemed ineligible as a target of satire and irreverent wit, a visible uptick in this trend occurs in eighteenth- and nineteenth-century Europe, especially in France and England. Much of the early modern period was absorbed in the so-called *Querelle des Anciens et des Modernes* (Quarrel of the Ancients and the Moderns), with Homer occupying a place of honor as the Ancient par excellence. For the Moderns, this meant that Homer was the scapegoat par excellence. The Quarrel's final phase in France, sparked by Dacier's new translation, was even dubbed "The Quarrel over Homer," so intensely did the contest of opinions turn around the poet's evaluation and devaluation.

Jonathan Swift's irreverent mock-epic in prose, *The Battle of the Books* (1704), stages the Quarrel as a war waged among the holdings in the King's Library, figured as a modern-day Alexandria of sorts, with each camp fiercely trying to erase the others' pages and Homer leading the charge of the ancients in what proved to be a fruitless skirmish. In 1716, Pierre Marivaux, moved to disdain by Anne Dacier's attack against his comrade in arms Houdar de la Motte, published a burlesque travesty of Homer's *Iliad* in verse (*Homère travesti, ou l'Iliade en vers burlesques*). His main brief was that "Homer is a terrible person; he ruins the reason of better minds." To prove the point, he rewrote Homer in the most vulgar language he could muster after consulting Homer's shade and securing its approval. In 1716, George Duckett and Thomas Burnet published *Homerides; or, Homer's First Book Moderniz'd* under the pseudonym of Sir Iliad Doggerel. The work was ostensibly an attack on Pope's new translation of the *Iliad*, but Homer was the collateral damage. In the same vein, Thomas Bridges's *A Burlesque Translation of Homer* (1762; 2nd ed., 1772), modeled as much on *Tristram Shandy* as on Homer, argued tongue in cheek that Homer had himself composed his poem as a burlesque and that a more "literal translation" than Pope's—his own—could prove the case beyond a shadow of a doubt. A few years on, Jacob Bryant published a learned but fanciful disquisition titled *A Dissertation Concerning the War of Troy and the Expedition of the Grecians, As Described by Homer; Shewing That*

*No Such Expedition Was Ever Undertaken, and That No Such City of Phrygia Existed* ([1796]).

In 1829, Constantine Koliades, a professor of Greek in Corfu, proclaimed in his *Ulysses Homer* that Odysseus was "the true author of the *Iliad* and the *Odyssey*," based in part on ancient anecdotes of the paraliterary kind and in greater part on specious reasoning. (Presumably *not* a factor in his judgment was his belief that his family enjoyed a direct line of descent from Odysseus's swineherd Eumaeus.) Throughout the remaining century, a parade of burlesques of Homer populated the stages and theaters of London with titles like *Melodrama Mad!; or, The Siege of Troy* (1819) and *Ulysses; or, the Iron-Clad Warrior, and the Little Tug of War* (1865), all of which stood out, in the words of a contemporary reviewer, for "the satanic glee [they showed] at the prospect of defiling Homer"—a glee that was shared by producers and audiences alike, as the productions were huge commercial successes.[38] Plainly, there was no shortage of wayward readings of Homer in the modern era, any more than there was in antiquity. And so, by the time the novelist and essayist Samuel Butler set pen to paper at the end of the century, the pump was primed for the next great and still unsurpassed exposé of Homer and the Homeric Question.

## Samuel Butler's Homer

In 1897, Butler published a curious and whimsical yet serious-sounding study with its mouthful of a title, *The Authoress of the "Odyssey": Where and When She Wrote, Who She Was, the Use She Made of the "Iliad," & How the Poem Grew under Her Hands*. Aimed at the late Victorian public, the book argued that the *Odyssey* was written by a woman who, "young, self-willed, and unmarried,"[39] had never left her modest home in Sicily and who strongly dissented from Homer's portrayal of the second sex. Butler had read classics at Cambridge as an undergraduate in the 1850s (in his preface he thanks those "men who taught me what little Greek I know"). At some point during the early 1890s he became obsessed with the *Odyssey* and decided to take on the classical establishment and all commonsense by making his case for female authorship, Homer notwithstanding. In 1892, Butler found a way to make "Homer" rhyme with "Humour" (in his essay "The Humour of Homer"). This was followed by other exploratory essays, such as "Was the Author of the *Odyssey* a Woman?" (1893). Then came the book itself. Some readers at the time considered the work a hoax, others believed it, and today scholars are unsure whether to write it off as a joke or to credit Butler with a serious if somewhat demented purpose. *The Authoress* is, however, anything but a serious work. On the contrary, it falls well within the recognizable genre of Homeric apostasy that originated in antiquity, drawing heavily as it does on several of these predecessors while parading its pseudo-scholarship of "subversive" intent (Butler's own term: 3). Butler prefaces his argument with a ninety-page "abridged" and "readable" prose translation of the *Odyssey*, which further aligns it with earlier efforts to whittle Homer down to size and turn him into prose. A brief look at Butler's method will give a taste of his particular form of mischievous madness.

Butler starts out from the ancient Separatist (266) and modern Analytic premises, which hold that the two epics were composed by two different authors and that each was no more than a patchwork of different sources and "strata" (251–59 and passim). Adding the ancient suspicion that the *Odyssey* was an inferior work and, for some, not by Homer at all (so the testimony of Proclus), Butler argues that the *Odyssey* has been "cobble[d]" together by an amateur. That amateur turns out to have been a woman who, largely ignorant of the world, hailed from a small coastal village in Sicily (present-day Trapani) and set out to fabricate a counter-epic in order to attack Homer's misrepresentation of women a century or more after the *Iliad* was composed. Bent on unseating Homer's authority without exposing her own identity, the Authoress was either careless or reckless or both, and the telling discrepancies show through at almost every turn. Butler claims to provide countless "proofs" that betray the female authorship of the *Odyssey* and concludes that "the writer is out of her depth, and knows it" (154).

As the writer's incompetencies mount, so do the offenses that are laid bare in what used to be Homer's second epic—its abundance of "anomalies, inconsistencies, absurdities, and small slovenlinesses," a charge that had been hurled at Homer since the fifth century BCE and was the chief source of evidence for the modern theory of Homer's orality. In Butler's hands, however, these faults are the telltale traces of the Authoress's aggressions against the epic tradition, which she succeeds in dismantling from within. Thus, offended both by Homer's disrespect for women and by "his utter contempt for the gods," the Authoress plays her *Odyssey* off against Homer's *Iliad* in a savagely contemptuous way, much to Butler's delight: "I think she was angry with him, and perhaps jealous" (247). The delight is heightened as Butler, from behind the scenes, proves himself to be the Authoress's eager co-conspirator. To give one instance of many, by "taking the water that was heated to wash the blood from the body of poor Patroclus ("Il." xviii.344 &c.) and using it for Ulysses's bath ("Od." viii.434–437)"—that is, by repeating a formula from the *Iliad* in another context altogether, thereby creating a horrific dissonance—she manages to produce a "disrespect . . . [that] is deeper than any that can be found in Homer towards the gods" (248, 251). Thanks to Butler's inane literalism, cheerfully carried out in the guise of simple earnestness, he and his Authoress succeed in turning Homer against Homer. The interpretive maxim of Alexandrian scholarship at its purest, "Explain Homer from Homer"—that is, on purely internal textual grounds—might as well now read "*Tar* Homer with Homer."

But this is just the beginning. Having proven his hypothesis about authorship, Butler scans the horizon for further targets: "Let us see what [else] the 'Odyssey' asks us to believe, or rather, swallow." What he discovers is rather startling. All the key persons and places named by the Authoress turn out, if we attend closely to the details, to be thinly veiled versions of one source and one location. The location is Scheria, the land of the Phaeacians, and the source is Nausicaa, the beguiling daughter of the Phaeacian royals who saves Odysseus's life in the central books of the *Odyssey*. It takes only one more imaginative leap to explain this coincidence. Because the Authoress never ventured away from Trapani, Butler reasons, her range of experience was limited to her immediate surroundings. Adopting the persona of Nausicaa as a fictive mask, she then turned to the remaining female characters' voices and identities, both human and divine, rendering them all variations of herself, as she only could. *Mutatis mutandis,* the same holds for the menfolk: "Nestor, Ulysses, Menelaus and Alcinous are every one of them the same person playing other parts" (205), which is to say, again given the limited circumference of her experience, that all four characters were based on the Authoress's own father, who is most immediately embodied in Alcinous, the Phaeacian king and father of Nausicaa in the poem. Likewise, all place-names in the poem, including Ithaca, are reducible to the local geography of Trapani, the only spot on earth that the Authoress ever knew. In a word, everywhere we look, "we find Nausicaa, all Nausicaa, and nothing but Nausicaa" (206). Plato's critique of Homeric mimesis (Homer's impersonation of his characters' voices and identities) here comes home to roost, but with a vengeance.

To prove the cogency of his discovery, Butler invites us to examine the frontispiece of his book, a portrait purporting to be that of Nausicaa (fig. 3.3):

> Let the reader look at my frontispiece and say whether he would find the smallest difficulty in crediting the original of the portrait with being able to write the "Odyssey." Would he refuse so to credit her merely because all he happened to know about her for certain was that she once went out washing clothes with her attendants?
>
> (207–8)

Butler asks the reader to imagine the original behind this portrait, as if one could. In fact, Butler reasons, one can. For although the Authoress is the epitome of an unreliable narrator ("We . . . know that we are being hoodwinked as far as the writer can hoodwink us") and a master in the *rifacimento* or reworking of inherited stories, she takes few pains to erase the traces of her own handiwork, not by ineptitude but by design. A case in point is her "whitewashing" of Penelope, which is done in such a way that "traces of an

FIGURE 3.3. Frontispiece to Samuel Butler, *The Authoress of the Odyssey* (1897). Credit: St. John's College, Cambridge.

earlier picture," blemishes and all—her "scandalous" reality and her "notorious profligacy"—"show up through the one she has painted over it" (123, 127, 136, 254). This is *rifacimento* as palimpsest, not as erasure: it exposes its own devices.

Consider the situation again. Faceless and anonymous (like Homer himself), the Authoress has inserted herself into her own tale by impersonating one of its lead female characters, Nausicaa. What is more, in doing so she has made a *rifacimento* of *herself*—not out of vanity, but out of the sheer pleasure she takes in the fiction and its mockery of the truth:

> At the same time I think it highly probable that the writer of the "Odyssey" was both short and plain, and was laughing at herself, and intending to make her audience laugh also, by describing herself as tall and beautiful. She may have been either plain or beautiful without its affecting the argument.
>
> (208)

And yet for all his nonchalance Butler keeps directing us to his frontispiece with a devious insistence: "my frontispiece, so mysterious, so imperfect, and yet so divinely beyond all perfection" (269). Butler might as well be speaking about Homer. In a real sense, he is.

With its thick, elaborate, and gold-painted wooden frame (a detail unmistakable even in the black-and-white photograph that serves as the book's frontispiece), the portrait has all the hallmarks of a modern masterpiece. As it turns out, the picture is a reproduction, owned by Butler himself, of an Italian forgery that dates from the early 1740s. Presented at the time as a portrait called *La Musa Polimnia* (*The Muse Polyhymnia*) that was found among the Roman rubble during the excavations at Herculaneum, the painting raised suspicions about its inauthenticity from the start, and the debates continued well into the nineteenth century.[40] Butler found the work hanging in the Museum of Cortona, where it is on display to this day, and he was plainly captivated by its explosive potential. In his preface, Butler describes the circumstances of the painting's discovery, though this is in fact a confabulation of his own making: "I was assured at Cortona that it was found by a man who was ploughing his field, and who happened to be a baker," and who decided to use it "as a door for his oven" until it could be "rescued and placed in the museum where it now rests" (x). This little *trouvaille* has now become Butler's Muse. In posting the controversial image at the front of his book, a copy of a copy with no authentic original lying behind it, Butler is advertising his book's own qualities, while also issuing a stern warning: *Caveat lector*. "There is not a trace of the *barocco* in my frontispiece," he later protests (208). The disclaimer merely foregrounds the suspicion he would deny. The forgery *was* made in the Baroque period, and Butler's use of it is baroque in every other sense of the word. Butler is selling his readers a bill of goods. The subliminal message is clear: his Nausicaa stands on no less stable a footing than any other portrait of Homer. Try and prove me wrong, Butler is saying under his breath—and prove yourselves wrong as you do.

Butler's emphasis on the *Odyssey* would be inexplicable unless it had a larger point, and it does. Just as the Authoress wrote the *Odyssey* in order "to rival, if not to supersede" Homer (251), the same can be said of Butler's own work, which does its best to upend the primacy and sanctity of Homer and all that this entails, from the myth of Homer in antiquity to the idea of Homer in contemporary classical scholarship. Simply to claim to be able to identify a concrete author for the *Odyssey* is to play havoc with the convention of Homer's anonymity and impersonality, if not his utter nonexistence, which was the premise of Homeric studies since d'Aubignac, Vico, and Wolf. To rebrand the author of the *Odyssey* as a woman—an unprovable hypothesis—is to expose the fragility of the Homeric Question with particular point. The Authoress, then, is a perfect foil for Butler. In resurrecting her resentments, Butler in fact spends a good deal of his book attacking the mythical status of the *Iliad* and its author. The two epics are, after all, cut from the same cloth and, for all their manifold differences, are both relics of a single canon. But just how different are they, in fact?

Butler's answer comes toward the end of his study. Encouraged by Homer's famous admission of ignorance about the facts of the Trojan War in book 2 of the *Iliad* ("We have heard only the rumor of it and know nothing"), Butler makes a startling surmise: Homer seems quite ignorant about the *fall* of Troy, and his silence is the proof. After all, the *Iliad* does stop short of narrating Troy's capture and destruction. Seizing on this fact, Butler draws the most perverse, literal-minded conclusion he can imagine. Homer's reticence, he writes,

> would point to a very considerable lapse of time—or else to suggest a fact which, though I have often thought it possible, I hardly dare to write—I mean *that Troy never fell at all,* or at any rate that it did not fall with the close of the Trojan War, *and that Homer knew this perfectly well.*
>
> (216; emphasis added)

This is one of the biggest bombshells of Butler's book, itself a book of bombshells, second only to his view about the *Odyssey*'s female authorship. Like the Authoress, Butler's Homer is an imposter. Far from being a Greek cheering on the Achaean victory, he was instead presumably an Asiatic of some kind who bore an ethnically motivated grudge against the Greeks he was catering to.[41] And by narrating his story as if Troy had fallen, Homer was, quite alarmingly, pulling the wool over the eyes of his intended Greek audience:

> [Homer], writing for a Greek audience whom he obviously despised, and whom he was fooling to the top of their bent though always sailing far enough off the wind to avoid disaster, would take very good care to tell them that—if I may be allowed the anachronism—Napoleon won the battle of Waterloo, though he knew very well that it was won by Wellington. It is certain that no even tolerably plausible account of the fall of Troy existed among the Greeks themselves; all plausibility ends with their burning of their tents and sailing away baffled ("Od." viii. 500, 501)—see also the epitome of the "Little Iliad," given in the fragment of Proclus. The wild story of the wooden horse only emphasises the fact that nothing more reasonable was known.
>
> (216–17)

The conceit that Homer despised his audience is lifted once again from Dio Chrysostom, who in his *Trojan Oration,* a work addressed to Trojan Greeks, complains not only that most of what Homer narrated "never occurred," not least of all "the story of the horse and the capture of Troy," as Homer knew full well, but also that "as his poem grew and he saw that men would readily believe anything, he showed his contempt for them" by defying the tradition and portraying the Trojans as the losers (11.34–35; trans. Cohoon). Homer's deceptions here seem no different in kind, and no more redeemable, than those of Butler's Homer or his Authoress, let alone Butler's own, skilled as he is in "always sailing far enough off the wind to avoid disaster," all the while remaining "one half laughing and the other half serious" (216, 259). In taking his revisionist suspicions about both epics to the limit, Butler implodes Homer from both ends.

So much for Butler's subversive *Authoress*. Lest we imagine that he has been inventing his plots out of thin air, we need to look back one last time into the antique past. Butler's debts are legion. The most obvious but least recognized of these is the hypothesis of female authorship itself. An explicit version of this idea is found in the third Sibylline oracle, which originated among Hellenistic Jews in the second and first centuries BCE and was written in Homer's dactylic hexameters with marked borrowings from Homer's epic diction. There, the Jewish Sibyl, a female prophetess who claims direct descendance from Noah and oracular knowledge from God, predicts that Homer will plagiarize her verses in his two poems and distort them with falsehoods, a charge that is repeated on the Sibyl's behalf by the roughly contemporary historian Diodorus of Sicily and by a number of later writers. This is a version of the "Homer lies" motif, now in the form of a *vaticinium ex eventu* (a prophecy made with hindsight), while further aspersions are cast on Homer's place of origin, which the Sibyl claims he has falsified. Indeed, just to flag up Homer's dependence on a Jewish oracle is to question his origins, if not his allegiances: his two epics are literally calqued on the Hebrew Bible, and the Jewish Sibyl is his Muse.[42]

The idea of female authorship received a new lease on life at the hands of Ptolemy Chennus (nicknamed "the Quail"), an Alexandrian grammarian and prankster from around the end of the first century CE and the author of several works on Homer. One of these was simply titled *Anti-Homer*, evidently an epic in twenty-four books. Elsewhere, in his *New* (or *Paradoxical*) *History*, Ptolemy claimed that Homer pinched the stories of both the *Iliad* and the *Odyssey* from two different women on two different occasions, one a certain Helen of Athens, daughter of the legendary ur-poet Musaeus, the other a certain Phantasia (Imagination) hailing from Memphis in Egypt (one of Homer's more exotic alleged birthplaces, though this may simply reflect the appropriation of Homer by the Alexandrian scholars), each playing the part of Homer's original female Muse.[43]

Ptolemy was doubtless inspired by earlier tradition and was pushing it to a new extreme. In his *Defense of Helen* (65), Isocrates had suggested that Helen visited Homer at night, possibly in a dream, and prompted him to compose the *Iliad,* thereby providing him with both the impetus and an outline. The conceit is introduced as a correction of Stesichorus, but Isocrates attributes the story to the Homeridae.[44] And behind everything stood the immovable fact of the Muses, which lay at the origin of all these suspicions and counternarratives and of Butler's own study. For, as he notes early on, both epic poems "begin with an invocation addressed to a woman, who, as the head of literature, must be supposed to have been an authoress, though none of her works have come down to us" (13). He is of course referring to "the Muse," but he might as well be referring to *La Musa.*

Butler's central hypotheses about the *Odyssey*, then, are hardly novel. Only his arguments are. While seemingly recondite to us today, none of this information would have seemed so in an earlier age, from the Renaissance down to Butler's present.[45] Being exceptionally learned in Homeric scholarship as he was, Butler would have had easy access to all of these details and more. Last but not least, in displacing Homer to the minor Italian shores and away from Greece, Butler was not only reigniting an ancient debate about whether Homer was familiar with Sicily (Thucydides took this for granted; Eratosthenes, the Hellenistic geographer and Homer-skeptic, disputed the fact), but he was also making a power play in the canonical geopolitics of classicism: he was literally deterritorializing the discipline. In short, Butler's *Authoress* is the Victorian counterpart to the ancient traditions that flourished around a mocked, defrocked, and debunked Homer. Far from inventing heresies out of the blue, Butler is bringing these hallowed traditions up to date.

## Cultural Power and the Hazards of Fame

Two lessons emerge from this all too brief sketch of Homer's literary afterlife. The first is that his success as a cultural presence over the millennia owed as much to his disputed merit as to his being *hors concours*. That is, his status always was, and continues to be, sustained as much by his station in the gutters and margins of the tradition as by his coronation in the official corridors of culture. This is a crucial point, because it suggests what is wrong with a purely laudatory vision of Homer, a view that exists in textbooks and remains the popular image of Homer even today. The best measure of Homer's standing in culture is neither his excellence as a poet nor his unequaled canonical status. Nor is it his persistent availability as an object of cultural consumption. Rather, it is his capacity to continuously *produce* culture in his wake. This is the truest mark of his staying power over time. Let's call this Homer's "cultural power." Homer's power to generate culture is distinct from his canonical power for the simple reason that the latter is only one version—one effect—of the former. Needless to say, the Homer in question here is not the poet and not his poems, but the very idea of Homer, which is irreducible to both.

A second takeaway follows from this last remark, and it has to do with Homer's identity. Homer cannot be equated with the divine Homer who sits atop the literary pyramid in the West, the way Zeus is perched above the human world in the Hellenistic *Apotheosis* sculpture. Nor is he equal to the displaced and mutilated Homer known from the persiflage of his most disgruntled readers. Rather, he is the total ensemble of his literary and nonliterary representations, high and low, sublime and ludicrous, reverent and disparaging. Homer is both edifice-like and permanently under construction, more so than any other ancient or modern author who comes to mind. Rather than stating that Homer never existed, we ought to recognize a variant on this troubling claim: Homer has enjoyed a *surplus* of existence. There was *no one Homer* in antiquity and later. Rather, there were "many Homers," as a late grammarian put it long before De Quincey—indeed, far too many Homers, all of them equal claimants to the title of being the one original "golden" Homer.[46] And for each of these several Homers there existed an exalted and a tarnished version of the same. The simplest confirmation of this is found in the list of works that came to be ascribed to Homer over time, which included, much to the chagrin of anyone who puts Homer on a pedestal, such disparate titles as the comic, scatological poem *Margites* (the *Idiot*), which even Aristotle took to be Homer's work, or the farcical *Battle of Frogs and Mice* that has been thought to feature in Archelaus's *Apotheosis* monument right alongside the personifications of Homer's two great epic poems. To ask whether these works were by Homer is meaningless. What matters is that they could be thought to have been works by the same Homer who created the *Iliad* and *Odyssey*.

How, one might well ask, is this possible? How could Homer occupy the center of culture and sit on the sidelines at one and the same time? The answer is that our conventional cultural maps have it all wrong. There is a seductiveness to the simple cut-and-dried distinction between canons and margins (or gutters) that needs to be resisted. Simply to couch literary history in terms of this opposition may be deeply problematic for a number of reasons. First, to posit the distinction presupposes a marginality where none may have existed or been felt. Second, margins have a way of shifting over time, as newcomers attach themselves to new centers of canon-making power and old standbys are asked, well, to stand off to the side. Third, while the process of transmission and reception might in one way create the illusion of a fixed canon, in another this process is constantly adjusting itself and its members in a kind of ongoing *rifacimento*: Homer was never the same figure from one moment to the next, or even at any single given moment, whether in the mind of an ambivalent reader or simply given the welter of contradictory features that continuously accumulated around him. Figures like Homer come to be overwritten like a palimpsest or a repeatedly reissued blank check. As a result, they are never entirely equal to themselves. That's the true force of literary and cultural memory: it stains as it burnishes, and it incites debate about its values. Lastly, criticism was built into the way Homer was always read, and Homer's fiercest critics were often attempting to adjust Homer's image, not to jettison it altogether. Even in those cases of wholesale revision, what justifies our assumption that all such revisions occur at the edges and margins of a canon, let alone that they are vented from the margins pure and simple? Much better is to recognize that Homer straddles both sides of the canon and margins divide. That is, we might say, a sign of his actual greatness.

All of which brings us to a final disturbing question. Whether he is elevated or brought low, can Homer ever *fail* to occupy the status he has? Is he too big to fail? Perhaps, though one suspects that this outcome is likelier to come about, in some future possible world, not through Homer's being shoved off into the margins in a definitive way but through his complete and utter neglect—marginalization in its most potent form—at which point the terms "margins" and "canons" will no longer signify, and Homer will be a forgotten name, neither a god nor a man, and not even a ghost.

# — 4 —
# What Did Homer See?

And the blindness—

—Giambattista Vico, *Scienza nuova* (1730)

In a letter allegedly composed by Aeschines, the fourth-century Athenian orator, the author describes some of his adventures on a sightseeing visit to Troy while he was in exile from Athens after a political setback at the hands of his rival Demosthenes. The letter is as much about his rambunctious traveling companion Cimon as it is about himself, and it begins like this:

> You can't imagine what that fellow Cimon made us go through in every town and harbor we visited, ignoring both laws and common decency. I had come to Troy eager to see both the landscape and the sea. But I'll keep quiet and won't write about what I saw there, since I would never have done with the topic, and I don't want to appear to be lacking in taste by filling your ears with empty prattle, like a poet. . . . After we spent several days at Troy and still hadn't had enough of gazing at the famous graves (my idea was to stay until I could see all the items mentioned in the epics and connected to the heroes), the day came when a host of Trojans were trying to arrange weddings for their daughters, at least those who were the right age.[1]

An erotic escapade follows, whereby "our fine fellow Cimon" makes lewd advances on an innocent young bride-to-be who was bathing in the river Scamander by disguising himself as the river god (this is an allusion to book 21 of the *Iliad*) and embarrassing Aeschines in the process. Aeschines complains that he would not be able to run through all of Cimon's tricks "even if I had ten tongues" (he is quoting from Homer's preamble to the massive Catalogue of

Ships in book 2 of the *Iliad*). Publicly exposed a few days later, Cimon defends his behavior to Aeschines in the following way: "I just had one pleasant conversation with a luscious girl I saw bathing in a river, escorted by her old slave. Anyway, it seems to me that the events at Troy aren't wholly horrible and tragic; we should make light of it all and stage *The Scamander Story* as a comedy!" The locals have a different opinion. When an angry mob approaches their door outraged by Cimon's antics, the two Athenians attempt to flee by sea but are stopped by an adverse wind (another literary allusion).[2] Aeschines continues, looking back on his adventures from a safe distance and now in league with his travel companion: "I suspect you'll find my story worth at least a chuckle." And there the letter ends.

The letter is a forgery, dating perhaps to the second century CE and belonging to a large corpus of fictional letters by famous personalities from the past. Its value lies not in its connection with Aeschines, who is no more than a device, but in its being an index of the grip that Homer's Troy could exercise over later Greeks and Romans. It was one thing to read Homer and quite another to visit the site of the Trojan War, to tour the landscape for oneself, making the rounds at the grave sites of the various heroes and heroines who were said to have been buried on the Trojan peninsula—Ajax, Antilochus, Patroclus, Hector, Paris, and Anchises each had a tomb; Achilles had as many as three or four tombs in the vicinity—and inspecting relics from the war, for example the wooden cult statue of Athena described in *Iliad* 6, weaponry of various kinds that was said to have belonged to different heroes, the lyre of Paris (but not that of Achilles, which was nowhere to be found), and so on.[3]

To visit Troy was to revisit Homer. It was literally to relive the now-dead past and to see the landscape as it must have appeared to Homer's eyes, and in this way to bring Homer himself back to life. But it was also to engage in what was a cliché even in antiquity. Describing Troy's environs was a topic that had been done to death well before the second century CE, although this did nothing to lessen the urge to take in the sights first- or secondhand or prevent the flow of future descriptions of Troy, real or imagined, from antiquity to the present. Readers, literary critics, tourists, antiquarians, political leaders, and archaeologists all had an equal stake in the prospect of picturing Troy.[4] Put simply, Homer could not be imagined without this prospect. And the reverse was equally true. The possibility that the one could validate the other was and remains today an overwhelming source of attraction. Indeed, the modern insistence that Troy must be brought out of myth into history and down from Olympus onto the Troad (the area surrounding and including the former citadel of Troy) would be unthinkable without the evidence of Homer. Behind this historicizing impulse lies the assumption that it is in principle possible to map Homer onto Troy. And to arrive at this kind of correlation between the two bodies of evidence—indeed, just to conceive its *possibility*—one has to ask, "What did Homer see?" The question, so simple in appearance and yet so central not only to the idea of Homer but to every idea of Troy in circulation then or now, has proved devilishly difficult to unpack.

## Being There

The question "What did Homer see?" has piqued and tormented the minds of Homer's audiences ever since Homer existed for those audiences. The reasons for this fascination and its frustration are several. The most immediate of these has to do with the nature of Homeric poetry. The Homeric accounts of the Trojan War and its aftermath were felt to be so vivid and compelling that they could transport audiences right to the scene of the action, rendering them firsthand witnesses to the events by proxy.

The trouble with this impression, as Plato in his dialogue *Ion* was quick to note (though he was hardly the first to do so), is that it is an illusion. There, Socrates interrogates the rhapsode Ion about his frame of mind whenever he is reciting Homer to his audience and picturing the events for himself and his listeners: "When you recite well and most amaze your audience . . . does your mind *imagine itself*, in its state of enthusiasm, *to be present* [more literally, "*to be there*"] *at the actual events you describe* (*para tois pragmasin . . . einai*)—in

Ithaca or at Troy or whatever the poem requires?"[5] Ion confirms the suspicion: he does imagine that he is being transported to Ithaca or Troy and visualizing events he has never seen whenever he recites Homer's verses. But when he is pressed further, he confesses that even in the throes of performance he is perfectly aware that he is manipulating his audience—all for money, as it turns out—and that he is carefully calibrating his voice and gestures to their tears or awe in the here and now. So much for divine inspiration! And as Ion falls victim to Plato's skepticism, so does Homer. The clear implication is that Homer, caught in the same chain of dependencies as Ion, is imagining and not seeing what he narrates.[6] And the same holds for the audience in his thrall. To listen to Homer, Plato insists, is not to see a thing. It is to be blinded by song.[7]

We can be sure that Plato has Homer and not only Ion in his sights because he is in fact glossing Homer's own language from the Catalogue of Ships, the same passage from which we saw "Aeschines" quoting a moment ago. Here is the full passage with the key phrases set off in italics:

Tell me now, you Muses who have your homes on Olympos—
for you, who are goddesses, *are there* (*pareste*; or "*are present*") and you know (*iste*; lit., "*have seen*") all things,
and *we have heard only the rumor of it and know* (*idmen*; lit., "*have seen*") *nothing.*
Who then of those were the chief men and the lords of the Danaäns?
I could not tell over the multitude of them nor name them, not if I had ten tongues and ten mouths, not if I had
a voice never to be broken and a heart of bronze within me,
not unless the Muses of Olympia, daughters
of Zeus of the aegis, remembered all those who came beneath Ilion.

(*Iliad* 2.484–92)

As the poet gears up to describe the battle raging around the Greek ships later on in book 12, he acknowledges once again that "it would be too hard for me to describe all these things as if I were a god" (176). Homer is emphatically not a god, but he does have the ear of the Muses, who are "there," present in their minds at the scene of the past, and so too present to Homer as he sings his song, which is also theirs. But once again, what did *Homer* actually *see*?

The most widely accepted answer in antiquity was that Homer saw nothing at all, at least not at first hand, and the verses just quoted were adduced as proof.[8] Further hints were extracted from elsewhere in his poetry, most prominently from *Odyssey* book 8, where Homer paints a picture of a bard named Demodocus who sounds very like Homer himself, or so one might wish to believe. (Eustathius, the twelfth-century archbishop of Thessalonica and Homerist, certainly does: he calls Homer's picture a "self-portrait."[9]) Blinded by the Muses in exchange for the gift of song, Demodocus sings at the court of the Phaeacians, who are said to live somewhere on the fringes of the known world and in complete isolation from the rest of humanity. Despite the remoteness of his location and his physical disability, Demodocus sings authoritatively about events at Troy. That authority is vouchsafed by Odysseus himself, who praises the singer for his uncanny knowledge: "You sing the Achaians' / venture, all they did and had done to them, all the sufferings . . . , / *as if you somehow had been there yourself* (*pareōn*) *or heard it* (*akousas*) *from / one who was*" (8.489–91). The line, a virtual quotation of Homer's appeal to the Muses in the Catalogue of Ships ("*you are there* [*pareste*], . . . we have *heard* [*akouomen*])," is good advertising for Odysseus, as the songs of Demodocus pertain to him, and even better advertising for Homer. Homer need not have been an eyewitness to the events he recounted. He might as well have been blind. And that is how most of antiquity pictured him.

## Homer's Blindness

Assuming that Homer's physical characteristics were invented after the fact ("posthumously," as it were)—an assumption I am happy to make—blindness seems a rather odd choice if the concern was to see in Homer a credible link to the past. Being blind may have been a mark of divine inspiration in some instances, prophecy first and foremost (Tiresias in the *Odyssey* is a prime example), but it was not an automatic feature of bards in antiquity, nor was it an automatically positive feature, generally speaking.[10] Of the several different singers we hear about in Homer, most of whom go unnamed, only two are said to be blind: Demodocus in the *Odyssey* and possibly Thamyris in the *Iliad*, whose impairment, whatever it was, came as a punishment from the Muses. (Later sources make him blind.) Hesiod, Homer's closest poetic relation, was sighted, as were all other Archaic poets known to us. And yet legend had it that Homer was blind.

Imagining Homer in this way created more problems than it solved. Whether or not Homer was an eyewitness to the events at Troy, he was a key witness, and indeed the primary witness whose testimony was consulted to verify historical and topographical details of the Trojan War. Was he really blind? That the question disturbed Homer's readers is apparent from the wavering of his biographers, who struggled to make sense of its implications, no doubt even before Heraclitus seized on the problem in order to ridicule the limits of what Homer could see and know. The net result of these struggles was a plethora of Homers, each equipped with a different life and set of circumstances that could variously be called upon to explain what could be known or never known about Homer and his world. For some writers Homer was blind at birth, for others he only gradually developed blindness, and for yet others he was never blind at all. It is probably significant that only a tiny handful of biographers insisted that he lived at the time of the Trojan War and so could act as an eyewitness to the events.[11] This circumspection (it can only be that) suggests more deeply seated doubts: Homer was for the most part considered at best a remote witness to what he sang. The analogy with Demodocus only went so far.

Other guesses about Homer's lifetime ranged from as few as two or three generations to as many as 400 years after the fall of Troy. The middle ground of around 160 years was the most commonly cited figure—168 years to be exact, according to one impressively confident account, but this too was just a stab in the dark.[12] The key factor in these reconstructions of Homer's life and circumstances was that the memory of Troy should still be fresh and that Homer should be positioned close to the events of Troy, both chronologically and geographically (his home was placed somewhere in nearby Asia Minor, whether Cyme, Smyrna, Chios, or Ios, and so on).[13] The debates raged as they did not only because local traditions were seeking to lay claim to the newly emerging Panhellenic Homer (a Homer who belonged to all of Hellas, as recent accounts have stressed), but also because the various claimants were responding to a problem that was palpable in the poems themselves—namely, the question of Homer's reliability in his report, or reportage, about Troy.[14] How trustworthy a narrator was Homer, in fact? The question was inevitably bound up with the problem of Homer's blindness, but that problem was in turn tied, often symbolically, to the larger and more pressing question of what Homer could ever have known about the places and events that he describes and appears to have seen. (We should note that the root meaning of the Homeric verb "to know" is "to have seen" and therefore to know, an ambiguity that plagues Homer's admission, "We have heard only the rumor of it and know/have seen nothing.") Modern scholarship typically assures us that Homer's knowledge was vouchsafed by the Muses and that ancient audiences needed little more of a guarantee than that.[15] Plato didn't buy this argument, and neither did others before and after him.

The simple truth is that antiquity conceived of Homer in a contradictory fashion, as someone who was both blind and sighted. Not only were the *Lives* divided on the matter, but so too was ancient portraiture. Visual representations of Homer could deceive the eye into believing that the blind bard could see, and a number of these portraits even show him reading. A late epigram in the *Greek Anthology*, dating to around 500 CE, underscores this confusion: "You would not think he was like a blind man to look at him."[16] Homer *must*, at some level, be able to see. This demand fed into other presumed facts concerning Homer's life that might be used to explain the reach, and limits, of his knowledge. He could be variously imagined as a traveler, a tourist, a poor itinerant beggar, or a "clever" and informed ethnographer with wide experience of the world who, blind or not, studied the people and places he visited through empirical observation and research (*historia*), "tracking down the truth" as he did, and who "probably also made written notes of everything" that he learned—and all of this, embarrassingly enough, simply to make up for his native *ignorance* about the past. In the process, the poet came to resemble no one so much as his own wandering, inquisitive, and observant Odysseus (a connection that was frequently drawn) or else, moving full circle in the other direction, the biographers themselves, who spent their lives conducting painstaking research (*historia*) into Homer's life and times, whether they traveled from their armchairs or by land and sea, no doubt taking copious notes as they did either way.[17]

Evidently, the real problem was not whether Homer was sighted or blind but how he came by his information. And here the various accounts were moved by a common impulse, one that would eventually lead to the modern experiment with Homeric archaeology. Let's dub this an impulse to "mundane empiricism." Later readers and critics repeatedly noted how the poet's descriptions of events, objects, characters, and scenes are produced with such elaborate detail that it seems "as if Homer were an eyewitness" or "as though he were there [or "present"]" at the scenes he records. The phrasing they use is lifted directly from Homer ("You sing the Achaians' / venture . . . / *as if you somehow had been there yourself,*" *Odyssey* 8.489–91), as is the notion that epic poetry presents a spectacle for an implied onlooker, be this Homer or an anonymous stand-in for the audience. Plainly, Homer has not merely anticipated his future readers and critics by luring them in. He has *produced* them.

The insistence on the empiricism of Homer is striking, but the same impulse can be detected in Homer himself. Demodocus may have his knowledge of Troy from the gods, but Odysseus is there to verify it. And as celestial as Muses may be, their job is not to serve as a conduit to recondite knowledge about the universe but to act as corroborating witnesses to facts on the ground: they can guarantee the truthfulness of Homer's account only because they were on hand to observe the events as they unfolded in time and which they can "now" recall. It was not enough that Homer should enjoy divine communications to compensate for his ignorance of epic reality. Homer and the world he depicted *must* be grounded in empirical reality, and the effort must be conducted with an emphatically *mortal* art. By the same token, Troy must be imagined to have been real, a place-name for an event that could be geotagged and situated in time, just as Homer must be imagined to have been himself a flesh-and-blood individual: the empirical impulse is at work in the biographical tradition too. The Muses may be divine creatures, but Homer had to be one of us—fragile, vulnerable, subject to human limits, and, finally, to death.

Of course, simply to state this is to stumble onto the greatest quandary that vexed the problem of Homer in antiquity and later on: for how could Homer's humanity be squared with his knowledge of the events at Troy, let alone at places as remote as Ithaca or Phaeacia? This lay at the root of the question "What did Homer see?" Readers, literary critics above all, recognized that Homer was by his own account as ignorant of the facts as his later readers were but also that he was no less eager than they to align his poems with reality, or at least with a *sense* of reality. He achieved this effect of the real through the sheer brilliance of his visualizations and by embedding a virtual onlooker into his scenes. At these moments (which is to say at every moment, including the scenes on Mount Olympus), the reader is invited, or rather *obliged*, to occupy the position of this internal spectator, to assume its point of view, and then to act as a witness or co-witness to the events being described. The resulting impression is one of copresence, immediacy, and intimacy.

Thus, when Hera soars over parts of Greece in *Iliad* 14, Homer gives her itinerary by running through the place-names of her fly-over in, as it were, real time. One of the later commentators writes, "The reader's mind, tracing Hera's path, is given over to an imagination and view of these places."[18] As if sharing the view of what Homer sees, the reader is made into a co-witness, if not a co-conspirator. This "as-if" quality is a powerful poetic device: it underwrites imaginative transferences but also safely disavows them. Readers and critics were well aware of the distance that separated them from the experience of the poems; hence the cautious nature of their observations above, which are hedged with caveats and hypotheticals ("as if" is the most frequent). This distance, too, was thought to have its mirror in Homer, who was conceived of as an artist—a *poiētēs* (poet/maker)—who created reality rather than merely reflecting it.

This is one reason why we can say that the later commentators are sly and not naïve readers. Homer for them was a master manipulator of poetic effects—as he must be if he did not directly witness what he describes. Sensitive to the charge that Homer seemed to know too much about what he never could have seen, ancient literary scholars typically rescued the poet from criticism by appealing to his plausibility, his realism, and his posture of restless curiosity about the world. Deliberate if skillfully achieved poetic illusion produced an "as-if" knowledge of the epic world. Wherever the cautious hypotheticals are dropped, balder statements take their place: "Homer wants to create in our minds the *appearance* [or "*illusion*"] (*doxa*) of truth."[19]

At times, achieving poetic illusion required Homer to work against, not with, the reader by concealing things from view, above all his own artfulness. A case in point is the so-called Greek wall of the *Iliad*. Thrown together overnight as a defensive measure during the last year of the war (this occurs in book 7) and spectacularly washed away after the war has ended (this is narrated in a flash-forward in book 12), the Greek wall is the single most conspicuous object in the poem, but also the most incoherent and inexplicable. It is repeatedly described from different angles and with different "looks." At times it appears to be a flimsy thing made of logs and stones that Trojan heroes can topple with their bare hands or breach with hurled stones. At other times it appears more like a city than a defensive structure, given its size and architectural details (it is equipped with towers—as many as seven in all—parapets, bastions, and bolted gates)—a veritable second Troy. The Trojan wall, by comparison, is a visual blank: beyond a few general labels ("steep," "windy," "well-built," fitted out with an unspecified number of "lofty towers" and "strong-built" gates), it is never given to us to see. Anomalous in every respect, the Greek wall has all the earmarks of an *ad hoc* invention that was added to the myth of Troy precisely to generate the kind of drama and deep mystery that it does. It was decided by the Alexandrian commentators that Homer wanted to hide the fact of this invention from his audiences lest someone in his own day should seek out the physical traces of the Greek wall, not find them, and suspect him of duplicity. The answer they hit upon is astounding to contemplate: like a guilty forger, Homer contrived to make the wall vanish without a trace. With the wall no longer visible, so too was all evidence of Homer's handiwork. A perfect crime![20] Here, we might say that the Greek wall was *too* vivid an object; it drew too much attention to the artfulness by which it was created and described. In order to hide his art, Homer had to conceal what he made lest the artifice be mistaken for an empirical reality—and what better way to hide the evidence than by destroying it? The result was a truly self-consuming artifact.

Less elaborate but no less revealing is the analysis of Achilles's near-fatal drowning in his battle with the river god Scamander, an implausible scene for a post-Homeric reader. Choked with blood and corpses from Achilles's most violent rampage in the poem, the river rises up against Achilles "in mortal likeness" (not unlike Cimon, who parodically impersonated Scamander at the start of this chapter), commands Achilles to desist, and then, "boiling / to a crest, muttering in foam and dead bodies" and "bellowing like a bull," threatens to overwhelm the defiant hero and bury him in an unmarked grave of sand, rubble, and water—the most unheroic death imaginable for an epic warrior (*Iliad* 21.212–341). Addressing the scene, ancient commentators observe how Homer secures the illusion of his reality: "The hearer has no opportunity to consider whether the description is true or not," so quickly and effectively does Homer's artistry work.[21] The conclusion to draw from these and other examples, and one that the ancient commentaries did in fact draw, is that vividness of description does not guarantee precision but at most an "as-if" precision.[22] Of course, the reader is ultimately a collaborator in these illusions: she knows better than to press the facts too hard. We may call this a readerly blindness.

As it turns out, Homer's blindness is rarely deemed an asset in the ancient traditions. Equivalent to a confession of ignorance if not of total fabrication and outright lying, Homer's being blind made him more, not less, vulnerable to criticism. To be "as blind as Homer" was a stock phrase of contempt in some quarters of antiquity, for instance in Lucian, who elsewhere has Zeus accuse Homer of being "a blind man and a fraud."[23] In one place, Lucian's predecessor Dio Chrysostom accuses those who are obsessed with Homer of displaying a kind of ophthalmia.[24] In another, he spells out what he means: as a remote witness to a past whose traces had all but vanished and about which "only an obscure and uncertain report (*phēmē*) survived," Homer had to resort to lies, while his readers could not see the true light either.[25] Not that his readers found lingering in the shadows of ignorance disagreeable in the least. There is a comfort to be taken in finding oneself deceived into not seeing or knowing, Dio observes shrewdly, or rather in *permitting* oneself not to see or know: "Humankind is hard to teach but easy to deceive. . . . They find the light painful, while the darkness, which permits them to see nothing, is restful and agreeable."[26] The remark closely echoes Heraclitus's critique of Homer for being as prone to deception as the rest of humankind, but it also brings to mind later skeptics of mythological hearsay from the fifth and fourth centuries on.[27] As it happens, the tradition in which Homer's blindness was not a badge of honor but a blemish stretched back even prior to Heraclitus. Let's connect some of these threads, first by revisiting Stesichorus quickly, not as a poet who radically revised Homer, as in chapter 3, but this time as a poet who was responding to the vexed question of what Homer did or did not see.

Stesichorus, recall, blasphemed Helen (or so he pretended) by falsely claiming that she had eloped to Troy, as Homer said, and then was punished by Helen with blindness for this lie. Upon recanting, Stesichorus regained his eyesight: he thus learned to see what Homer never did. This sly but explosive innuendo, implied already in Plato, is made explicit in the Roman *Life of Homer* and in Proclus: it was *Homer's* blindness that Stesichorus had revealed.[28] With this full-on assault on Homer's poetic authority, Stesichorus set a mighty precedent. His accusation was repeated with countless variations by Homer's many detractors (Plato and Dio among them), as was the pejorative connotation of blindness. Behind everything was a lingering problem. Homer's fame rested on the striking visual clarity and absolute immediacy of his descriptions. And yet, how could the experience of his poetry be reconciled with the fact of his blindness? The concern was real, and neither the appeal to the Muses nor the example of Demodocus sufficed to put it to rest. Instead, the question "What did Homer see?" proved to be an exasperating problem with no clear answer. Stesichorus was exploiting this uncertainty.

The countertradition to which Stesichorus belongs is vital and strange, but it consistently recognizes that Homer's blindness is both symbolic and physical. Homer's legendary disgrace at the hands of the fisher boys who teased him with a riddle about invisible lice is an early example. This episode probably circulated in popular form long before Heraclitus gleefully retold it at the end of the sixth century, and it continued to flourish long after Alcidamas made it canonical in the fourth century, as we saw in chapter 3. The story mocks the limits of what Homer can see and therefore know. Wherever the riddle is repeated or mentioned, as it frequently is, Homer is presented as a mere hapless mortal (the encounter with the fisher boys occasions his depression and death) and as anything but a fiduciary with solid ties to the divine. Physical and mental or epistemic blindness were genuine concerns, and they reflected the troubled conscience that came with experiencing Homer. Homer must give us a window onto reality, but how much trust could one place in what he claimed to know and see? The worries are mirrored elsewhere. The point is that Homer's blindness was one of the more conspicuous ways in which these concerns bubbled up to the surface: it was a metaphor for what he did not know and what his readers could never verify—in other words, for "readerly blindness."

A few more examples will help to reinforce the point. According to one of the *Lives*, Homer developed his eye ailment in Ithaca, a somewhat inauspicious coincidence as it turns out. While he was convalescing, he "enquired into and learned about the story of Odysseus" from the local inhabitants and then grew blind.[29] Here Homer's knowledge brings about blindness. Is it not a *form* of blindness? According to a somewhat darker version of the same story, the answer is yes. In this account, Homer summoned from the dead the shade of Odysseus himself by means of a blood offering, hoping to learn about the Trojan War from a firsthand witness who still had a fresh recall of the facts, as newly departed souls evidently do. The price that Odysseus extracted for this precious information was a promise from the poet to aggrandize the hero, even if this meant promulgating "alternative facts" about him. The *Odyssey* was the result.[30] This is one more instance of the "Homer lies" motif, cleverly reworked now as a Faustian bargain made by the poet to compensate for his ignorance of epic reality. Once again, Homer's knowledge is symbolically paid for by his blindness—though the ultimate victim is not Homer but his audiences. We might note that the Muses are irrelevant in these tellings of Homeric inspiration: Homer's Muse has now been replaced by active fieldwork (*historia*) or by the ghost of Odysseus.

As the traditions grew, the reservations deepened. According to another *Life,* Homer visited the tomb of Achilles like a tourist and asked to behold the hero just "as he was" when he donned the armor of Hephaestus. "When Achilles appeared, Homer was blinded by the dazzle of the armor." In return, he was honored by Thetis (Achilles's mother) and the Muses with the gift of poetry.[31] On the surface, we can see a clear parallel to Demodocus, who had to forfeit his vision in exchange for a higher calling. But this anecdote has a hidden sting. Here we see enacted before our eyes the same lesson that Plato so astutely made in the *Ion* and that is hinted at in the earlier anecdotes about Homer's encounters with the source materials of the *Odyssey*: the nearer you approach Homeric reality and the more vividly it appears to you, the less of it you will be able to see. We are all tourists whenever we step onto the Troad, Homer included. Epic poetry blinds with its brilliance.[32]

To be sure, not everyone agreed with Stesichorus and Plato or their Second Sophistic progeny: denials of Homer's blindness could be as vehement as the accusations they were meant to fend off. Toward the end of antiquity, Proclus, the great Neoplatonist philosopher, sought to defend Homer against the charge: "Those who have stated that Homer was blind seem to me to be mentally blind themselves, for he saw more clearly than any man ever." What Proclus had in mind, however, was Homer's 20/20 metaphysical vision, not his talent for empirical perception, which he did not rate highly in any case.[33] Not to be outdone, and wishing to cover his bases, Lucian declared he had empirical proof that Homer was *not* blind, "as people say." He could tell at a glance when he first laid eyes on Homer in the Underworld. Because the answer was self-evident, he did not need to ask. Instead, he could save his breath for more urgent Homeric questions, such as where he came from ("This point in particular is being investigated even yet at home"), whether the lines bracketed as spurious or suspect by the Alexandrian editors were his (they were; knowing this, Lucian "pronounced the grammarians Zenodotus and Aristarchus guilty of utter nonsense"), why he began the *Iliad* with the word "wrath," whether he wrote the *Odyssey* before or after the *Iliad* "as most people say," and other sundry items.[34]

The debates about whether and what Homer saw are a sign of how troubling and irresolvable the question actually was. Whatever its origins, we can be sure of one thing: Homer's blindness was a sign not only of what Homer may never have seen with his own eyes but also of what his audiences could never ascertain. The idea of blindness was a way of capturing the gap between what Homer knew or said in his poems and what could be known by a reader. The source of endless anxieties, that gap was inescapably real and could never be completely closed, not least because Homer's blindness, or indeed any other fact about him, could not be established with any certainty. In other words, Homer's legendary blindness was a *topos* rather than a fact, and its purpose in life, so to speak, was to index the range of uncertainties and doubts that stubbornly collected around the figure of Homer. In this light, we can say that Homer's being blind was not an accident of the tradition. On the contrary, it incarnated the most sensitive issues that came with hearing and reading Homer. The real question was not whether Homer was blind but to what extent *we* are blind whenever we view the past through the eyes of Homer.

## The Trojan Question

Compounding these uncertainties and inseparable from them was another complex of problems—as intractable as the Homeric Question in its ancient form—that we may call the "Trojan Question." Like its Homeric counterpart, the question about Troy was really a bundle of interrelated problems that were subject to relentless speculation and debate at least from the second half of the fifth century and that continue to be debated today: Where was the Homeric Troy located before it was destroyed? What, if anything, was left to be seen of Troy's citadel and its fortifications in the centuries after it fell? And, finally, could Homer ever have actually *seen* Troy?[35] To these questions, modern archaeology added one more: Can Homer's Troy be identified with the Bronze Age site that was unearthed by Heinrich Schliemann at Hisarlık in 1870 and formerly known as Ilium?

Much hung on these questions, the more so since, as far as we know, it was Homer's *Iliad* and not the poems from the so-called Epic Cycle that was the ancient gold standard for fact-checking the Trojan landscape, and it remains so today. The reasons why Homer's poem could have claimed this privilege are unclear, but they are not hard to imagine. One factor surely has to be the combination of rich "empirical" detail and the extraordinary degree of descriptive vividness (*enargeia*) that appears to have been a hallmark of the *Iliad* and to have set it off from other epic poems. The impression of "being there" would have been a natural and virtually inevitable outcome of the fact that Homer, again uniquely in the epic tradition (or so it appears), tarries over events that take place along a narrow strip of land for a period of some fifty-odd days in the roughly 16,000 verses of his claustrophobic *Iliad*. This feature of Homer's poem helps to explain why so many of the later sources depend almost entirely on his accounts of the Troad. The reliance on Homer as the best and earliest source on the topography of Troy made it all the more imperative that his testimony should be consulted and validated, or simply trusted blindly, by later generations. Eustathius, the Byzantine Homerist, expresses the predicament of later readers well: "It is not obligatory that all the cities and towns that the poet records have to be found. He names what existed in his own day, but time has obliterated many of them."[36]

Which brings us back to the question "What did Homer see?" or rather "What was left of Troy for him to see?" For either Troy was still standing at the time when Homer produced his songs or else it had fallen and was in ruins. The choice was stark but also momentous: if Homer did not see Troy fall and was truly operating from hearsay (or less), what could anyone really know about Troy? A treacherous circularity resulted: knowledge about Troy could not be confirmed without knowledge about Homer, while each threw some light and considerably more darkness on the other. This circularity heightened the attraction and value of Homer, who came to represent what Troy's destruction also came to represent: an idea of something that could no longer be seen and that remained permanently lost to culture—whether we call this the splendor of the Greek Bronze Age, a mythical Heroic Age, or just a vague sense of some irreparably lost past.

As if by attraction, Homer was himself often felt as a strange loss, as grand and distant as Troy, and it was only inevitable that he should assume mythic proportions. The result was a curious overdetermination. On the one hand, Homer became a proxy for the witnessing gaze of his later hearers and readers, someone who stood closer to their experience than to the heroic era he portrayed. On the other, Homer's poems became the most precious relic of this past, a past to which he himself belonged as one more all-but-vanished relic that was indissolubly linked to the violent destruction of Troy. Indeed, in some stories about the emergence of the Homeric corpus mentioned earlier in this book, the poems, once whole, were said to have been scattered by natural catastrophes on a massive scale until they finally resurfaced in random quantities like so many archaeological finds. Homer may have been partly salvaged from obliteration (to what degree was never entirely clear), but the destruction of Troy was complete, or so it was portrayed. This last was something of an overstatement—traces of the citadel remained—but it nonetheless accurately captured the emotional reality of Troy's demise, which left behind a traumatic memory that still burns today. In sum, what Homer testified to was the very fact of this loss far more than the loss itself, which was all the harder to bear precisely because it had no clear contours or boundaries. Homer's Troy was the backdoor entrance to an unthinkable trauma that lay behind each of his two epics.

## *Aphanismos*

Troy had two connotations in antiquity. It was known either as Homer had described it—as a vital, flourishing civilization, albeit one pitched on the brink of disaster—or as it appeared in dim memory and on the ground in the form of large but inexplicable ruins said to belong to Troy, a fact that could only be established by making reference to its *aphanismos,* or "disappearance" through near-traceless obliteration.[37] Needless to say, there was a problem with this way of getting at things, for how do you prove an absence? At the extreme, not only did Troy disappear in the ancient imagination, but every trace of its obliteration had to disappear too. "Even the ruins [of Troy] have perished," Lucan would famously write centuries later (*Civil War* 9.969). This oddity of logic, captured by the idea not only of loss but of *the very loss of loss,* troubled every aspect of the Homeric poems. It also troubled the way Homer came to be imagined given how he was completely identified with the fate of Troy.

The loss that Troy represents makes itself achingly felt in both epics, not nostalgically but hauntingly, horrifically, and most impressively of all in the way that Troy appears and disappears in Homer's poetry like a flickering light. Homer's tactic of continually alluding to but avoiding Troy's final hour is a signature feature of his version of the myth of Troy. The device is all the more effective for being so chimerical and oblique. Earlier epics told the tale to which Homer only indirectly alludes, and one, the *Sack of Troy* from the Epic Cycle, is devoted entirely to this event. By contrast, the destruction of Troy in Homer operates like *un grand absent*—a great void—at the heart of both of his poems: it is that which they are forbidden to visit but around which each poem circles, warily. It is never actually given to us to witness or see except *in absentia*, through hints and occasional but imperfect foreshadowings. And yet, *in that form it is ever present to mind*. The overall effect in the *Iliad* is less one of anticipation than of unparalleled poignancy, and the same is true for the *Odyssey* too. Without this sense of destruction, the *Iliad* would lack a future and the *Odyssey* would lack a past. With it, both poems are endowed with an aura of tragic, or just desperate, finality.[38]

There are two apparent or near exceptions to this policy of reticence, one in each poem. Both are worth a quick glance. The first, an apparent exception (though it really is not one), comes in seven brief lines from the *Odyssey* in which the sack of Troy is said to have been retold by the bard Demodocus (8.514–20): "He sang then how the sons of the Achaians left their hollow / hiding place and streamed from the horse and sacked the city and / he sang how one and another fought through the steep citadel." But this is a compressed periphrasis of an action, not its visualization or description, as ancient readers were well aware. There is no burning city, no battles are shown, and no deaths are recounted, at least not for us: we are not told what Demodocus actually sang. Instead, the narrative jump-cuts to Odysseus as he reacts to the song. In a surprising turn, he is compared to "a wife"—any wife—who weeps over the body of her dying husband after he "fell fighting for her city and her people"—again, any city—and then is dragged off, tearfully, into a life of misery and slavery (521–31). The latter image, even more so than the prior mention of Troy's sacking, is generic, not specific, which adds to its pathos (we are invited to reflect on the human toll of warfare in general), while both passages seem designed to pique and then defy our expectations. Hoping to get a vivid account of what the *Iliad* failed to deliver, we learn little more than what we already knew: "The city was destined to be destroyed" (8.511). The apparent exception from the *Odyssey* thus proves the rule: Troy's fall cannot be shown but only suggested. Homer has not missed an opportunity here. He has exploited it in keeping with his overall policy.[39]

The second instance occurs in the *Iliad*. A near miss rather than an apparent exception, it has an even greater impact than the occurrence in the *Odyssey*. Although the *Iliad* studiously avoids putting the fall of Troy on display, the poem does offer one brief but derailing glimpse of the future destruction of the city and its people, namely, at the dead center of the poem. At the start of book 12 we see how, after Troy's capture, the area surrounding the battlefield undergoes a complete obliteration at the hands of the gods. The scene is at once strange and ghastly. Depicted is an empty landscape that is being emptied still further. The war by now had taken its full toll: "All the bravest among the Trojans / had died in the fighting, and many of the Argives had been beaten down, and some left" (*Iliad* 12.13–14). The Greeks had sailed away, leaving behind their defensive wall. Poseidon, Apollo, and Zeus conspired to devastate the wall, and they did so in style. Together they spent nine days unleashing the combined forces of eight rivers, an earthquake, and the sea to clear the battlefield of all prior traces of the war and restore the plain to its pristine natural origins. The place was "made all smooth again," and the beach was "once again piled . . . under sand" (12.14–33). In its sheer vehemence, scale, and utter finality, this passage is unparalleled in the *Iliad* or in any other work from the classical tradition for that matter.[40]

The purported aim of all this mayhem is the destruction of the curious Greek fortification mentioned a few pages ago, the defensive wall that was erected overnight in book 7. But that wall is merely an ersatz for the Trojan wall, whose destruction could not be shown, as the ancients recognized, or rather surmised from Homer's conduct as a poet.[41] True to form, by demolishing the wall as horrifically as he does, Homer gives us an ersatz destruction of Troy itself. Their fates are linked together for us in lines 11–12 of the same passage: "So long as the citadel of lord Priam was a city untaken, / for this time the great wall of the Achaians stood firm." When the one disappears, so does the other. But it is the radically disproportionate nature of the event that points to its truest meaning. Where other poets may have sung the capture of Troy, Homer presages its complete burial. Adding to the horrors is a further fact about the Greek wall that needs to be mentioned: it was built over a massive "tomb" (*tumbos*, or "burial mound") that contained the "indiscriminately" mingled ashes of fallen Greek warriors (*Iliad* 7.333–38). Macabre in every way, and forecasting the fate of its Trojan counterpart, the Greek wall is traumatic simply to conceive. But then so too are the walls of Troy, whose bitter fate it shared.[42]

As a poetic moment, the passage from book 12 is arresting, not least because it unaccountably ruptures the temporal flow of the narrative, as if disobeying the conventions that the epic has set for itself by reaching beyond its self-appointed temporal horizon into a distant future. For in a marked departure from custom, the poet here relinquishes his role as a contemporary eyewitness of the war and momentarily looks back on his narrative from the retrospective view of a later, nonepic present day. From this vantage point, the heroes of the Trojan War appear, for the first and last time in either poem, as "the race of half-god mortals" (*hēmitheoi*). The phrase is charged but also fraught. With it, Homer is invoking a perspective that is found only in the most drastic of epic moments, notably in Hesiod, who announces Zeus's intention to annihilate the race of "half-god mortals" along with much of the human race. The Trojan War is the means to this end.[43] The effect is spine-chilling. In later thinking, Troy's sacking signaled the irrepealable division between immortal (mythical) and mortal (historical) time. It was conventionally used to mark the ground zero of recorded human history, the way Democritus, the fifth-century atomist, dated one of his writings to "730 years after the capture of Troy."[44]

Whether or not the distinction between mythical and historical time was available in the eighth century (and it probably was not), there is no question that for Homer, as for later authors, the Trojan War heroes appear to be already legendary, a different breed of creatures. Sprung from the mating of mortals and gods, enjoying direct communication with the latter and nearly divinized themselves, they are henceforth walled off in a remote past, having been detached from the present through a violent rupture of immeasurable proportions. Ancient and modern commentators have struggled to make sense of the sudden intrusion of this seemingly alien perspective in the *Iliad* 12, but their worries are probably overdrawn. The *Iliad* and *Odyssey* are colored by this kind of temporal pathos from start to finish. Everything that transpires in the poems issues from a long-gone era, reminding us of a past that is unimaginably prior and unreachable—or rather, that is *only* imaginably prior and reachable, since access to this past had to be gained through the experience of the poems themselves. So what, then, is to be made of this radically ruptural moment that is foregrounded in *Iliad* 12 but palpable everywhere else in the poem? A quick speculation is worth pondering.

## The Theory of Systems Collapse

The plain fact is that Troy loomed far greater in the ancient imagination than it did on the ground. Its ruins survived, but little more. Troy was a mystery to behold. It was linked to an irreparable but also inexplicable loss. And Homer partook of that loss, representing in his own person and in the legendary scattering of his poems by fires, flooding, or earthquakes a fate that was as traumatic as the event around which his two poems were built. No other ancient author—and few places—enjoyed this kind of catastrophic fame, not even Mycenae, Tiryns, or Pylos, three of the great palatial centers of the Mycenaean Age, for which Troy could conceivably stand as a screen, its fall representing the collapse of these and other great eastern Mediterranean centers at the end of the second millennium.

This possibility is worth pausing over, as it is not sufficiently considered in the literature.[45] It is well known that a massive "systems collapse" swept across the Aegean and Mediterranean East sometime around 1200 BCE, wiping out Bronze Age palaces on the Greek mainland (Pylos, Mycenae, Thebes, Tiryns, and others), on Crete (Knossos and elsewhere), on Cyprus (Enkomi), in the Levant (Ugarit, Megiddo, and so on), and in Asia Minor (Hattusa, Troy, Miletus), and ushering in an era of steep decline that threw these civilizations back into a prehistoric state, what was once called a "Dark Age" and is now known as the "Early Iron Age." Palatial centers were ruined, whether burned or overtaken, and then abandoned or reutilized on a diminished scale. Political and economic structures were destroyed, populations migrated or resettled in smaller concentrations, international trade ground to a near halt, and knowledge of writing and other technologies in the arts and crafts all but disappeared. Greece would not recover for a half a millennium. How such massive changes could have come about in so many places at once and in so short a time—seemingly in a blink of the eye, though it probably took decades—is one of the great mysteries of the ancient world. Warfare was involved, but the evidence points primarily to destruction by natural and not man-made forces, earthquakes and fires first and foremost, followed by droughts, floods, and drastic climate changes.[46]

The evidence from what today is known as Troy falls into the identical pattern. The site is a time capsule composed of nine layers or strata with several substrata or subphases, ranging from the Archaic to the Roman period on top (Troy VIII–IX), where Ilium, or rather "New Ilium," was located, to the Early Bronze Age (Troy I, 3000–2500 BCE) at the bottom (fig. 4.1). Schliemann, a wealthy German entrepreneur who traded professions to become the first archaeologist of Troy in 1870, identified a palace on the site from 2300 BCE (Troy II), a good millennium too early to match up with a fortification that could have been attacked by Mycenean Greeks—though he did not know this at the time. Schliemann subsequently recognized that he had overshot the mark but insisted that he had discovered the site of Homer's Troy. Later archaeologists have refined the picture but have come no closer to finding Homer's Troy than Schliemann did.

Aligning the evidence of the excavations with that of the poems has proved difficult to do. The relevant middle layers (Troy VI–VII) make for a poor fit with the expected chronologies. With its imposing façades, high, angled walls, and grand physical dimensions, the layer known as Troy VIh best matches Homer's description of Troy. It was destroyed around 1300, but the causes of its

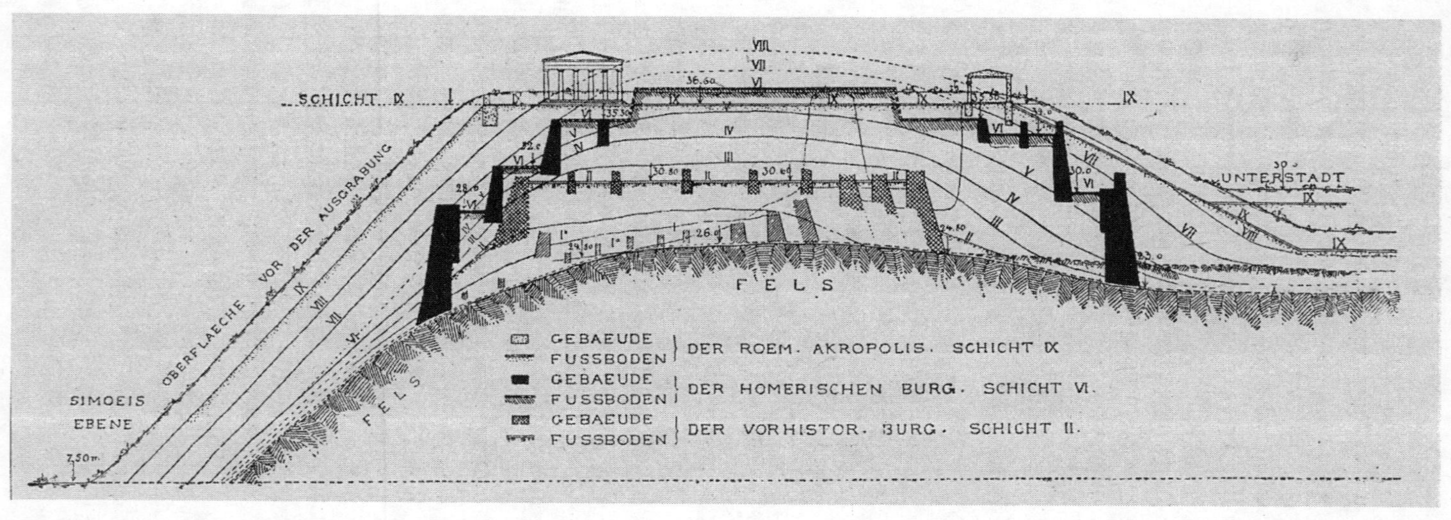


FIGURE 4.1. Stratigraphy of Troy. From Wilhelm Dörpfeld et al., *Troja und Ilion: Ergebnisse der Ausgrabungen in den vorhistorischen und historischen Schichten von Ilion, 1870–1894* (1902) 1:32.

destruction appear to have been natural. The next phase, Troy VIIa, seems to be a city that was rebuilt in the aftermath of this event. Much poorer and shrunken, it hardly suits the "steep" and "windy" city of Troy known to Homer. Troy VIIa was probably destroyed by fire alone and not by war (evidence for the latter is scant and ambiguous), and its life came to a halt somewhere between 1230 and 1180, decades after the Mycenaean palaces had been destroyed and hence too late to be attributed to an invasion by Greeks. Three more phases of destruction followed (the causes of which are unclear), and then the site was reoccupied with an infusion from a new population—possibly from Thrace, the Balkans, or the lower Danube—around 1100 BCE. The area was absorbed into the Greek world through a gradual process of acculturation, at which point the inhabitants of Troy became Greeks. Thereafter, in the seventh century, the site became known as "Ilion" in a tribute to its epic past.[47]

The question remains, Which phase of Troy—if any—corresponds to Homer's Troy? And the answer is equivocal: none quite exactly fits the bill, but any or all of these phases before 700 BCE could have contributed to the image or memory of Troy in its former glory and later demise, including, one should add, the remains unearthed by Schliemann, as these formed the Early Bronze Age ancestor of the Late Bronze Age citadel. It is possible that the myths surrounding Troy preserve a confused memory of the events that took place at Troy, if they reflect any of them at all. And perhaps this is where we should leave things too. In sum, Homer's Troy is likelier to be an amalgam rather than a true-to-life portrait, just as Homer's poetry is itself an amalgam reflecting disparate temporal layers and memories. On both of these points, current scholarship has reached a consensus, whatever other differences of opinion remain.

But amalgam of what? Mesmerized by Homer, a number of modern archaeologists and historians have insisted that the Trojan War must be real, at least in its kernel if not in the exact form that we have from Homer. M. I. Finley's view is paradigmatic: "We may take it for granted that there was a Trojan War in Mycenaean times; more correctly, that there were many Trojan Wars."[48] Very likely there *were* many wars resembling to a degree what may have occurred at Troy. But signs of destruction through war do not fit the chronology of "our"—that is, Homer's—Troy, and multiplying the Trojan War into many other, similar wars is no more satisfying an answer to the "Trojan Question" than proliferating Homer into a plurality of Homers is to the Homeric Question. Homer *may* be telescoping the memory of several different historical wars into one powerful symbol of the destructiveness of warfare. But if so, he is doing more than just embellishing freely, and for all we know his poems encompass a farrago of places and images, each laid over the other so as to produce a single and coherent but purely imaginary city: Troy.[49] Near Eastern literary predecessors from the third or second millennium, be they Hittite, Mesopotamian, or Luwian (representing the native language and culture of Western Anatolia), all document various sources of urban collapse, including war (an ever-compelling theme). They cannot be ruled out as influences on the Homeric conception of Troy, but neither do they render Homeric Troy more historical: they merely add further literary and imaginative overlays.[50] And once we acknowledge the contribution of the imagination to the Homeric picture, the door opens wide again to a different kind of memory from that which has transfixed readers of Homer, as well as a different approach to what the Trojan War represents.

Suppose for a moment that Homer is recording not a singular event in history but rather a singular *inexplicability*—an unaccountable loss with no known but only an imaginable origin. To anyone living near Troy after 1200 and down to 700, Troy would have presented the ghostly vestige of a once remarkable civilization. Massive Cyclopean stonework, even in its ruined state, never ceased to attract marvel, which gave rise to the suspicion that its builders were themselves larger-than-life individuals belonging to a magnificent but now vanished race. Objects recovered from the ground likewise provoked interest and puzzlement.[51] The Trojan War would have been a perfect way to commemorate this end as it might have appeared to a Greek in the early Iron Age, transfigured now in the imagination. Cult activity is attested from the twelfth century into the eighth century, though little more is known about the site, which never recovered its earlier splendor.[52] If we add to this a further suspicion that must have been available to survivors after 1200 BCE—namely, that Troy was not alone in undergoing complete destruction, but that palace centers across the Mediterranean, once networked together, had fallen as well—then a larger picture will have loomed into view for Homer's earliest audiences. Troy was among these casualties. Might it be a stand-in for them the way the Greek wall is a stand-in for Troy?

The suspicion is palpable in the epics too. A hint that we are on the right track is found in book 4 of the *Iliad*, where Hera darkly offers Zeus a trade: Zeus may "sack utterly" "Argos and Sparta, and Mykenai of the wide ways" (her "darling" cities) whenever he likes so long as he agrees now "to visit horrible war again on Achaians and Trojans" (4.50–56). Bored more than interested, Zeus gives his consent. Like children swapping marbles, the gods plan to visit destruction on what Homer is presenting as four great palaces from the past, each of which did in fact leave behind impressive and suggestive ruins after their destruction around 1200, ruins that remain visible to this day.[53] And as we saw, the destruction of Troy in Homer is bound up, obscurely, with the memory of a natural holocaust involving earthquake storms, flooding, and silting that was capable of rendering the landscape unrecognizable. What *Iliad* 12 preserves, then, is not the memory of an event but the burial of a memory, the effect of a cataclysmic loss that was all the more traumatic in that it could be traced to no known cause (apart from the arbitrary whims of gods) and, so too, could have no rational explanation, let alone be coherently witnessed after the fact.

Lurking behind all of this, according to some of the ancient commentaries, is the myth that the Trojan War was caused by Zeus's desire to eliminate the populations that were weighing heavily upon the earth, with Helen as bait: such was the meaning of the obscure "plan of Zeus" that is announced five lines into the first book of the *Iliad*.[54] Needless to say, a prospect like this puts the war in a disturbing, Malthusian light. The Trojan War, then, was Zeus's attempt to lighten the load of the earth through radical depopulation, but it came with an epoch-making twist. Henceforth, mortals and immortals would be rigorously separated, and the race of semidivine mortals would be extinguished. At stake is no longer a conflict between two peoples or the end of a city but a traumatic event in the history of humankind, unfathomable except as a myth about the end of mythical time itself. Further hints are detectable in the *Odyssey*, which in many respects appears to cap off a remarkable mythical era and to return us to a more mundane present reality, one that is closer to Homer's Iron Age contemporaries than to the Bronze Age of the Trojan War, which was no more.[55]

The Catalogue of Ships is another reminder of this vanished presence. It is a virtual map of what historians today refer to as the Mycenaean world (the term is something of a misnomer), albeit hazily and badly reconstructed.[56] Highly stylized and poetically designed, the Catalogue betrays the political geography of a later Archaic Age and jumbles up that of the earlier Bronze Age: it is a *mélange* of data that are at once inherited and anachronistic.[57] For these reasons, the Catalogue is suggestive but not indicative of any historical reality. On the contrary, it bears all the signs of a projection that was organized around the anachronistic myth of a Panhellenic assault on Asia Minor, one that was conceivable only starting in the late eighth century, when the notion of Greekness was just beginning to take shape. (Homer's Greeks have not yet learned to be "Greek."[58]) Like an anamorphic image, or a screen memory for that matter, the Catalogue contains in its very distortions the truth of its traumatic core.[59] Homer's Troy, meanwhile, is the place where all this significance gets collected and condensed, and then in turn deflected onto the Greek wall, which represents, in its crumbling and finally vanished materiality, a distorted memory of Troy, while both come to stand in for an irreparable and unknowable loss, a loss that could barely be imagined.

This is the way ancient commentators remembered things: the battle around the Greek wall was a substitute for the battle around the walls of Troy that the poem, for whatever reason, could not permit us to view.[60] And this is also how Eustathius remembered things when he observed that the "Homeric" wall, by which he meant the

Greek wall that is obliterated before our eyes in book 12 long before Homer ever could have lived to see it, is "more famous" than the wall of Troy. Eustathius was pointing to the irony that the patently fictional wall, which he took to be Homer's own invention, was in some ways more real than Troy, just as Vico would later hold that Homer's fictions were themselves more real than Troy, and for the exact same reason as Eustathius puts forward: Troy had vanished, while Homer's poems never did. A similar mood would prevail into the next century. In a letter from 1820, Goethe expressed disdain for contemporary illustrations of the Trojan landscape: "The overview of the plain of Troy ruins the *Iliad*," which exists only for the imagination.[61] The same thought occurred to Johann Gottfried Herder, Goethe's contemporary, who couldn't give a fig whether Troy ever existed on earth or not: Homer's triumph as a poet was to trump reality itself.[62]

Whether a Trojan War such as Homer describes had any historical reality is secondary to the effects that its memory—the very idea of Troy—had in the subsequent history of the Greeks. The Trojan War became the founding myth of the Hellenes, around which they forged a sense of shared identity and a unity of purpose and opposed themselves to non-Greek barbarians. As for the question why it was Troy and not other Bronze Age palaces in Greece that was singled out as the proxy for the event we refer to with the notion of a general systems collapse (a question that could be put in antiquity and occasionally gets asked today), the answer, I suggest, is that it was easier for early Iron Age Greeks to "explain" their historical predicament by offloading it to a place outside of Greece and to remember it as a Greek conquest rather than as a Greek catastrophe.[63] This is the case whether "the tradition of the Trojan War . . . originated among the refugees from Mycenaean Greece who settled along the Aegean shore of Asia Minor" after the disruptions on the mainland or, less dramatically but perhaps more plausibly, whether the Trojan War tradition resulted from an adaptation of local and other traditions among the populations who congregated along the eastern Aegean seacoast in the post-Mycenaean period and eventually became Greek.[64] Either way, the bargain struck by Hera hints at a truer picture that, although heavily recessed, gives the lie to this no doubt unconscious mythical compromise with the past.

A close parallel is found in the stories of Exodus and the conquest of Canaan as these are told in the Hebrew Bible. Featuring many of the same elements that we find in Homer—Cyclopean, megalithic ruins suggesting an earlier, grander, and more powerfully endowed race of heroes, historical displacements, and a traumatic past that never occurred in the way it was imagined—these stories appear to have been fashioned in response to the same Late Bronze Age crisis that swept across mainland Greece, Asia Minor, and the rest of the Mediterranean around 1200 BCE. Just as the Trojan War provided a charter myth for nascent Greeks who henceforth would learn to be Greeks, so too did the biblical stories provide Israelites with a myth of ethnic origins and a new collective identity as they emerged out of the ashes of the same series of destructions.[65] And although the narratives of both cultures appeared to describe a transition out of myth into history, in fact the opposite took place. In each case, one myth merely replaced another.

## The Invisible City

Representing a loss that could not be confirmed but only imagined, the Trojan War could be doubted at least in its details if not as a whole. Modern scholars tend to deny that the historicity of Troy was ever questioned in antiquity, but the facts tell a different story. Stesichorus radically reimagined the Trojan War. Early allegorists from the sixth to fifth century could dismiss the *Iliad*'s surface narrative as a pretense: the poem for them was not about war; it was a map of the physical and moral universe. Lucretius insisted that historical events, strictly speaking, are not real (*per se*) existents (atoms and void) but only ephemeral accidents with a qualified claim to reality, and he gave as his star examples the abduction of Helen and the Trojan War. The Roman Stoic Epictetus dismissed Homer's poems as being about "things which neither exist nor ever will," much as a later philosophical commentator, Hermias, would do on Neoplatonic grounds in the early fifth century. What Dio

Chrysostom thought about the historicity of the Trojan War is unclear, but his dim view of Homer's veracity speaks for itself: turning the plot of the *Iliad* inside out, Dio declared Homer's poetry to be "a kind of dream, an obscure and vague one at that."[66]

Was Troy no more than a dream? Whether or not it was, its traces were conjectural at best. And yet despite this logic, or more likely because of it, tourists, travelers, and scholars flocked to Troy in search of what Homer's poems describe, the way "Aeschines" and his companion did in the fabricated letter discussed at the start of this chapter: the letter may have been false, but the desires it projected were real. The thirst for a tangible relic of the Homeric past was insatiable. Mapping the topography of the Trojan battlefield was, and continues to be, an ever-tempting and elusive quest. Over the centuries Troy became more than a destination for disaster tourism: it became something of a theme park-*cum*-museum, with mythical objects trotted out for visitors to gaze upon and hero cult shrines erected for the purpose of venerating the epic dead on both sides of the war with personal offerings. Eventually, an entire Homer-industry rose up around the problem. Writers from the fifth century to the end of antiquity scanned Homer's text for pointers to the past, whether to produce a mental map of the Troad or simply to establish the much-controverted location of ancient Troy.

The height of this activity occurred in the Hellenistic period during the first half of the second century BCE, when three scholars—Aristarchus at Alexandria, Crates of Mallos, and Demetrius of Scepsis—studied the Troad in an effort to visualize the battlefield in relation to the Greek encampment and to pin down other topographical details. Aristarchus wrote a monograph on the Greek camp with a "diagram" of some sort, and Crates, based in Pergamon not far from Troy, drew up an opposing picture of his own. Where most scholars argued from their armchairs, Demetrius did not. He was an inhabitant of the Troad and was driven by local politics. Combining conventional philology, autopsy, and polemical fury, he wrote a massive commentary in thirty books on a mere sixty-two lines of the Catalogue of Ships (the Trojan portion: *Iliad* 2.816–77) disputing the claims of the Ilians, and those of the late fifth-century antiquarian Hellanicus before him, that Ilium occupied the former site of Troy. In his experience of the place, Demetrius found Ilium to be a shabby settlement unworthy of the grandeur of Troy. Strabo agreed. But then where was Troy?

If the former citadel of Troy could not itself be seen beyond the remnants of its damaged fortification walls and the elevation where it once stood, the landscape was a consoling presence, being the most permanent marker of the past. Mount Ida was indisputably itself, as were the several rivers named by Homer (though some of their names had changed; the Scamander was not one of these) and the Great Pine, a magnificent conifer some 225 feet in height and 24 feet in girth that served as a fixed landmark and may have enjoyed tenuous links to Homer according to one of the *Lives*. One could visit the spot where the Judgment of Paris was said to have occurred. But not all landmarks were permanent, and not all of them matched Homer's text unequivocally. Thanks to river deposits, the shoreline had silted up and changed shape and position, as the female scholar from the early second century BCE known as Hestiaea—a notable anomaly in the otherwise male-dominated world of Greek erudite letters but otherwise a cipher—was the first to recognize, based on firsthand observations (she was a native of the region); the hot and cold springs named by Homer in *Iliad* 22 proved elusive; the Greek wall had been washed away along with much else, as Homer himself says; and so on.[67] The harder one looked, the more the discrepancies mounted.

Modern archaeologists fell under the same spell, placing all their bets on what Homer saw and often looking for the identical objects that drew the ancients to Troy, though deep down they knew better, as did Strabo long ago, when he complained in a moment of exasperation that "Homer . . . leaves us to guess about most things."[68] Schliemann sought out the identical landscape markers as his ancient forebears (including the famous hot and cold springs) and was equally disappointed, though he believed that he had found the buried ruins of Troy. He hadn't, and he was forced to make the painful concession that had agonized so much of antiquity:

> Homer can *never* have seen Ilium's Great Tower, the surrounding wall of Poseidon and Apollo, the Scaean Gate or the Palace of King Priam, for all these monuments lay buried deep in heaps of rubbish, and he made no excavations to bring them to light. He knew of these monuments of immortal fame only from hearsay, for the tragic fate of ancient Troy was then still in fresh remembrance, and had already been for centuries in the mouth of all minstrels.[69]

As the Cambridge classicist Richard Claverhouse Jebb noted at the time, Schliemann was caught in a logical bind: he recognized the truth and yet could not "shake off the opposite belief, that Homer is an historian describing things as they were." Schliemann's attitude, typical of all those who rely on Homer to gain access to Troy, is a perfect example of fetishistic disavowal, as his thoughts ran something like this: "*I know very well that Homer never saw Troy*, that it was all just 'hearsay,' that 'at his time, and probably ages before his time, the city he glorifies was buried beneath mountains of *débris*,' and that he was 'magnifying [Troy] with poetic license'—*but I will treat him as a historical witness just the same*."[70] Such was the power of Homer's delusive *enargeia*.

That was in 1880. Over a century later, Schliemann's modern successor, Manfred Korfmann, would make the same assumption: "I regard Homer as a 'contemporary witness,' that is, as reporting on whatever the condition of Ilios was in about 700 B.C." as it could be "seen by eyewitnesses at the time."[71] But if Bronze Age Troy lay under a mountain of rubble in Homer's day, what value can the poet's observations have? The reliance on Homer by the archaeologists is striking, though they are hardly alone. Martin West, Homer's most recent editor, indicates how tempting it can be to identify Homer with what Homer saw: "As I sat amid the ruins of Troy on a beautifully clear day in September 1994 and surveyed the landscape—the Dardanelles, Imbros with Samothrace towering behind it, Tenedos, and a very obvious Batieia on the horizon, halfway to the hidden beach of Beşik Bay—the conviction grew stronger: *he composed it here*."[72]

Convictions like this have brought us to the point where we

are in our understanding of Homer today. This is not to deny that doubts can be heard elsewhere in the profession or even outside of it. It is merely to indicate the seductive prospect of occupying the place where Homer stood and then of seeing what the poet saw. What is most problematic about this desire is not that it is founded on an impossible impulse but that it does not sufficiently acknowledge its actual source: it springs from a more fundamental disorientation and serves a compensatory purpose, one that is every bit as symptomatic as the ancient responses to the trauma represented by Troy. For at the center of the two Homeric epics lies not a splendid citadel but its complete destruction and the empty waste it left behind, at the place "where much ox-hide armor and helmets had fallen / in the dust, and the race of half-god mortals" and that was then "made all smooth again" and "piled . . . under sand." If we want to ask what Homer saw, the answer is not nothing, as was widely feared or suspected, but the absence of everything, which is to say *less than nothing*.

## The Immortal City

The simplest way to remedy Troy's erasure was to rebuild the city, whether in the imagination, on the ground, or both. Epic poetry was, of course, the place where Troy was resurrected in all of its magnificent, if fantasized, original glory. The physical site of Troy followed suit. From around 1150 BCE down to the Hellenistic period, Troy was continually remodeled, always with an eye to creating links with the sacred remains of the Bronze Age citadel. Though at first these links may or may not have been connected to Homeric Troy, once Homer's poems emerged around 700 BCE the connections became programmatic and all-dominant. Even so, Troy was never actually rebuilt. Instead, it was built over and around, redesigned, and reimagined, its surviving Bronze Age fortification walls forming backdrops to the new structures, its mound shaved off, and its remains quarried for building materials where needed. Thus for a thousand years Troy was in effect made into a living museum, a place where the memory of Homeric Troy could be enshrined even as the physical site was altered beyond recognition and made usable for each new present.[73]

As the political center of gravity shifted from Greece to Rome over the next several centuries, so too did the concern with Troy's legacy. Indeed, the Romans staked their identity on the prospect of a rebuilt Troy, having claimed direct descendance as a race from the Trojan hero Aeneas. But to remember Troy was to remember its ruin. Small wonder that the poet who retells Troy's traumatic destruction in a way that Homer never could is also the poet who announces the fantasy of a resurgent Troy.[74] Vergil's *Aeneid*, composed in the final decades of the first century BCE, is obsessed with this architectural problem. In it, Troy is reimagined and rebuilt several times over and at different locations across the Mediterranean in a string of replicas and miniatures. Each is a shadow of Troy, and each foreshadows Rome, Troy's most illustrious reincarnation, made possible by Aeneas's final conquest of Italy in a second Trojan War. And yet this final stage, too, marks a doubling back to lost origins and an erasure. The old Troy must be obliterated by the greater glory of the Latin race whence it first arose, at least according to the myth that Rome told itself and that Vergil enshrines in his poem, Rome's first and greatest national epic: "Troy has fallen. Let it go along with its name" (12.828). In this way, Rome set the template for a new political mythology that imprinted itself on the West, with each new empire laying claim to the Roman lineage and to a piece of Troy, if not to being the site of a new Troy altogether, as the city of London was fabled to be in the early twelfth century when it was dubbed "Troynovant" (New Troy). (The sobriquet survived in the popular and poetic imaginations well into the nineteenth century.) Troy lived on, a perpetual fugitive of its conflicted past. Such was the strange logic of the idea of Troy.

The perplexities of this logic and its intertwining with the idea of Homer are perhaps nowhere better captured than in a short story by the Argentine writer Jorge Luis Borges, "The Immortal," which was first published in 1947 and reprinted in the collection *El Aleph* (1949). A compressed fable in five "acts" and spanning a mere fifteen pages, "The Immortal" is a frame narrative (a story within a story) of bewildering complexity. The outermost tale, set in London in 1929, concerns a manuscript that was found in the last volume of a rare first edition of Pope's translation of the *Iliad* and sold by a certain antique dealer, Joseph Cartaphilus of Smyrna, shortly thereafter deceased.[75] The manuscript, narrated in the first person, tells the tale of a wanderer who sets off on a fabulous odyssey through space and time in search of "the secret City of the Immortals," a place that was washed by a river "whose waters grant immortality" (106). It is unclear whether the wanderer is after immortality or just a glimpse of the City of the Immortals, or if to attain one of these goals he must attain the other. When he finally reaches his destination, it turns out that the river is the dark "Aisepos" that runs down from Mount Ida into the Troad (108). Mentioned in the Trojan Catalogue in the *Iliad*, the Aesepus is also one of the eight rivers used by the Olympian deities to flood and erase the Trojan plain after the war has ended in book 12 of the *Iliad*. The vertiginous City of the Immortals must therefore be Troy (a possibility that has surprisingly escaped critics). But the narrator has yet to find the City. He has merely found where it must lie. Nor has he yet discovered the truth of his own identity, which emerges only once he locates the City itself.

The narrator of the inner story at one point identifies himself as Marcus Flaminius Rufus, a Roman tribune stationed in Egypt. Having learned of the City of the Immortals, he heads off in a westerly direction to look for it and eventually finds himself wounded in a desert. He hallucinates "an exiguous and nitid labyrinth" and then awakens only to find himself lying with his hands bound behind his back at the foot of a mountain, where he repeats, "inexplicably, some words in Greek: 'the rich Trojans from Zelea who drink the black water of the Aisepos'" (107–8). He is quoting from the *Iliad* without recognizing the source of his words. Later on, the narrator, speaking about himself from an alienated third-person perspective, confirms this for us by way of a learned gloss: "These words are Homeric and may be sought at the end of the famous catalogue of the ships" (117).[76] Obsessed with being able to glimpse the City but unable to do so from above, Rufus takes refuge in a circular chamber below, where by chance he encounters the City in its subterranean bowels. The spectacle is Escheresque:

> I went down; through a chaos of sordid galleries I reached a vast circular chamber, scarcely visible. There were nine doors in this cellar; eight led to a labyrinth that treacherously returned to the same chamber; the ninth (through another labyrinth) led to a second circular chamber equal to the first. I do not know the total number of these chambers; my misfortune and anxiety multiplied them.
>
> (109)

Eventually, Rufus finds an egress and seems to behold a "palace" above, though what he actually sees is an object that refuses to come into focus. Surrounding a little courtyard, "a single building of irregular form and variable height," heterogeneously adorned with "different cupolas and columns," soars upward (110). Mirroring the labyrinth of its foundations below, it too is an "inextricable palace" of senseless complexity and "of enormous antiquity," abounding "in dead-end corridors, high unattainable windows, portentous doors which led to a cell or pit, incredible inverted stairways whose steps and balustrades hung downwards," while other stairways clung "airily to the side of a monumental wall" (110–11). The City now fills the narrator not only with boundless fascination but also with "sacred horror" (109). He rightfully describes the structure as "mad" and as "a kind of parody or inversion and also temple of the irrational gods" who built it (113). Reflecting on the experience later on (the story is this reflection), the narrator no longer knows whether the details he remembers having seen are "a transcription of reality or of the forms which unhinged my nights" (111). With this confession, the narrator indicates that he has been assimilated to the inhabitants of the City and fully "habituated to this doubtful world" (109). But the key to the City of the Immortals does not lie in its present. It lies in its past.

Nine centuries earlier, we are told, the original city was razed by the Immortals themselves, who then proceeded to erect it again "with the relics of its ruins" on the advice of one of their members

(113), the narrator's companion and guide at the City. The latter becomes increasingly central to the story. The narrator refers to him at first as a "troglodyte" (Greek for "cave-dweller," "one who enters holes"), a designation he shares with the rest of his tribe ("infantile in their barbarity" and "of slight stature[,] they did not inspire fear but rather repulsion," 108–9), then as Argos, owing to his sorry looks (this is the name of Odysseus's aged dog at Ithaca, who sits on a pile of manure waiting for his master to return), and finally as Homer, for that is who this creature reveals himself to be (113). That the plan to rebuild the original city was the brainchild of the troglodytic Homer "should not surprise us," for "it is famous that after singing of the war of Ilion, he [this same creature] sang of the war of the frogs and mice. He was like a god who might create the cosmos and then create a chaos" (114). The reference is to the pseudo-Homeric mock-epic poem, the *Battle of Frogs and Mice,* and Borges appears to be weighing in on the canonical disputes about Homer's oeuvre, though it is not at all clear why he should. We can, however, speculate about his interest in the poem, which shadowed Homer well into early modernity.

George Chapman, Homer's first great English translator, translated the poem in 1624, calling it "the crowne of all Homers workes." Thomas Parnell discussed its merits and authenticity in his introduction to Pope's *Iliad* in 1715. He then retranslated the poem in 1717 at Pope's request, and the work was appended to later editions of Pope's translation. Given the centrality of Pope to his story, Borges would naturally have been drawn to the poem and been tempted to make something of it. And that he did.

Disorienting as the details may be, the pattern fits together beautifully: just as the parodic second *Battle* is the chaotic undoing and remake of the first, so too is the City of the Immortals the grotesque afterimage of a ruined Troy, while its architect is a strange and repulsive afterimage of Homer. Tying the various pieces of this puzzle together is one last detail that needs to be mentioned: the name of the Immortals, and of this Immortal as their representative-in-chief, is surely fashioned after Troglodytes, one of the characters, a mouse, in the *Battle of Frogs and Mice,* who dies and then is a "symbolic" character and that Troy never existed may be Vico's (Vico is named twice in the story), but the phenomenon is a fact of Homer's many lives and afterlives.[82] And as Borges shows with his story, the life of Homer is the afterlife of his poems, for these are indistinguishably the same.[83]

Borges's pastiche of Homer(s) would be incomplete were we to fail to take up one more troubling speculation. The fact that Borges composed "The Immortal" just after the Second World War can hardly be an accident. This was a time when the *Iliad* was being read as an allegory of the Nazi destruction of Western civilization, and of Jews in particular, by such Jewish writers as Max Horkheimer, Theodor Adorno, Erich Auerbach, Simone Weil, and Rachel Bespaloff, to be discussed in the next chapter. Borges himself abhorred the anti-Semitism of the Fascists, both in Germany and at home, and he did so publicly and vocally even before he was called out by the Fascist Argentine journal *Crisol* for keeping his "Jewish ancestry maliciously hidden"—a legacy he regretted being unable to claim ("I, a Jew," 1934).[84] A spate of pro-Jewish and anti-Nazi writings followed, some of them allegorical in nature.[85] Might "The Immortal" belong to this set of writings?

Confirming the suspicion is the fact that Borges's opening pro-gonist, the antiquarian bookdealer Joseph Cartaphilus, bears the ame given by legend to the Wandering Jew, that accursed creature ho cannot die and is condemned to walk the earth from the Cru-ixion to the Second Coming.[86] On the other hand, Borges's ver-n of Cartaphilus, whose name aptly means something like "lover papyrus, paper, or books," also happens to have been a native Smyrna (105), one of Homer's several alleged birthplaces. He is her said to have died at sea while returning to his homeland as assenger of the *Zeus*" and to have "been buried on the island of (105), the traditional location of Homer's final resting place. His siognomy, as described by the Princess, is no less telling: "He she tells us, a wasted and earthen man, with gray eyes and gray d, of singularly vague features (*de rasgos singularmente vagos*)" ). This is a perfect description of Homer as he appears in his nt and then modern portraits—as someone who is both singu-



is resurrected and continues to fight, and for this reason appears to incarnate a parody of epic immortality. Immortality appears to vouchsafe nothing, not even for the Immortals, for once they destroyed and then rebuilt their city, they promptly "forgot it and went to dwell in the caves"—all this in order that they might "live in thought, in pure speculation." Thus "absorbed in thought, they hardly perceived the physical world" (112–13). So much ado about nothing! And yet the logic, Borges suggests, is fully Homeric.[77]

What, finally, are we to make of the Immortals' City? It is Troy, but not exactly. Rather, it is the vertiginous *idea* of Troy. And it is this inasmuch as it contains, in its heaping confusions, every possible version of Troy, past or present, amalgamated into one—a disturbingly overrich "memory-trace" that is immortal, not in the divine sense but in this exact human sense. As Freud writes in his *Civilization and Its Discontents* (1930), "In mental life nothing which has once been formed can perish"; "everything is somehow preserved."[78] But how different, in fact, is this from Homer's Troy? Homer's Troy, too, is either a physical place that has been made into a mental construct—an imagined idea—or a mental construct that has been assigned to a place and put into the form of an architectural image. In other words, Borges's construct is the image of Troy as Troy is reflected in Homer's mind and in the minds of all those who have come after him.

The parallels are unavoidable, and they are clearly marked out for us. Homer's Troy begins its life when it vanishes. Thereafter, Troy must be reconstructed out of the relics of its ruins, which are made not of stones but of ideas, imaginings, and words. Freud is once again helpful here: taking Rome, "the Eternal City," as his analogy for the mind, Freud produces from it a palimpsestic image, one that is cluttered with ruins, albeit not "ruins of themselves but of *later* restorations made after fire or destruction."[79] One has to wonder whether Borges hasn't at some level calqued Freud's Rome onto Homer's Troy. Whether or not he has, every reader of Homer performs this act of reconstruction by playing the part of an archaeologist, that is, by burrowing into time, literally climbing down into the vaults and chambers of the site of Troy, recreating an image of the past on top of these foundations, and finally inhabiting it mentally in what we might call a Homeric "archaeo-poetics."

Archaeologists are of course readers too, but with one difference: they literalize what readers of Homer perform in their imaginations; their labors are a materialization of a commonly shared fantasy. A materialization, but also a nuancing. The Troy of the archaeologists, as we saw, has been divided into nine subterranean strata, each one a doorway to a different Troy (Borges himself speaks of "nine doors"), while those layers have been subdivided into further and finer strata: Troy II with its seven sublayers; Troy VIa-h; Troy VIIa; Troy VIIb1–3 and possibly b4, with some of these further analyzed into "early" or "late," as in "VIIb3 late," and so on. All of this complexity is likewise reflected in Borges's dizzying confusions, and rather accurately at that. Most of the stratigraphic divisions just named were in place after Carl Blegen's excavations at Troy (1932–1938), and so they would have been familiar to Borges in 1947. Since then the number of "Troys," each representing a different "destruction horizon," have only proliferated further. These additions were foreseen by Borges too; his image is incalculably complex.

Inverting the logic of space and time, but in the end more faithful to the illogic of both, the City of the Immortals is the embodiment of a painful anachronism: it contains within itself all of its constructed traces and layers in a bewildering simultaneity, but it nevertheless remains constitutively open to further exploration, construction, and division. The City of the Immortals may be an anachronism, in the same way that the "rich *Trojans* from Zelea who drink the black water of the Aisepos" are in Borges's Spanish original called *teucros* after Vergil, but if so then the City is no more of an anachronism than what goes by the name of Troy today. The name is itself the most fragile possession or accident of the place: "Troy" or "Ilion," as applied to an inhabited city, could easily have been derived from the vocabulary of myth or epic (for instance, from Homer) and then applied by the inhabitants to a conjectured location in the Troad. In this way, a mythical Troy could have been assigned to a local geography, though never without controversy. As time wore on and as the speculations about Homer and his po-



ems grew in number and complexity, the complexity of "T
ramified and grew ever more difficult to pin down to a
time or place: Troy, Ilium, New Ilium . . .

Just as each of the proliferating layers or levels crea
ent Troy, so too does each of the many possible Troys
to one or all of the many possible Homers: the Home
around 700 BCE; the Homers (bards) of oral traditi
after this time, some of whom may have seen the Br
of Troy (if this was ever its real name); the blind Ho
ing Homer; the Homer of Vergil; the Homer of Ale
the Homer of Schliemann; and so on. This profu
ers is reflected in Borges's fiction too. Nearly every
scribed by him in any detail—on my count, five
candidate for being Homer, while the lines dividin
Homers are equally obscure, for ultimately they ar
each other. The series includes Cartaphilus, the a
dealer in London, who turns out to be the intern
118n1), and thus Homer; the troglodytic Immor
turns out to be Homer (a fact about himself that
and only now, slowly and dimly, remembers; 11
and bloody horseman" who comes from the ea
the City of the Immortals that send the narrato
(106), but later appears to be the internal nar
were, in reverse, from the other end of the story
back on itself (107); the internal narrator, who
guises throughout time (116), only to reveal in
is a version of Homer: "I have been Homer; s
One, like Ulysses; shortly, I shall be all men; I
(I leave aside a character who is named in the
will come back to him in a moment.) Wheth
tor belongs to this series is harder to determi
the more so if he is a proxy for Borges. N
the modern bard afflicted with near blindn
finity with the figure of Homer.[80] And nee
as much an anachronistic construction, pr
*post festum*, as is Homer's Troy.[81] The und

lar and generic, which is to say both a token and a type, as we saw in chapter 2. But the phrase "singularly vague features" is a paradox in its own right: it captures with diabolical precision the problem of visualizing Homer at any time. Cartaphilus, we now realize, is the internal narrator of the work that we are reading, which is to say that he is every incarnation of Homer that he chronicles for us with his life story. The work we are reading is thus—another paradox—an autobiographical *Life of Homer.*

But now back to the final wrinkle in our story. As an avatar of Homer, Borges's Cartaphilus combines at least two roles: that of an eternally reborn Homer and that of a Sephardic Greek-Jew who is fluent in "Salonika Spanish" (a dialect approximate to Ladino, the Judaeo-Spanish language spoken by diasporic Jews throughout Europe and the Ottoman Empire) and who wanders the globe in various guises and reincarnations. His life extends forward to 1921, at which point, landing in Eritrea facing the Red Sea, he reclaims his mortality again (116), and then to 1929, when he is said to have died at sea and been buried on Ios, thus ending the cycle of incarnations—or else commencing them once again.

The Jewish connection is obviously central to "The Immortal." Lest it be overlooked, in 1950 Borges added a fictitious "Postscript" to the story that purports to describe a critical commentary on Cartaphilus's narrative by one Nahum Cordovero in a work that was "biblically titled *A Coat of Many Colors* (Manchester, 1948)" (118). Cordovero's apparent namesake, Moses ben Jacob Cordovero, was a sixteenth-century Cabalist of Spanish or Portuguese extraction. This genealogy matches Cartaphilus's own to a tee. The latter's languages included "an enigmatic conjunction of Salonika Spanish and Macao Portuguese" (105). Thus "The Immortal" is the story of two mythical and inexhaustible identities, each the half-forgotten identity of the other, that merge and diverge over time: part golem, part revenant, Cartaphilus is Homer, the Wandering Jew. "Jewgreek is greekjew. Extremes meet. Death is the highest form of life" (Joyce). And the place where these extremes meet in Borges is in the labyrinthine ruins of Troy, which exists as a kind of Second Temple in the mind.[87]

To conclude, Borges may be faithfully recapitulating the Homeric tradition, but he is not improving on it in any way, not even with the notion that Homer was a Jew, or at the very least a Judaizer, for this was likewise part of Homer's identity at least from the mid-seventeenth century on, for instance in Zachary Bogan's *Homerus Hebraizon* (1658) and then Gerard Croese's *Homer the Hebrew [Omēros Hebraios], or, The History of the Hebrews According to Homer* (1704), a work that takes the standard comparison of Homer and the Bible, found already in Longinus, to new heights.[88] One source of the comparison may well be the third Sibylline oracle, in which Jewish, Greek, and Roman catastrophes merge in a fantastical sequence of dire imaginings, with Homeric Troy serving as a harbinger of the Greek destructions yet to come, and with Homer exposed for having appropriated the Sibyl's oracular wisdom.[89]

Borges is not rewriting the tradition. Rather, it is the tradition that writes Borges, with the result that his Homer is, very like the Homer of antiquity, a poet who lives on in the shadow of catastrophe. Catastrophe multiplied Homer into a scatter of fragments, each one tied to the remains of Troy. The *Lives of Homer,* Borgesian in their own right, reflect this scatter by presenting Homer as a multiform of himself. Borges's Homer seems to follow this same process in reverse: seeking himself, he must do so among multiple strands that, in the end, dissolve into discrepant fragments of a life that are finally collected together again in the baroque afterimage of an eternally ruined and eternally resurrected Troy. A *Life of Troy* has not yet been found, but Borges's story is as good a candidate as any. "The Immortal" thus demonstrates what we already know: that Troy and Homer have no life but only an afterlife, and that neither one nor the other can be coherently imagined, let alone seen. Of each of these entities "only words remain," words that have been so profusely overwritten—all in the name of seeing what Homer saw—that they are no longer individually legible.

# — 5 —
# Why War?

The *Iliad* is a poem of war, and the *Odyssey* is shaped by war's aftermath. Of the more than 15,000 verses of the *Iliad*, around a third—some 5,000—are devoted to battle scenes involving carnage on a massive scale, much of it graphically detailed and of the grimmest imaginable sort.[1] War can bring glory, but it is also said by Homer to be "destructive," "deadly," "dreadful," "abominable," and "a cause of tears." One classicist recently compiled a further list of terms from the *Iliad* to make the point: war in Homer is "bloody, wretched, baneful, cruel, harsh, piercing, and 'burning hot,'" a source of fear, terror, panic, "pain, exhaustion, sweat, dust, and noise."[2] Deaths in the *Iliad* are frequent. They are also particularly gruesome. Brains run "from the wound along the spear by the eye-hole, bleeding" or are "spattered forth." Severed heads spin on the ground like balls gone astray. Tongues, eyes, and teeth are shattered at the root.

Whatever else we may want to say about the *Iliad*, it can be a horrifically violent poem. And while the *Iliad* is scarred by depictions of war, the *Odyssey*, the *Iliad*'s PTSD offspring, is by no means free of these wounds. Heroes in the *Odyssey* weep uncontrollably at the mere remembrance of the sufferings they experienced at Troy, while the combat scenes that it does contain are styled after those of the *Iliad* and can be every bit as gruesome as the battles that take place at Troy: they, too, occur under the aegis of Ares, the god of war.[3] Given the looming presence of war in both poems, it is inevitable that war should affect how Homer has been viewed. As it happens, the fact of war does not produce predictable readings of Homer. Instead, it complicates them.

The most urgent questions are also the most obvious: What perspectives on war do the poems invite us to see? Is Homer sanctioning, ennobling, or condemning war? How clear, unclear, or just ambivalent are his views? Where a reader stands culturally, ethnically, and historically will determine how questions like these come to be answered, or even whether they get posed at all. This last point is worth stressing. War in the poems may be difficult to ignore, but its distasteful aspects can be suppressed or palliated. And there are strong pressures coming from different sides to do just this.

## The Pleasure of the Text

The first and most powerful of these pressures is aesthetic. The poems are exquisite works of art that delight the ear and engage the imagination. Their beauty is undeniable. It can also be distracting to the point of obliterating all other considerations, much like the fabulous lotuses consumed by Odysseus's crew or the bewitching Sirens of the *Odyssey*, both of which harbor hidden mortal dangers. The German literary critic Erich Auerbach saw this clearly. In an influential essay—the opening chapter of *Mimesis* titled "Odysseus's Scar," written at a time when a war of more recent vintage was raging about him (1942)—he insisted that to read Homer is to take one's mind off present realities and immerse oneself in a different world altogether: "Between battles and passions, adventures and perils, [the poems] bewitch us and ingratiate themselves to us" with their "savory present." Homer's "reality . . . ensnares us, weaving its web around us. . . . And this 'real' world into which we are lured exists for itself, contains nothing but itself."[4]

Self-absorbed and devoid of any hint of depth, darkness, and suspense, the Homeric poems in this reading, which I believe is deliberately provocative, though it is typically taken at face value, reveal a brightly lit world that passes before us like a parade of images across a single plane. Auerbach calls this a "procession of phenomena" (7). "The Homeric style," he writes, "knows only a foreground, only a uniformly illuminated, uniformly objective present" (7). We think of style as a literary device, but for Auerbach it is much more than that: it is a symptom of how reality comes to be registered in a text. Its synonym in *Mimesis* is *Auffassungs- und Darstellungsweise,* which is to say the text's means and manner of comprehending and representing reality. To read immersively is to adapt ourselves to this reality. To read critically, the way Auerbach does, is to stand back and evaluate what a style seeks to accomplish. As Auerbach proceeds, his critical purchase becomes more apparent. Homer may seek "to make us forget our own reality for a few hours," but in doing so he also somehow manages to make us forget his poems' own reality in the process (15). As a result, an oppressive and destructive reality recedes into the background. Brilliant appearances take its place.

Auerbach was epitomizing but not endorsing an approach to Homer that became canonical in the age of Weimar classicism during the late eighteenth century, though it existed earlier and it continues to flourish today. For Goethe and Schiller writing collaboratively in an essay titled "On Epic and Dramatic Poetry" (1797), around which Auerbach builds his own essay, Homer's poems provided quiet, peaceful, and durable aesthetic experiences. Calming and soothing, the poems, they felt, are designed to maximize tranquil aesthetic absorption, a goal that is incarnated in the figure of the rhapsode: "[The poet] appears as a sage who casts a calm eye on the events he narrates; the goal of his delivery is to soothe the audience so that they will gladly give him an extended hearing." Goethe and Schiller are not blind to the narrative content of the poems; they simply read this content in a singular light. The epics, they note a short page earlier, feature "battles, voyages, [and] every kind of activity that promotes a certain sensual breadth."[5] Comforting entertainment and sensual expanses eclipse bloodshed and danger.

In the same way, Winckelmann, writing nearly half a century earlier (1755), could insist that Achilles is "distinguished" not by his terrifying prowess or by his manslaughtering deeds but "above all by his lightness of foot," a trait that better suited Winkelmann's promotion of "noble simplicity and quiet grandeur" as the hallmark of Classical Greek art.[6] A few years later, in 1768, Herder could enthuse, "In Homer one can slumber as pleasantly and enthusiastically over the philosophy of the earliest time as in the temple of poetic Apollo."[7] Goethe and Schiller were obviously expressing clichés, and that is how their opinions lived on. In 1801, C. G. Heyne,

Friedrich August Wolf's teacher and a Homerist, could lament, "Unfortunately, the main subject matter of epic poetry is war and murder." But a consoling thought was not far behind: "Be that as it may, in Homer . . . everything is a matter of ideals" and "ideas" that have been "put into a visible form." Homer is a model of sublimation, and therefore also of forgetting.[8]

Two centuries on, one can still read how "the Homeric bard remains, above all, a 'singer of tales' . . . , a purveyor of pleasure (*terpsis*), and a preserver of traditions," or how "'the contemplation of death is the single factor that makes us long for immortality,'" or indeed how a hero's bleeding wound (in this case, Menelaus's) "is an object of art to be contemplated in part for its beauty" by "displacing the violence and transmuting the war scene into a source of aesthetic contemplation."[9] Plainly, the aesthetic imperative—the privileging of form over content—has a way of banishing all other considerations from view. The roots of this perspective lie in antiquity itself, as will be shown in detail below. And while dissenting views did exist in that earlier time, whether in Greek tragedy or among some of the philosophers, they tended to be drowned out by the dominant aestheticizing approach to Homer that was canonized by ancient literary criticism, with an impact that continues to be felt even now.

It was only on the threshold of modernity that the mingling in Homer of the beauty of art and the violence of warfare, and the disturbing proximity of civilization to barbarity, came under intense critical scrutiny for the first time, starting with Julius Scaliger in the sixteenth century. Scaliger found nothing but crudeness in Homer: his poetry, Scaliger believed, is as uncivilized as the manners he depicts, and war and its metaphors are the proof. Completely implicated in the violence of his poems, Homer is now guilty on both moral and aesthetic grounds. This view was repeated widely in some quarters, especially among the advocates of the Moderns in the early modern Quarrel. But it was not the only alternative to dreamy classicism. Vico, Nietzsche, and German and French writers from the Second World War, among them Auerbach himself, offer some of the most compelling arguments against the one-sided reading of Homer that Scaliger inaugurated for the modern era, in addition to constructing powerful arguments against the classicizing view that he was opposing. The chief target of these critiques was, for the most part, not Homer but rather the critical blindness of his readers. There will be more to say about these wartime critiques in the final pages of this chapter.

## Homer the Philhellene

A second factor that has seduced readers into overlooking the violence of warfare in Homer is closely allied with the first—namely, the sheer weight of the poet's standing as an original and unsurpassed monument of Greek culture, a view that, like the aesthetic reading of Homer, first took root in antiquity. As such, Homer was felt to be not only a symbol of Hellenicity but its finest incarnation: he was the first citizen of Greece. And the true job of a citizen is to defend his homeland. Such a view was possible only once the idea of "Greece" emerged, which is to say a Panhellenic identity among Greek-speaking peoples that was grounded in shared ethnic and cultural traits and that transcended local identities. Vague and inchoate in the eighth and seventh centuries, the idea gradually crystallized over the next two centuries, especially after the Panathenaea was reorganized to feature full-dress performances of Homer's two epic poems. And as the notion of Greekness began to form, so did the notion of a Panhellenic Homer, a Homer who belonged to all Greece. Whether the emergence of these two ideas was a coincidence or a single phenomenon (the details are too sparse to support anything but speculations), the consequences were momentous. From this point on and forever after, the idea of Homer was soldered to the idea of Greece. And from here it was just a short step to the next major transformation in Homer's identity: the view that Homer was a patriot who had championed the Greek and European invasion of barbarian Asia in what could now appear as a titanic clash of civilizations.

Homer was enlisted in this cause *post festum*, for it was only after Greece stopped the Persians in 480 BCE that the poet came to be imagined in this light. The cocktail of art and ideology proved intoxicating. Homer could now be understood not only as a Panhellenic but also as a philhellenic author: in Greek, he was called a *philellēn*, or "Greek-sympathizer"—literally, a "Greek-*lover*." Once it was stated, the conceit of Homer's pro-Greek and anti-Trojan sympathies took hold of the Western imagination and was extended to any number of further ends: Athens' political hegemony over Greece under Pericles, the conquest of the East under Alexander the Great, the culture wars of later antiquity (whether between Greece and Rome or between pagans and Christians), the appropriation of the Greek heritage by modern Europe, or the racialized ideologies of Fascism.

We can be certain that any reading of Homer along these lines is a misreading, for the simple reason that each of these concepts—Greeks, Europe, patriotism, barbarians, and Asia—would have been unintelligible to a Greek living at the time when the Homeric poems were created. As Thucydides noticed, probably not for the first time, Homer lacks a comprehensive word for Greeks ("Hellenes" are a tribe from Thessaly united under Achilles), and he has no corresponding word for "barbarians": the similarities between the Achaeans and the Trojans far outweigh any dissimilarities they may be thought to have (they worship the same gods, bear the same kinds of weapons, address each other in the same language, and share other deep cultural and other connections).[10] And while Trojans suffer incomparably more than Greeks in the *Iliad*, at least statistically, Homer's evident sympathies for the Trojans both on and off the battlefield more than cancel out the impression that Homer was an unqualified champion of the Greeks.[11] In all other respects, he appears to be an impartial witness to what he describes: war visits calamities on both sides of the conflict in equal measure.[12] If there is any object of loathing in Homer, it is war itself—a verdict that is agreed on by Greeks and Trojans alike.

Later writers were capable of equally searching reflections, but they tended to sound their objections from the margins. Aeschylus's *Agamemnon* questions the costs of the Greek victory over the Trojans: "In place of men, urns and ashes return to the homes of each"

(434–36). Euripides in his *Trojan Women* from 415 BCE has Hector's wife, Andromache, decry the fact that it was the *Greeks* who had "invented" barbaric evils (764); he is reflecting on the ongoing Peloponnesian War but revisiting Homer in its light. He was not alone. Euripides's contemporary, the orator Antiphon, likewise denounced the mutual destruction of Greeks by fellow Greeks during the same war in identical terms: "In this we have become barbarous to each other."[13] Nevertheless, ideology has a way of shaping reality, and so comments like those made by Isocrates in the fourth century express the dominant Greek perspective from the fifth century onward:

> We are so naturally hostile toward the Persians that even in our stories (*mythoi*) we devote most time to those about the Trojan Wars and the Persian Wars, which tell about their troubles. . . . I think even the poetry of Homer has a greater reputation because it celebrated *those who fought well against the barbarians*, and because of this, our ancestors wished to give his art a place of honor in poetic contests and in the education of the young, *so that we might hear his words many times and learn the fundamental hatred we have toward them*, and in admiration of the courage of those who fought against the barbarians, we might *desire to emulate their deeds*.
>
> (*Panegyricus* 158–59; trans. Papillon; emphasis added)

Identified with "Persians," Trojans were now enemies of the Greek state. Identified with "barbarians," they were enemies of Greek culture.

## Intimate Encounters

Attitudes like those shown by Isocrates translated directly into reading habits.[14] Greek readers and critics saw themselves as Homer's kindred spirits, while Homer was read in turn as a pro-Greek poet who was speaking to fellow Greeks, a philhellene. So, for example Philostratus, writing in the third century CE, saw Homer as someone who behaved "not like a poet of fiction but as if he were himself one of the Greeks at Troy" and "a fellow soldier."[15] To read Homer was an occasion for intimate confraternity and for luxuriating in shared emotions, which at times could be tribal. In itself, this is nothing new. It is an extension of a deeper tendency that, as we have seen, runs through virtually every aspect of contact with Homer: the feeling of "being there" and sharing the view of what Homer sees in his poems, whether as a co-witness or co-conspirator; the feeling of standing where the poet stood as he surveyed the landscape of Troy, the way tourists, travelers, and archaeologists did; or the sensation that one could survey Homer's own thoughts and on that basis extrapolate facts about his biographical person and his physical appearance, as contributors to the *Lives* and producers of the visual portraits of Homer did.

Among literary critics, this illusion of shared intimacy, a form of blindness in itself, was also an occasion for reading meaning out of the very poetic form by which Homer shared his thoughts. No feature of his poems, however small, was immune to being understood as telling a tale about Homer's personal views and political leanings. The implications for literary analysis were immense. In the hunt for meaning, critics exposed levels of detail never before imagined to exist in his poems, least of all by Plato, who made this kind of analysis conceivable for the first time when, as discussed in chapter 3, he developed the distinction between Homer's first- and third-person utterances, behind both of which lay what Homer really "thought." But to locate what Homer really thought one had to imagine Homer thinking, and so the circle of interpretation easily became self-confirming.

Some of the most extreme examples of this newfound attentiveness to Homer come down to us in the ancient commentaries on Homer known as scholia. Given their compilatory nature (they are warehouses of information), they reflect attitudes to Homer from the earliest known treatments of the poet to the Hellenistic Age—when scholarship on Homer reached its zenith and the commentaries first came into existence—into the late antique and Byzantine periods, when these corpora were recompiled and, alas, progressively abbreviated. Assuming the form of textual notes and comments, albeit on a massive scale and spanning many thousands of pages, they run through Homer's poems line by line and word by word, dissecting everything from grammatical forms to larger narrative patterns. Despite their technical character, they are some of the best clues we have to ancient reading practices, and it pays to listen to them closely, the more so as the Alexandrians were particularly sensitive to the problems we have been discussing and were unusually inventive in finding ways to resolve them, at least to their own satisfaction if not to ours.[16]

Why, it was asked, does Homer hurry through some battle scenes and not others? Because, the answer runs, lengthy accounts of the disastrous sufferings of the Greeks would be too painful to bear, both for the poet himself and for his Greek audience. Homer was sparing his readers—"He made the battle brief because he did not wish to draw out the misfortunes of the Greeks"—but also himself, since he "suffers along with the Achaians."[17] Why at different points does Homer limit the list of Greek heroes who are beaten back to just a few names? Because it is disagreeable "as a philhellene" to dwell on these losses, and so "he runs through the difficult parts quickly" and in this way manages to "disguise the disgrace" of the Greek setback.[18] Why does Homer hint at the final capture of Troy even as Zeus is emboldening Hector to rout the Greek forces and set them into a panic? He does this to "comfort the reader by intimating the sack of Troy to come. For who could bear the spectacle of the Greek ships being set ablaze or of Ajax on the run without knowing in the back of their minds that the perpetrators of these deeds will be defeated?"[19]

Who indeed? If the pathos of these critical moments is astonishing, no less astonishing is the continuum of sympathetic feeling they presuppose, which runs without break from the anxieties of the Achaeans to Homer and from there to his readers. Homer acts as an emotional bridge that turns the reading experience into a fully mimetic loop. That such a loop was felt to exist from early on is clear from Plato's dialogue *Ion,* where the rhapsode Ion boasts to Socrates that he occupies a privileged place in the transmission of Homer's intended meanings: a chain of dependencies runs from the Muses above down to Homer, then further down to Ion, and from there to the thronging crowds assembled at the festivals in Socrates's day, who could be moved to ecstasy, panic, or tears in response to the rhapsode's own identical, or rather feigned, emotional states.[20]

In the later scholarship, Homer is once again being imagined as a medium and a conduit, not only for the eternal Muses above but also for the Greeks in their various sufferings or triumphs on the battlefield in the mythological past, and then, like a livestream cable transmission that could be replayed at will, for audiences centuries later who, now at the receiving end of a text rather than a rhapsodic performance, are permitted to witness the events taking place at Troy through Homer's eyes. If the critics are unable to disentangle their own identity from that of Homer, this is because Homer is decidedly a "philhellene" just like the critics themselves, who in turn are more than happy to stand in for the Greek reader at large—non-Greek readers are inconceivable—as they imagine him (never "her") to be. Thus, by showing Hera taking pity on the Greeks and then being moved to take action that might aid them in their direst of straits, "Homer again keeps us in suspense [by diverting us] from the present circumstances, unwilling, as a pro-Greek (*philellēn*), to set out in detail the misfortune of the Greeks."[21] The use of "us" in cases like these tells all we need to know about the kinds of identification that are at work in the Homeric commentaries. Ever solicitous of his audience, Homer is careful to protect them from distressing events on the battlefield, here by evoking the fond sympathies of Hera: "for the poet is *always* pro-Greek," just like his readers.[22]

Notable in all of this is not only the commentators' ability to detect philhellenic sympathies in Homer, however forced such judgments may seem to us today, but also, and more significantly, their sensitivity to neuralgic moments in his poetry, which were clearly hard for an ancient reader to bear. It seems evident that readers had trouble dealing with pain on the battlefield, and Homer's poems had plenty of pain to deliver. The commentators, insofar as they took on the role of literary critics, were acting like life coaches or even therapists for readers: by diving head first into symptomatic readings of Homer's texts, they taught readers how to cope with fears, anxieties, and other powerful emotions—including more pleasurable feelings, since enjoyment, admiration, and astonishment make for excellent antidotes to pain, and they may even be pain's ultimate reward.

A question to ask is whether these scholars were exposing readers to Homer's poetry or shielding them from it. Not that the scholars were in any way exempt from the difficulties they sensed: they were practicing self-therapy as well. Even the suggestion that Homer was a philhellene, a near redundancy in itself, is symptomatic of the same anxieties; it masks the concern that Homer might be differently construed. Given his exotic, often savage, otherness, was Homer even Greek? The thought did cross the minds of some ancient readers. Dio Chrysostom's encounter with the "barbaric" and warlike avatars of Homeric Greeks in the Scythian heartland, as narrated in his *Borysthenian Discourse* (*Oration* 36), is one such example. Stripped of the trappings of epic fantasy, these creatures are not a welcome sight. And Homer, whose *Iliad* they adore and know by heart, falls prey to the same shattered fantasy. Just as these barbarian Greeks no longer speak Greek distinctly (*hellēnizein*), a further mark of their barbarity, so too could Homer's command of pure Greek (*hellēnismos*) be challenged among the Homeric commentators, as it was by Zenodotus, Aristarchus's predecessor and rival. In any event, the Homeric commentators are useful reminders that to read Homer was not without risks. His texts were not simply beautiful objects. They were dangerous minefields that could threaten one's sense of identity and intactness.

A case in point is given by Eustathius. At one point in his massive commentary on the *Iliad*, he treats a particularly bloody moment—the mayhem of deaths that brings book 4 to an end—by turning his attention not to Homer but to a reader's experience of the poetry. The verses in question read:

There no more could a man who was in that work make light of it,
one who still unhit and still unstabbed by the sharp bronze

spun in the midst of that fighting, with Pallas Athene's hold on
his hand guiding him, driving back the volleying spears thrown.
For on that day many men of the Achaians and Trojans
lay sprawled in the dust face downward beside one another.

(*Iliad* 4.539–44)

Now Eustathius:

> The reader of Homer would be a spectator of this sort [of the sort that Homer describes in line 539: the warrior who "focalizes" the reader's identifications], someone who experiences none of the evils of war, but enjoys the beautiful spectacle of the war narratives in his mind, visiting different parts of the battle without any risk of danger and without having to fault or disparage any of Homer's verses—and all the more so if the Homeric Pallas [viz., Athena, representing Homer's divine artistry] should guide him . . . as she turns the pages of the Homeric book with her hand, and in this way fends off the blows of the weapons.[23]

Eustathius is describing an instance of what literary critics call Homer's immersive or engaging style of narration, which features both vivid clarity (*enargeia*) and emotional involvement. Longinus had found Homer's *Iliad* to be both "dramatic" and "exciting," and therefore sublime (9.13). Eustathius uses this same language a few lines earlier, when he makes the rather extraordinary claim that it is no less "glorious, grand, and exciting" to narrate a battle than it is to engage in one,[24] a thought that is, however, no less strange than the transformation of the warrior in line 539 into a figure for the gentle reader.

But now consider what Eustathius makes of this trademark feature of Homer's narrative style. Eustathius's reader is able to enjoy Homer's descriptions of warfare in a pain-free fashion from the comfort of his chair, wading into and out of the fray without experiencing any of its evils. For the reader, war is just a "beautiful spectacle," like a film projected onto a screen, and a constant source of "surprise and applause." The last quoted words come from Alexander Pope, who is drawing directly on Eustathius here, as can be seen from his own commentary on the same scene in his *Essay on Homer's Battels* from 1716: "Whosoever should be guided thro' [Homer's] battels by *Minerva* . . . would see nothing through the whole but Subjects of Surprize and Applause." So viewed, war as spectacle can be enjoyed in the imagination without any risk of harm or injury: aesthetics defends the reader from the horrors of the war. Pope had eyes only for "the Poetical Beauties of the Author," and the same is generally true of Eustathius.[25]

Eustathius's commentary makes for an unusually frank admission by an ancient critic. But beyond what we have just seen, it is the phrase "without having to fault or disparage any of Homer's verses" that gives pause. It is not entirely clear whom Eustathius had in mind: possibly Plato, perhaps Zoilus (one of Homer's fiercest fourth-century critics), or simply his own bad conscience. The point is that Homer's poems harbored a potential for moral harm and injury. They could be enjoyed, but that enjoyment needed justification. Much ancient literary criticism existed in order to provide this justification. Eustathius stands out for making this defensive posture as explicit as he does.

## Why "Wrath"?

The risks of reading Homer were apparent from the word go, starting with the *Iliad*'s opening line: *Mēnin aeide thea,* "Sing, goddess, the wrath of Achilles." Few words generated as much critical wrangling in antiquity as the very first word of the poem: *mēnin,* "wrath" or "anger." A raft of scholiastic comments, many dating from the Hellenistic period accumulated around this one word, which the grammarian-critics took to be *dusphēmos* (ill-omened, slanderous, shameful). But the first to highlight the significance of *mēnin* was Homer himself. He calls Achilles's wrath *oulo<u>menēn</u>* (accursed, wretched)—an off-rhyme, set off by a strong enjambment, that is lost in Lattimore's rendering, "Sing, goddess, the anger of Peleus's son Achilleus / *and its devastation*"—and immediately glosses the reason why:

[The wrath of Achilles] put pains thousandfold upon the Achaians
hurled in their multitudes to the house of Hades strong souls
of heroes, but gave their bodies to be the delicate feasting
of dogs, of all birds, and the will of Zeus was accomplished.

(*Iliad* 1.2–5)

As the ancient scholars, scandalized by what they read, zeroed in on the opening verse of the *Iliad*, each of their comments proved more ingenious than the last as they struggled to explain away the poem's troubling first word. The mention of "wrath," they wrote, brings on an emotional catharsis of sorts. It immediately heightens the reader's attention and prepares him to focus on the grandeur or sublimity of the poem, which (readers expect) will end in a pleasurable release—a "characteristically Greek" way of managing the soul. It habituates "us" to bear our emotions more nobly, especially because Homer "is going to narrate wars and the deaths of heroes"—*Greek* heroes, that is. It makes Homer's praise of the Greeks more convincing because his praise is not absolute—he will eventually show the Greeks winning the war, but it is more plausible to do so without favoring them from the start. Achilles's anger is the premise of the action that follows. But it is the anger itself, not Achilles, that Homer is in fact blaming, good patriot that he was. It is not even the anger (*mēnis*) so much as the abundant "battle-spirit" (*menos*) possessed by Achilles that is "baleful" (*oloos*) and hence branded as "accursed" (*oulomenēn*), and so on.[26] In their totality, the explanations recall nothing so much as the "kettle logic" that Freud took to govern the illogical behavior of dreams, whereby each new justification erases the premise of the last. The commentators were truly exercised by the problem, and no consensus was ever reached. Not even the appeal to magic and numerology could put an end to the debates. Apion, the first-century CE grammarian discussed in chapter 2, is a case in point. Lucian, with his characteristic wit, would deflate all of this academic desperation with a single deft stroke in his fantastically conceived *A True Story*. Faced with the opportunity to interview Homer in the Land of the Dead, "I next asked him why he began with the wrath of Achilles; and he said that it just came into his head that way, without any study."[27]

The antiquity of the problem of the *Iliad*'s first word (*mēnis*) is vouchsafed by Aristotle in his *Poetics*, who reports that Protagoras, the premiere sophist from the previous century, blamed Homer for misunderstanding the gender of *mēnis*, which in Homer and everywhere else is feminine but which here designates a masculine act: the anger of Achilles is, after all, acknowledged to be "destructive" and "baleful" in the next line. Protagoras was quite plainly wading into a preexisting debate about the word, and he was facetiously turning to his advantage the criticisms and defenses that the mention of *mēnis* invited. (He was in fact making a novel contribution to linguistics by flagging the gendering of Greek nouns.) Aristotle would weigh in on the problem in his *Rhetoric*, where he noted how the poet has Apollo blame Achilles for not relenting in his anger toward Hector "once he was dead. The poet said it well: 'for he is outraging senseless clay in his wrath' [*Iliad* 24.54]."[28] The reference is to the way Achilles pierced Hector's feet, threaded them with a thong, and dragged the body behind his chariot with his head trailing in the dust, first before the gates of Troy (book 22) and then three times a day for several days afterward around the tomb of Patroclus (book 24).

Aristotle, to his credit, recognizes there is a problem here. He simply restricts his observation to a comment on psychology. (Elsewhere, he excuses Achilles's behavior as a custom of the times that has persisted even down to Aristotle's own present in Achilles's native home of Thessaly.[29]) Plato, for his part, denied that an atrocity like that committed by Homer's Achilles could ever have taken place: no Greek hero would perform such an act, and certainly not one who was the "son of a goddess and of the wise and temperate Peleus, himself third in line from Zeus"; Homer was maligning reality itself. As outraged by Achilles as Plato may have been, he did not object to the fact of warfare in Homer. It was not on those grounds that he banished Homer from his ideal city-state, but because Homer depicted Achilles, Priam, and others as emotionally overwrought, unseemly in their conduct, at times weeping like women and not warriors, or else moved by material considerations but not by virtue or decency. Dragging Hector's dead body behind a chariot overstepped the boundaries of propriety for a hero like Achilles. Killing Hector did not.[30]

The controversies surrounding the *Iliad*'s opening word, *mēnis*, or its dedication to slaughter never completely went away. The problem was still alive and well in the fourth century CE when the orator Libanius composed a pair of demonstration speeches about Achilles. In one, he condemned the hero for being "bitter, grievous, and like a wild animal," steeped in "wickedness," and motivated by an uncontrollable and unreasonable display of anger, above all in his outraging of Hector's corpse: "From what sort of barbarians did Achilles learn to do this? Who taught him that it was proper to wage war even on the dead?" In the other, he wrote a eulogy to the hero that begins, "Homer made me a lover of Achilles."[31] Libanius was not confused. He was faithfully reflecting the divisions of antiquity itself, which in its most honest moments registered the disturbances caused by Homer's poems.[32]

## Homer among the Literary Critics

In the generation after Aristotle, literary criticism of Homer took on a life of its own. What stands out in this genre of writing, which evolved outside the tradition of formal commentary on Homer but in parallel with it, are less the poet's pro-Greek attitudes than those of the critics themselves and, by proxy, the reader. Nevertheless, common to both strands of ancient criticism were a number of beliefs and practices: the presumptive value of Homeric poetry, which was thought to be quintessentially Greek and of unrivaled stature; a recognition of the intensity of his poetry; and the defensive maneuvers that were required to navigate around the ever-troubling nexus of art and war. In short, Homer presented a conundrum that was easier to dodge than to confront: How can the greatest of Greek poets be appreciated when his poetry is so very troubling? The literary critics rose to the challenge less by presenting new and different answers than by skirting the problem in different ways.

The simplest way to avoid the more gruesome aspects of Homeric carnage was to overlook them altogether, which was frequently done. The next best line of defense was to shift attention to the artistry by which these details are conveyed by the poet and to celebrate their astonishing perfection, poetically speaking. These two approaches, deflection and celebration, often amounted to the same thing. An example of this conflation is found in the essay *On Style* by a certain Demetrius, possibly dating from the second century BCE, whose treatment of Homer's forceful style is a forerunner of the Longinian sublime. When Demetrius fastens onto a phrase from book 13 of the *Iliad*, "the battle shuddered" (339), what he sees is not a battle, although he recognizes that it is part of the image's background noise ("the clash of spears and the low, continuous sound they make"), but rather a vibrant personification and vivid metaphor that "represents the battle shuddering *as if it were alive*" (§82; trans. Innes, modified; emphasis added). This is a nice touch. And it is easy for any reader of a text like *On Style* to get caught up in the excitement that poetic language provokes whenever it attracts to itself features of the object-world. Here, the attraction lies in the lively personification of inanimate objects (the weapons of war and, by extension, the battle itself) through metaphor (thus anticipating today's criticism in the vein of vibrant materialism, but also presaging some of its limits). Consequently, the deadly battle is, in Demetrius's hands, more alive than the corpses that are strewn in its wake. Force on the epic battlefield is assimilated without remainder into Homer's forceful style.

Demetrius was by no means the first to acknowledge that inanimate, death-dealing objects take on a poetic life of their own in Homer (he thanks Aristotle for the insight). Nor was he the last. Consider how the Augustan critic Dionysius of Halicarnassus appreciates "those lines of Homer in which Achilles is made to outrage Hector after his death" in *Iliad* 22. Dionysius quotes the verses in full (all sixteen of them), only to marvel at their literary qualities and above all their rhythms: "This is the way in which a *noble body and terrible sufferings* should be described by men of sensibility and intelligence. . . . In the passage of Homer *there is not a single undig-*

*nified or undistinguished line*" that would cause a reader any "pain," and the rhythms are perfect.[33] The physical and moral outrage that Homer brings to the fore is instantly eclipsed by his poetic technique. As with Eustathius, reading and literary criticism are here made into a defensive practice: they are a way of averting the gaze.

The author of the treatise *On the Sublime*, known to us as Longinus and usually dated to sometime in the first century CE, perfected this practice of aversion. For Longinus, Homer is never more sublime than at the deadliest moments of his poetry. He thrills to scenes of combat and the way "the gale of battle blows hard in Homer," particularly in the *Iliad*, which shows the poet at "the height of his powers, dramatic and exciting," thanks to the "outpouring of passions crowding one on another" and to his "versatility, realism, [and] the abundance of imagery taken from life."[34] Larger-than-life gods and heroes in Homer command jaw-dropping wonder—they are sublime, aesthetically speaking—but one will look in vain for any criticism by Longinus of their doings on the battlefield. The real source of the sublimity, however, does not lie in the poetry. Rather, it lies in the experience of the reader who, as in Eustathius, *flirts* with the danger of warfare without actually being touched by it. Where Eustathius is eager to divert the reader's gaze from this danger, Longinus hurls readers headlong into its midst. The shared intimacies between poet and reader that we find in the scholia are available in Longinus too. They simply exist on a more intense scale.

The Longinian sublime is a vast sympathetic system: it registers the vulnerability of a reader to the dangers of Homeric poetry, which come in jolts as potential shocks and wounds but are then deflected through a sublimation. Consider the image that Longinus famously analyzes at the start of his lengthy chapter on Homer, namely, the picture of Eris, the goddess of strife, as she appears in *Iliad* 4, the same book that Eustathius was commenting on above and a mere 100 verses earlier. It is one of the more terrifying passages in the poem because its theme is nothing other than terror itself. Homer shows Ares, Athena, and a threesome of ungodly divine presences visiting horrors "equally between both sides" of the battlefield—namely, Terror, Fear (Panic), and Strife, "whose wrath is relentless, . . . the sister and companion of murderous Ares [the god of war]." Strife starts off as a tiny creature, as quarrels usually do, but quickly evolves into a cosmic force: she "grows until she strides on the earth with her head striking heaven" (*Iliad* 4.439–44).

Longinus seizes on this maximized version of Strife and then translates the image into his own idiom. In occupying and thereby symbolizing "the gap between earth and heaven," Strife marks the height of sublimity. Stunned into admiration, Longinus adds, "One might say that this gap is the measure not so much of Strife as of Homer" (9.5). The move is significant. Homer is equated with Strife, a startling thought under any description, but then he is instantly made to assimilate all her vast and ungodly powers into his poetic art, which is itself immeasurably great. Our attention passes from the causes of war to the sublimity of its depiction, and it is this latter that gives the true measure of Homer. In short, Homer truly is a poet of war for Longinus. But, as with Goethe and others in later epochs, war in Homer can be appreciated only once it has been transformed into an aesthetic object (a "picture," "image," or "appearance"—a collection of *phantasmata*, 9.6) that can be experienced in its own right, and then into an emblem of Homer's poetic art. And although Strife is said by Homer to visit both sides of the battlefield equally, it is Homer, not Strife, whose appearances need to be saved. This transformation is possible because of the underlying system of Greek values that validates the experience of reading Homer from a philhellenic perspective—for "we are pure Greeks, with no barbarian blood" (23.4, quoting Plato). Whether or not Homer is being understood as a philhellene, Longinus certainly projects himself as one. There is no way to disentangle the art from the ideology that surrounds and supports it.

The upshot of this all-too-rapid survey of ancient literary critics on the topic of warfare in Homer may come as an unwelcome surprise. Not only were they utterly unequipped to confront the horrific violence of the poems and quick to avert their gaze from this element in epic, thereby turning criticism into an uncritical defensive maneuver, they were also all too eager to become outright *apologists* for Homeric violence, whether by aestheticizing the gore, condoning it, or sidestepping it altogether. Nor are the ancients alone: too many modern critics follow cheerfully in their footsteps.

Looking briefly ahead, we can say that the habits of reading that were established in antiquity, above all the conceit of shared intimacies, shaped how Homer would be understood by later readers. Shelley's Romantic slogan from 1822, "We are all Greeks," is an expression of this same solidarity. The way to Homer's appropriation by the moderns was prepared for by the ancients at a most basic level of experience: he was always imagined to be one of "us," and "we" were always one of "them." His lasting reputation was built on these shared structures of feeling, which served as textual escorts and helped guide the reception of Homer. In fact, what was passed down over the millennia were not Homer's texts alone but these very structures of feeling. This inheritance was, however, divided. Homer had his critics, and even Homer's greatest admirers developed the same neuralgic sensitivity to the troubling dimensions of his depiction of war that was felt in antiquity. The question that ought to matter most to us today is how successful the glorification of war by inattention could ever be. As it happens, the impetus to this question is found not only in the critical traditions of antiquity but also in the Homeric poems themselves to which these traditions were responding—or from which they were recoiling. Here I can only sketch the outlines of a path forward to a differently attuned reading of Homer.

## War Music

Rather than pretending that the *Iliad* and *Odyssey* are unproblematically great works of art and unrivaled paradigms of cultural value, it is perhaps better to acknowledge that the Homeric poems are at bottom contradictory objects that present hard problems and no easy solutions, not only because the epics are blood-soaked but because any pleasure or solace they present is tainted by the horrors they depict. Extricating pure, untainted cultural and aesthetic or ethical value from Homer is an impossible task. I believe we can go further and say that this kind of extrication was never meant to be.

But to recognize this requires that we acknowledge and not bury the "uncomfortable dissonances" that run through both poems.[35]

We need look no further than the opening lines of the *Iliad*. The first verse sets the tone: "Sing, goddess, the anger of Peleus's son Achilleus." The opening two words of this verse are, as we saw, *mēnin aeide*, "wrath [or "anger"] sing." Together, they mark the founding and ineluctable paradox of the poem, which, to be sure, is a song, but a song that commemorates bloodshed and its horrific consequences, as we hear in the continuation, which is worth quoting for a second time:

Anger sing, goddess . . .
and its accursed devastation, which put pains thousandfold upon the
  Achaians,
hurled in their multitudes to the house of Hades strong souls
of heroes, but gave their bodies to be the delicate feasting
of dogs, of all birds.

(*Iliad* 1.1–5; trans. slightly modified)

The implications of this opening prayer to the Muses cascade through the rest of the poem, touching every aspect of it, not only at the level of theme but in the actual delivery of the poetry, which is both oral and formulaic: it is formed by repeated patternings of sound shapes that are governed by an insistent meter and rhythmical cadence, be this at the level of a phrase, a line, or an entire block of verses conveying either messages or actions. The simple repetition of arming scenes (a subset of so-called type scenes), in which heroes elaborately arm themselves for battle with gleaming weaponry, turns warfare and the act of killing itself into a ritualized occurrence with a peculiar aesthetic rhythm of its own. War literally becomes formulaic, just like the poetry that conveys it.

The point is not that bloodshed is the stuff of which Homer's poems are made, although statistically this is true, but that the stuff of the poems is inseparable from the way in which it is heard. Every mention of pain, destruction, death, burial, and decay occurs in rhythmic verse, the six-footed dactylic hexameter—each foot comprising two short syllables and a long syllable ( – ˘ ˘ ) or their equivalent ( – – )—that is sung to a lyre. Homeric beauty is painful to perceive, and aesthetic pleasure cannot be detached from the harshness of Homeric realities; hence the troubling dissonance of *mēnin aeide* ( – ˘ ˘ | – ˘ ), "wrath | sing," or, in a later gloss, "War Music," which is the title of Christopher Logue's remarkable rendering of the *Iliad* (1959–2005).

Perhaps there can be no more vivid illustration of the paradox encapsulated by these pairs of words than a short excerpt from *Zeno Writing* (2002), an eleven-minute film montage that later formed part of the exhibition *Smoke, Ashes, Fable* (2017–2018) by the South African artist William Kentridge. The film closes with a disturbing sequence of images and sounds: documentary footage from World War I with explosions hurling debris into the air, blasts of ordnance issuing from artillery and tanks, a pair of charcoal arcs tracing figure eights on a piece of paper that dissolves into footage of two biplane fighters chasing each other in the same pattern, troops advancing and retreating before a line of further blasts, buildings ablaze and engulfed in billowing smoke above, with fiery smoke-laced wreckage below, all set against the background of a South African choir hymning music that recalls a canticle, a liturgy, or a dirge. As the images fade away and the choral music reaches a moving lento, all that remains is a text, cursive and handwritten in charcoal pencil, that contains a quotation from Marcus Aurelius's *Meditations* (12.27) on the vanity of human enmity. Repeated in two stanzas, the text resembles a poem more than it does the prose original:

[a line of decapitated letters]
Smoke, Ashes, Fable?
Where are they all now?
Perhaps they are no longer
even fable. –
Smoke Ashes Fable? Where
are they all now. Perhaps
they are no longer even smoke –
[a trailing line of half-legible text follows]

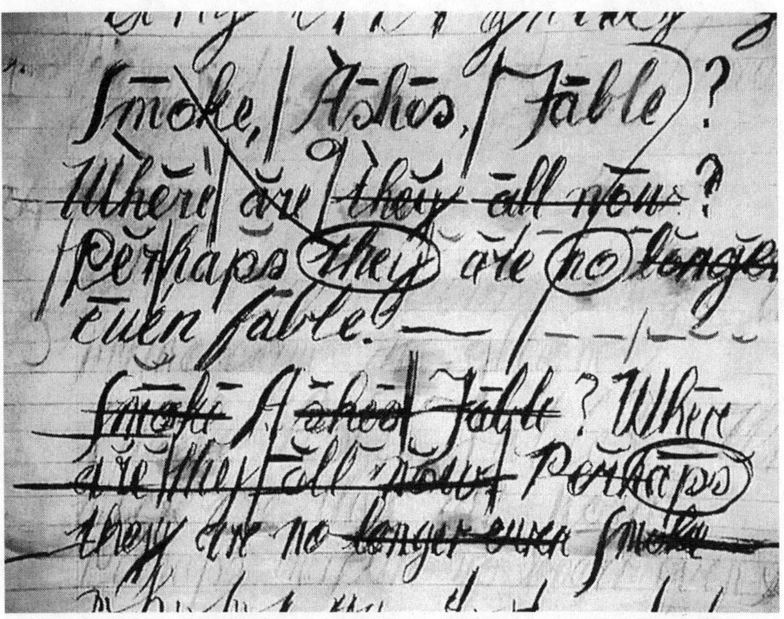


FIGURE 5.1. William Kentridge, *Zeno Writing* (2002). Still from the 35 mm film. Based on charcoal drawing on paper and transferred to video. Copyright and courtesy of William Kentridge.

Seconds later, the text is overwritten, smudged, and erased like a living palimpsest. Marks appear over the letters, long vertical bars plunge between the words, and half the text is crossed out with thick horizontal gashes (fig. 5.1).

At first, the marks appear to be stress accents of a sort. As the sequence progresses, it becomes clear that they belong to a special kind of scansion system that marks long and short durations ( – ⏑ ), with the durations divided into "feet" or measures by means of vertical bars ( | ). The measures are, in fact, dactylic hexameters, the verse form of epic poetry that was used by Homer and later, in imitation, by Vergil.[36] After a few seconds the words are erased, leaving only the bare metrical symbols, which are mostly unchanged from the earlier images. Set against an empty background and rendered naked and exposed, they now appear strangely distorted (fig. 5.2). The measures seem to be suspended in midair, but once again this is an illusion. They are in fact falling, possibly into place

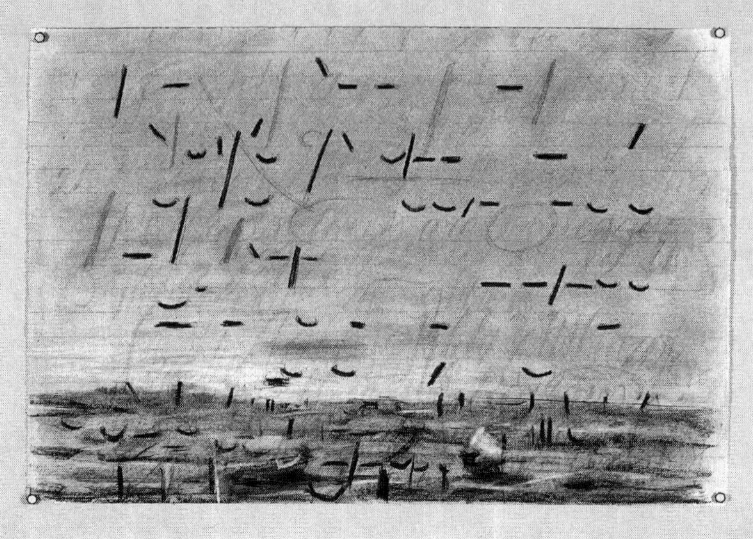

FIGURE 5.2. William Kentridge, *Zeno Writing* (2002). Drawing made for final frame of the sequence to which it belongs. Charcoal on paper, transferred to video. Copyright and courtesy of William Kentridge.

(momentarily), then apart—as if exploded—and onto a barren landscape littered with the broken feet of verses. Formerly slanted metrical bars now impale the ground like javelins hurled from the heavens. Are the metrical signs being blown to bits by bombs? Or are they *themselves* the bombs? Whatever the answer, war has been set to music, to the distortion of both.

Wrath Sing. *Mēnin aeide*. War Music. An abyss stretches between the words, and yet the poem unfolds around this very abyss. Readers of Homer have always struggled to bridge the gap, but the poem insistently keeps the gap open from start to finish. But why worry about these two words? The first word of the poem generates the problem on its own. *"Wrath" is itself sung*. The command to "sing" is otiose. And the same is true of every other word, image, or scene that resounds in Homer's poetry. A more productive analysis would want to consider how Homer's epic style works to resist and trouble what his language conveys. Style, in this view, would exist in order to "make forms difficult" (as the Russian Formalist critic Victor Shklovsky would have said)—not only difficult to perceive (this was Shklovsky's point) but difficult to accept on their own or any other terms.

Two quick examples will help to reinforce the point about Homer's self-resistant poetics of war. In book 3 of the *Iliad*, Menelaus (Helen's husband) and Paris (Helen's paramour) face off in a duel that could easily put an end to the war. A ritualized arming scene opens the sequence. The weapons, elaborately described, are at once brilliant and terrible to behold. Eventually the two come to blows. Having exchanged vain spear casts, Menelaus reaches for Paris's helmet, grabs it by the chinstrap, and nearly takes his life then and there: "The broidered strap under the softness of his throat strangled Paris, / fastened under his chin to hold on the horned helmet" (3.371–72). Paris's life hangs by a thread, as does the fate of the epic itself. But the strap breaks, thanks to the workings of a divine hand, and Menelaus hurls an empty helmet angrily to the side. Paris disappears (Aphrodite removes him from sight), and the war proceeds as planned. No more than a breath held in suspense, the two quoted verses are built on an exquisite contradiction: a beautiful object, itself an instrument of war, is bringing death to a beautiful hero. We admire the scene along with the internal audience ("Amazement seized the beholders"). But the greater part of the tension comes from the collision of beauty and danger that is built into this moment but is characteristic of the entirety of the poem. To catch oneself admiring the beauty is to ask about its justification in the context of war.

Now to the second example. *Iliad* book 9 finds Achilles withdrawn and sullen, sitting by the seashore, "delighting his heart in a lyre . . . /, and singing of men's fame" (186–89). The moment is disorienting: those brutal hands strumming a musical instrument? The ancient commentators have trouble making sense of this scene too. Achilles is the last character in the poem one would expect to find performing a song, let alone this kind of song, which defines the genre of epic poetry itself. At one level, then, the moment strangely contains itself: an epic song is being performed within an epic song, and it is being performed by the protagonist for whose sake the song that is the *Iliad* exists. But the scene goes beyond marking the self-reflexivity of Homer's poetry. Achilles and song ought not to belong together—certainly not in this way, and perhaps in no way at all. And yet they obviously do. The moment from *Iliad* 9, then, repeats the paradox of the first two words of the poem: "Wrath sing." It seems designed to underscore the abiding, because constitutive, paradox of "war music." But the problems mount as we look more closely.

Achilles's lyre is described as "clear-sounding, / splendid and carefully wrought, with a bridge of silver upon it" (186–87). It is a delicate, beautiful work of art, much like Paris's finely embroidered chinstrap, that produces still more art (music) when it is strummed, just as Homer's poem is a well-crafted artifact that produces more art whenever it is brought to life by a singer, but also just as Paris's chinstrap, when pulled asunder, threatens to produce more death. Then, in the next words, a bombshell: "which [lyre] he won out of the spoils when he ruined Eëtion's city. / With this he was pleasuring his heart, and singing of men's fame" (188–89). The lyre comes courtesy of the spoils of war won through the rough hands of Achilles, whose very same hands now strum it tunefully. But that is not all. Eëtion, the Theban king, was the father of Hector's wife, Andromache. And it was Achilles who killed Eëtion along with his seven sons, taking the queen captive and later releasing her for a ransom. (The tale is retold for us by Andromache herself in book 6 of the *Iliad*.) The lyre, then, carries a heavy load of suffering indeed.

Achilles's mood is difficult to gauge. He seems at once melancholic, vulnerable, pleasurably diverted, and strangely detached from reality—a perfect mirror of the unstable collocation of song and warfare. A string of associations comes to mind at this moment: Apollo "angrily" making his entrance early in book 1 with the shafts in his quiver clanging noisily at his shoulder strapped along with his bow, which he will use to lay waste to the Greek camp; the Achaean troops "chanting a splendid hymn to Apollo" in an effort to appease the god (*Iliad* 472–74) as he is raining a pestilence down on their camp and ravaging the men, their mules, and their dogs (*Iliad* 1.49–52, echoing and in part fulfilling the forecast of *Iliad* 1.4–5); Apollo plucking his "beautifully wrought lyre" to the accompaniment of the "sweet sounding" Muses on Mount Olympus at the close of book 1—the very same Muses that Homer invokes at the start of his poem when he utters his prayer, "Wrath sing"—as though nothing had happened in the interval.

Song and warfare make for a disturbing problem, and the *Iliad* seems determined to unsettle the reader at every conceivable turn, and where we least expect it.[37] Examples of Homer's self-resistant poetics could be multiplied, and the sample could be extended to the *Odyssey*: the Sirens, who would lure Odysseus to his death with their song of men's deeds and sufferings at Troy—song that is, in essence, epic poetry itself; Odysseus weeping like a bride of a slain hero in *Odyssey* 8 upon hearing the song about his own exploits at Troy; the rejection by Penelope of Phemius's epic song about the heroes' "bitter homecoming" in *Odyssey* 1, the *Odyssey* being itself one such song; Odysseus stringing his great bow, which he will use to slay the suitors, the way a lyre-player tunes his instrument; and so on. But it is not just that song and warfare make for a disturbing problem. It is that these two things are antagonistically opposed yet formally conjoined. The Homeric songs often appear to be extended threnodies convulsed by their own themes, as if designed to produce unease and critique rather than to celebrate heroic triumphs. Do we possess the critical tools to assess this dilemma of judgment?[38]

It would, in any event, be a mistake to claim that either poem celebrates war. On the contrary, they *problematize* war, the *Iliad* above all, since war is its theme. A poem about war, the *Iliad* is also, and perhaps to an even greater extent, a poem about the *frustrations* of war. The entirety of its design is staked on this premise. The Trojan War, as Homer presents it, has no beginning and no end. Instead of a linear plot that culminates in a clear goal, the *Iliad* spectacularly confutes this perception through repeated delays and virtual refusals of any teleology, with circular motions that are more salient than any forward motions that the narrative throughline suggests and with all of its actions frustrated from within. Heroes press on with their heroic missions in a complete expenditure of life that in one light may seem beautiful, and has for this reason earned the epithet from modern scholars "the beautiful death," but in another appears useless and empty.

Occupying the center of the poem from start to finish, Achilles is the most conspicuous example of this kind of countermotion, which in his case assumes a certain *vis inertiae*. He sits out the war for the bulk of the poem, rejecting the war's premise, and remains a reluctant participant in its doings until this position becomes untenable in the face of the death of his companion Patroclus: "I for my part did not come here for the sake of the Trojan / spearmen to fight against them, since to me they have done nothing" (1.152–53); "Yet why must the Argives fight with the Trojans?" (9.337–38); "I wish that strife would vanish away from among gods and mortals, / and gall, which makes a man grow angry for all his great mind" (18.107–8). At a stroke, Achilles's wishful thinking undoes two of the prime movers in the plot of the poem: the rage of war and his own anger. And in the Underworld in the *Odyssey* he reflects on his fate, remarkably announcing that he would gladly choose the life of a serf laboring the land in thrall to another over the life of a glorious shade (11.488–91).[39] Heraclitus, the philosopher who declared as the governing principle of reality the notion that "war is father and king of all" (fr. 53 DK), would never forgive Homer for this blanket critique of strife, which he quoted and refuted, according to later testimony.[40]

Nor is Achilles alone. In book 12 of the *Iliad*, Sarpedon, the Trojan offspring of Zeus, muses on the pointlessness of glory won in battle; his imminent death as it is portrayed four books later is the proof (see the next section below). In book 6, Glaucus, another Trojan fighter, observes how human life is like a scatter of leaves blown to the ground by the wind. He then parts from his Greek opponent with a mutual agreement not to engage in a duel to the death. This quiet despair about the futility of conflict later appealed to Pyrrho of Elis, the philosophical skeptic from the Hellenistic period, who was fond of repeating Glaucus's remarks whenever he could. Pyrrho "also admired Homer because he likened men to wasps, flies, and birds," all insignificant creatures in the larger scheme of things.[41] (He was alluding to Sarpedon's death in *Iliad* 16.) These are not isolated aberrations. Across the board, on both sides of the conflict and even among the gods, fighting is not regarded as a desirable activity in and of itself. On the contrary, it is feared and hated. Warriors pray to the gods that they will "escape death and the grind of Ares," the god and symbol of "horrible" war (*Iliad* 2.401, 4.14, 4.65, 5.379, etc.; *Odyssey* 11.314, 24.475). Ares is himself the "most hateful of all gods who hold Olympos," and this judgment comes from none other than Zeus (*Iliad* 5.890). The list of examples could be extended, but the point is sufficiently clear. Thoughts like these, repeated with extraordinary insistence in the poem, throw into doubt the validity and meaning of the war, and of war *tout court*. Taken together, they add up to a single question: Why war?

## A Beautiful Death?

The usual answer is *kleos aphthiton*, "imperishable glory," the memory of heroic valor performed in battle, ending in what has been called "a beautiful death." The most eloquent modern spokesperson for this strange idea is the French classicist Jean-Pierre Vernant. The idea has deep roots in German humanism and classicism in all of its manifestations, including its Nazi variants, but it was Vernant who popularized it. Vernant describes heroic death as a liberation from the physical limits of the human condition: "Death [for a hero] is not a simple demise, a privation of life; it is a transformation" into real life, which is conferred by recognition, memory, and postmortem honors. "A bloody death is beautiful and glorious when it strikes the hero in the fullness of youth; it raises him above the human condition and saves him from common death by conferring sublime luster on his demise."[42]

While it is unquestionable that epic poetry confers this dignity on the war dead by remembering them through song, it would be a mistake to say that epic privileges this ideal above all else. There is *nothing* beautiful about the death of a hero per se. Quite the contrary. For in the moment of death the greatest of heroes are made ugly or, what amounts to the same thing in the world of epic, unrecognizable, as happens to Sarpedon when he perishes at the hands of Patroclus:

No longer could a man, even a knowing one, have made out the godlike
Sarpedon, since he was piled from head to ends of feet under
a mass of weapons, the blood and the dust, while others about him
kept forever swarming over his dead body, as flies
through a sheepfold thunder about the pails overspilling
milk, in the season of spring when the milk splashes in the buckets.
So they swarmed over the dead man.

(*Iliad* 16.638–44)[43]

How "beautiful"—how aesthetically satisfying—is this scene? Most readers gloss over such moments as the price one has to pay in order to validate an aesthetically satisfying Homer, much as Vernant does. Heroic memory is in fact *premised* on this kind of forgetting and disavowal. To be sure, seductive counterarguments exist and are typically made. Isn't the imperishable glory that Homeric heroes enjoy ratified by the poems themselves and a function of their own ideology? Isn't the mere survival of the songs the surest sign that death has been transcended and finally made into a memorable object of beauty? Nevertheless, to assent to readings like these is to engage in circular reasoning. It is to presume that the poems, just because they are sung, are a thing of beauty and that their own qualities as song are transferred directly to every aspect of the poems. And yet this is exactly what critics do today whenever they take up a redemptively tragic humanist stance: they enliven the dead. And the same is true of critics whenever they adopt a posthumanist stance that celebrates the vivacity of objects at the expense of the thingliness of human death: enlivening (aestheticizing) objects, they reify the human realm. This is not to say that more realistic and disenchanted readings of Homer do not exist. They do, and these will be touched on below. It *is* to say, however, that calling the *Iliad* a thing of beauty is not simply falsified by the poem. It is a dodge.[44]

Warfare in Homer is a deeply ambivalent act. It is undergone both willingly and reluctantly by epic heroes, while the *Iliad* as a whole likewise both affirms and resists the value of warfare. We might say that the aesthetics of the heroic ideal makes "the beautiful death" a compelling value but that the ethics of the poem puts this ideal into question. A sounder approach would be to say that Homer uses beauty not to make war palatable but to make it questionable. Homeric epic is always also counter-epic. It enchants and disenchants at one and the same time. It is not the attraction of a beautiful death but rather the sheer expenditure of life in its fullest flowering that draws us to epic heroes. This waste fascinates. Epic attracts by problematizing itself. There is no way to eliminate the essential and deep ambivalences of epic around the horrors of war, for these are arguably what epic is about, just as the plot of the *Iliad* is not governed by the capture of Troy but by the obstacles that are strewn in the path leading to this outcome. As Euripides would later say in his play about the same war, "I think it makes small difference to the dead, if they / are buried in the tokens of luxury [i.e., with funeral honors and in tombs]. All this / is an empty glorification left for those who live" (*Trojan Women* 1248–50; trans. Lattimore).

## Phantasms of War

Euripides was echoing a sentiment that is best captured by the tradition, inaugurated by the Archaic lyric poet Stesichorus, that the Trojan War was fought over an empty phantom. That phantom (*eidōlon*) was Helen herself. According to Stesichorus, Helen's phantom image was conveyed to Troy, while the real Helen resided elsewhere. But as spectacular and daring as this version of things was, the inspiration for it lay in Homer himself. In *Iliad* book 5, Apollo rescues Aeneas from the battlefield and puts in his place a phantom (an *eidōlon*) around which the Greeks and the Trojans are seen to be "hewing at each other" in vain (*Iliad* 5.449–53). *Eidōlon* is the Homeric word used for dream images, which are typically delusive and sent by the gods, and for Underworld shades, which are without substance and life. Aeneas's figment is both dreamlike and ghostly, and so too is the warfare around him. So much fury, and so little to gain! Nor is this the first or last time that phantom images haunt the Trojan battlefield. Later accounts describe how the ghosts of Homeric warriors could be seen and heard at a now-deserted Troy, a phenomenon that was at once terrifying and alluring. In this light, Stesichorus's version of events looks less like a rewriting of Homer than a particular *reading* of Homer: it brings out the phantasmal, ghostly character of the epics as they appeared to post-Homeric audiences, a point that Lucian would later stress in his own reimagining of the *Iliad* as a "battle of the *shades* of heroes," as we saw in chapter 2.

The tradition of the Trojan War's having been fought over nothing, a mere phantom, took on a life of its own, and it quickly became one of the most compelling counterreadings of Homer. Herodotus, Euripides (who devoted a play to this theme), Isocrates, Plato, several Greek authors under Rome (Dio Chrysostom and Philostratus), and one of the Homeric *Lives* all drew on it. From there this counterreading passed into later antiquity and then into contemporary modernity, most notably in H.D.'s *Helen in Egypt* (1954) and in Derek Walcott's *Omeros* (1990), featuring a dark-skinned Caribbean Helen who, when viewed through a classicizing prism, appears as little more than a wreath of smoke and a shadow of her former self, and about whom the narrator states, "You were never in Troy." Released from this prism, she is something else altogether.[45] In this way, a strand within epic's own resistance to itself was made into an anti-epic tradition in literature.

## Modern Disenchanted Readings of Homer

If this study has shown nothing else, it is that Homer has appeared in an ambivalent light from his earliest mentions. Modern readings of Homer are no exception, and if anything the ambivalences have only deepened. As the earliest preserved literary connection to the past in the West, Homer gave precious testimony to what the West once was. His literary brilliance was beyond all doubt. But that brilliance was mired in bloody warfare, and the society he depicted was at once strange and familiar. Some of the shrewdest responses to Homer on record are the most sensitive to this contradiction and the unease it caused, or ought to have caused, in readers who celebrated Homer as a pinnacle of literary perfection. Thucydides is a case in point. Ever the clear-eyed observer of reality, he was unafraid to say about Homer's world, "Indeed, one might point to many other respects in which the customs of Greece long ago resemble those of the barbarians today."[46] He might have added what Euripides and others said, namely, that the contemporary Greek world had proved to be little more advanced in its customs. Plainly, Homer was vulnerable to demystification and disenchantment from an early date.

Later writers echoed Thucydides's sentiment, among them Dio Chrysostom, as we saw, as did the moderns. Robert Wood, the great admirer of Homer from the mid-eighteenth century who toured the Troad on foot with a copy of the *Iliad* in hand, was willing to concede that "most of Homer's heroes would, in the present age, be capitally convicted, in any country in Europe, on the Poet's evidence." Wood abhorred "the horrors," the "cruelty, violence, and injustice," and the "insolent triumph of the conqueror over the vanquished[,] which form so many disgusting pictures in Homer" and in other "barbarous" cultures. Wood attributed these flaws to the "primitive wit" exemplified by Homer and the world he depicts, which Wood found to be "strangely divided" between its displays of brutality on the one hand and generous and sympathetic "acts of humanity" on the other.[47] Worrying about these complications, which were not unknown to antiquity, turns out to have been a genre unto itself in modernity.

The second edition of Vico's *New Science* (1730) announced a "discovery of the true Homer." With this work, Vico entered the culture wars that had raged around Homer ever since the Italian humanist Julius Caesar Scaliger promoted the refined Vergil over the bumbling, primitive Homer in 1561. Scaliger's views are plain enough: Homer's depictions of "extremely offensive butchery . . . do not comport with heroic majesty."[48] The next wave of controversy broke out in France during the Quarrel of the Ancients and the Moderns in the late seventeenth century. In this context, Homer was either championed as the unsurpassed poet of antiquity or attacked on religious, moral, and poetic grounds. Opinions about

Homer's depictions of and attitude toward war were likewise divided.[49] Agreeing with the parties to the several disputes, Vico confuted them all. Vico's Homer, like Nietzsche's in the next century, is an amalgam of contradictions. On the one hand, he is conceded to be a "celestially sublime" poet, even "the most sublime of all the sublime poets" (§§807, 825).[50] On the other, he is also recognized to be a supremely violent and primitive poet, a barbarian in every respect, as his poems reflect: they are full of coarseness, volatility, irrationality, cruelty, butchery, rapaciousness, wildness, inhumanity, and savagery (the terms are all Vico's). Examples include Odysseus's poisoned arrows, corpses left "prey to dogs and vultures," and Achilles's dragging of "the naked corpse of Hector . . . three times around the walls of Troy" with his chariot (§781).

Vico is not content merely to allow these two sides of Homer to run their separate courses. They must be taken together. The defects of Homer's cultural development, his barbarity, and his "weakness" of mind are paradoxically what give rise to his unequaled grandeur. His similes, though "taken from beasts and other savage things," are "incomparable," despite what Scaliger believes. (Vico pointedly names him here.) And "the truculent and savage style in which he describes so many, such varied and such bloody battles, [and] so many and such extravagantly cruel kinds of butchery," in fact "make up all the sublimity of the *Iliad* in particular" (§§785, 787). That is the crux of the matter: Homer is sublime to the exact extent that "the frightfulness of the Homeric battles and deaths . . . gives to the *Iliad* all its marvelousness" (§827). And yet Vico's argument carries a hidden sting. For if what he says is true, what does this say about the sources of *our own* admiration for Homer? As the model not of human perfection but of human imperfection, Vico's Homer literally stands on a cracked base. That is how he appears in the frontispiece to *The New Science*, as a flawed statue that represents human imperfection, above all the imperfection of those who would worship him like a god.

Vico's arguments went largely unheard, but the pattern of his critique lived on. Here, Nietzsche proved to be Vico's true successor. He independently arrived at similar conclusions, which could now be directed at a new consensus that had formed around the classical revival heralded by Winckelmann, Herder, Goethe, and Schiller, a block of opinion that had shaped so much of nineteenth-century thinking about Homer and that Auerbach would likewise challenge in 1942, as we saw earlier in this chapter. One of Nietzsche's abiding criticisms of classical culture in antiquity is that it stands in the shadow of a darker past that was a never-ending source of horrific attractions and denials among the ancients—much like modernity itself. He calls this past "pre-Homeric," which is a somewhat misleading qualification, because the pre-Homeric element that inhabits all subsequent Greek culture as its inner "id" is in fact detectable already in Homer. Differently put, the pre-Homeric represents everything that Homer and the rest of antiquity are supposed to have extricated themselves from but never fully did or could.

Nietzsche introduces this concept in an essay titled "Homer's Contest" (1872). There, he invites the reader to look into everything that "lies *behind* the world of Homer" but is by the same token "the womb of everything Hellenic":

> The Greeks, the most humane people of ancient time, have a trait of cruelty, of tiger-like pleasure in destruction, in them: a trait which . . . must strike fear into us when we approach them with the emasculated concept of modern humanity. . . . Why did the Greek sculptor repeatedly have to represent war and battles with endless repetition, human bodies stretched out, their veins taut with hatred or the arrogance of triumph, the wounded doubled up, the dying in agony? Why did the whole Greek world rejoice over the pictures of battle in the *Iliad*? I fear we have not understood these in a sufficiently "Greek" way, and even that we would shudder if we ever did understand them in a Greek way.[51]

Nietzsche fetches up vivid images for the reader to contemplate: Alexander the Great piercing the feet of Batis, the military commander of Gaza, and dragging his live body behind a chariot in imitation of Achilles, whose own action taken against Hector "has something offensive and horrific about it" even "for us" (Nietzsche has quietly borrowed this precise pairing of the two torture scenes from Dionysius of Halicarnassus);[52] statuary that recalls the Aegina marbles from around 500 BCE depicting warriors from Troy in various states of jubilant victory or dying defeat, and the Laocoön group in the Vatican that portrays another violent scene from the Trojan cycle, one that famously attracted Winckelmann's eye but not his ire; and finally, the atrocities committed by both Athens and Sparta at the time of the Peloponnesian War. In each of these cases, "we look into the bottomless abysses of hatred," which is to say into "that pre-Homeric abyss of a gruesome savagery of hatred and pleasure in destruction." As the list of examples makes evident, the pre-Homeric is not tied to any specific time or place; it can resurface in any age almost at random, whenever a culture "becomes evil and cruel, vengeful and godless, in short, 'pre-Homeric,'" which only contributes to the horrific quality of the notion.[53] In later writings, most famously in *On the Genealogy of Morals*, Nietzsche expands the list to include "the Roman, Arabian, Germanic, Japanese nobility, Homeric heroes, [and] Scandinavian Vikings," all of whom are summed up in the iconic figure of the "blond" and "Aryan" "beast of prey." Nietzsche is touching on the phantasmatic core of violence and "naïve barbarism" that lies behind modern civilization and continues to inform it.[54]

When Nietzsche asks the question, "Why did the whole Greek world rejoice over the pictures of battle in the *Iliad*?" he is also asking the question's corollary, Why does the whole modern world *continue* to rejoice over these same pictures? Nietzsche has in mind the classicizing view of Homer that deflects attention away from violence by means of aesthetic absorption. A critique of this classicizing response is found in *The Birth of Tragedy* from 1872. There, the veil of the Apollonian, the symbolic principle of the beautiful, which is to say everything that Goethe and company reveled in when they looked at Classical art, assuages the guilty conscience of the observer who takes in, as through a scrim, the uglier, turbulent, and violent Dionysian reality that resides beneath the unruffled calm of beautiful appearances. Homer is the place where these two forces originally collide and are finally sublimated, by means of a disavowal. Through our "delight in semblance and redemption through appearance," the "epic-Apollonian" principle of beauty "casts a spell over even the most terrifying things before our very eyes," thanks to the "calm, unmoved gaze" with which the rhapsode beholds his materials: he is a model of aesthetic disengagement and distance *à la* Goethe.[55] Vico was making the identical point when he asked what it means to declare that Homer is "the most sublime of all the sublime poets." What has to be *ignored* in order to pronounce this aesthetic judgment? By what criteria does anyone call Homer the cradle of Western values and humanity?

Nietzsche's ultimate target is not Homer but the very idea of humanity that guides present-day perceptions of Homer—and of our own hapless voyeurism, if we can bear to admit it.[56] He is opposing modern recuperations of Homer as exemplified by Goethe and Schiller but also by Herder, whose essay "On the Humanity of Homer in his *Iliad*" from 1794 paints a rather rosy picture of the *Iliad* as a poem that beams forth "the gentle ray of humanity"—it shows "all of its characters to be equally humane and gentle"—and, luckily for its readers, ends before the real "atrocities of the Greeks" can be put on display in the final conquest of Troy. Herder is giving a novel twist to the tried-and-true gesture of avoidance that was earlier perfected by the ancient literary critics: whereas they located their own disavowal in Homer's style, he is inscribing disavowal within the plotline of the *Iliad* itself.[57] Nietzsche, of course, knows better: the Homeric poems are violent to the core. It is not the ancients who are primitive, but the moderns, and most of all when they pretend to be modern and too refined to take pleasure in bloodlust.[58] His view is entirely consonant with that of Vico, for whom Homer is a product of the "barbarous peoples of Greece (who are held to have spread humanity through the world)" (§781), the key term here being "held" (*creduto*), not "humanity." He too knows better than to adopt this overly cheerful ideal of modern humanism.

Nietzsche inspired half-hearted followers, most notably the Cambridge ritualists, who were attracted to his baring of the ancient primitive core of Greek culture so long as it was safely confined to ritual practices. One of their founding members was Gilbert Murray, whose ambivalence toward Homer's texts was the starting point of this book. Murray sought to blunt the impact of violence in Homer by treating it as part of a mythical or actual prehistory that had been more or less purged from the poems: "Yet the spirit of [the poems] is not savage. It is chivalrous. No enemy is ever tortured. No prisoners—with one exception . . . —are ever maltreated." This is a remarkable set of denials. Murray may wish to believe that the *Iliad* marks an advance over earlier, "rude [and] unexpurgated" versions of the story in which Hector "was still alive" when he was being dragged behind Achilles's chariot. Yet he cannot wish away the poisoned arrows of Odysseus that troubled Vico. He simply declares the *Odyssey* to be "*less* expurgated" than the *Iliad*.[59]

Later writers continued and intensified the Vichian and Nietzschean line of disenchanted readings of Homer during the Second World War, among them Simone Weil (*The Iliad, or, The Poem of Force*), Erich Auerbach ("Odysseus' Scar," in *Mimesis*), Rachel Bespaloff (*On the Iliad*), and Max Horkheimer and Theodor Adorno ("Odysseus or Myth and Enlightenment," in *Dialectic of Enlightenment*), all of whom composed their essays between 1939 and 1942 and published them during or shortly after the war.[60] It is safe to say that it was the experience of the war above all that produced these deep rejections of classically "safe" readings of Homer around the troubling nexus of art and war and replaced them with dissonant readings of the poems.

Simone Weil's celebrated essay is best known for its opening line and main thesis: "The true hero, the true subject, the center of the *Iliad* is force."[61] At a stroke, Weil radically decenters the focus of conventional readings of Homer, thereby dispossessing his poetry of its classical allure, its humanity, and its canonical literary virtues. For Weil, there is no beauty to be found in Homer—no beautiful deaths, no shows of power that are not self-vitiating and horrifically empty, "no consoling prospect of immortality," no *kleos* or glory for the glittering heroes, "no washed-out halo of patriotism" that might "descend" "on the hero's head" (4), no redemption from the brutal logic of force that turns living men into inanimate things whether they are victims or so-called victors. "The cold brutality of the deeds of war is left undisguised; neither victors nor vanquished are admired, scorned, or hated. . . . Those comparisons which liken them to beasts or things can inspire neither admiration nor contempt, but only regret that men are capable of being so transformed" (32).

Homer's similes, which were understood by his literary admirers as supremely poeticizing and by his opponents like Scaliger as demeaning flaws, are for Weil divested of all aesthetic value: they neither move nor repel. Instead, they take on the equivocal status of force itself. What *is* distinctive about the *Iliad* is the way the poem exposes to the glare of daylight the fundamental facts of force and of human vulnerability, mostly along two axes: whenever epic heroes try, in vain, to ignore these facts (the poem strips away those pretensions with a ruthlessness that is rare in literature) or whenever force appears to have been put on pause however briefly (though in reality it has not been), as in the excursions to the baths of Troy, the scenes of daily life shining through the scenes of war, the moments of reflection before a spear is hurled or a knife implanted in a breast, all of which descend on the action like so many "moments of grace," only to vanish as quickly as they arrive (30).

Weil's is a resolutely disenchanted and disenchanting reading of Homer, and it is typical of others by her contemporaries. Bespaloff explicitly speaks of a "radical disenchantment" of force in Homer.[62] Horkheimer and Adorno dissect the mechanisms of enchantment. And all five of the twentieth-century critics in question here perform this disenchantment with their readings. In stripping Homer of his aura, each of these writers is doing more than simply subverting the canonical interpretations of Homer in the Western tradition. They are also directly challenging the appropriation of Homer by European and especially German nationalists that culminated with the Nazis. The roots of this movement, they recognized, ran deep in modern culture, where the study of Homer had played so immense a role in fashioning that culture's sense of identity. Speaking of Wilamowitz's *Die Heimkehr des Odysseus* (*The Return of Odysseus*) from 1927 and sundry other writings by this influential scholar and Nietzsche's mortal enemy, Adorno and Horkheimer write that these "are among the most striking documents of the German intermingling of barbarism and culture, which is fundamental to modern Philhellenism."[63] At issue is not Homer but its modern reflection, what the authors call "the Homeric spirit," which seeks to banish the horrors of what it depicts by consigning them to the soothing oblivion of a mythically enchanted past, but whose gesture backfires and burns the horrors all the more indelibly into the mind.

To return to where this chapter started and to complete our rapid tour of modern disenchanted readings of Homer, we can take up "Odysseus' Scar," Auerbach's lead essay from *Mimesis,* one last time. The whole of the essay is dedicated to a single proposition: Homer's narrative is brilliantly illuminated by a superficial source of light. All foreground and no background, with not the slightest hint of layers of recessed obscurity, darkness, or depth, Homer's narrative style maximizes entertainment and minimizes critical reflection. And although the epics narrate difficult scenarios, the style used to do so serves to distract listeners from what they are given to see, in large part simply through the clarity and vividness of the presentation.

In praising the brilliant surfaces of the Homeric style, Auerbach was giving a new spin to an old critical trope. Ancient literary critics adored Homer's vividness. But in Auerbach's hands, this critical insight comes not as praise but as a reproach. Homer's much-touted poetic vividness, his *enargeia,* succeeds not by illuminating objects but by removing them from view. And his aesthetic operations in general exist not to convey action but to distract us from its own narration—a useful device given the troubling scenes that he presents in both poems.

I say "both poems" because, the title of his chapter notwithstanding ("Odysseus' Scar"), Auerbach has surprisingly much to say about the *Iliad.* The first example he chooses to discuss is not taken from the *Odyssey* but is rather a dire moment from book 16 of the *Iliad,* where Trojan fires are threatening the ships of Achilles and his Myrmidon troops with complete destruction. "Though it be in the thick of a battle," Homer somehow finds time to distract us with "the wonderful simile of the wolf," "the order of the Myrmidon host," and "a detailed account of the ancestry of several subordinate leaders"—all of which he takes to be hallmarks of Homer's leisurely digressive style. Examples of this technique that are adduced by Auerbach include the exchange between the Cyclops and Odysseus (before and after Polyphemus is blinded), that between Odysseus and the suitors "when [Odysseus] begins to kill them," and the long speeches by Hector and Achilles "before battle and after" (5–6).

There's much talk in the poems, but also "much that is terrible (*viel Schreckliches*)" (6). These two things go hand in hand. The poet's goal is not merely to distract us (to entertain us and to "bewitch us" into "forget[ting] our own reality for a while") but also not to "disturb" us. And language is the means of this distraction: it reminds us that we are in the midst of a highly stylized world that is defined by language even at its most terrifying moments. All of Homer's "garrulousness," the expansive descriptions for which his poems are famous (his so-called *epische Breite*), soothes and comforts, but it does so *through the ceaseless flow of epic language itself.*[64] Thus, "no speech is so filled with anger or scorn that the particles which express logical and grammatical connections are lacking or out of place." Everything is orderly, "delimit[ed]," and legible; all the logical connections are "brought to light in perfect fullness, so that a continuous rhythmic procession of phenomena passes by." Such is "the basic impulse of the Homeric style" (6). The poems remain surface images—appearances—that can never be ruffled even by the violence that runs through them both. There are no depths to plumb in these Homeric mirrors—if, that is, we permit ourselves to stop at their surface, as the poem encourages us to do. Between the lines, Auerbach is quietly invoking Nietzsche's Apollonian principle, the veil of beautiful appearances, and its source in Weimar classicism, in relation to which Auerbach's own essay has been conceived. But by the same token, he is further reminding us that these brilliant Homeric surfaces exist to divert the eye from that which lurks beneath them, namely, all "that is terrible" in the poems, what Nietzsche described as their Dionysian undertow and, in his own essay on Homer, what he called "the pre-Homeric abyss" of savagery and destructive violence. In short, Auerbach is conveying a message that is diametrically opposed to the one for which he is most widely known and misunderstood. Homer's poetic surfaces are disguises. They do not tell the whole story.

As proof, we need look no further than Auerbach's most celebrated example, the foot-washing scene from book 19 of the *Odyssey*, which gives his essay its title. Representing a moment of recogntion in the narrative, the scene is also a moment of thinly veiled violence and aggression. A quick reminder of the context will be useful. Odysseus has just arrived at his own palace disguised as a beggar and seeking revenge. The aged Eurycleia, his childhood nurse, begins to wash his feet on orders from Penelope. As Eurycleia sets to work, the identifying scar on his thigh comes to light. She immediately cries out for joy, nearly thwarting his plans. Odysseus then springs to action to eliminate the threat. Auerbach describes what happens next: "Even in the dramatic moment of recognition, Homer does not omit to tell the reader that it is with his right hand that Odysseus takes the old woman by the throat to keep her from speaking, at the same time that he draws her closer to him with his left" and threatens her with death if she overturns his plans. And yet, for all its heightened danger and drama, the scene in its entirety "is scrupulously externalized and narrated in leisurely fashion" (3). The narrative surface and Homer's style are not only at odds with what they convey but they also actively work to redirect attention away from it. Most readers today probably do not even remember the repressed violence of the foot-washing scene, while Auerbach's critics conveniently overlook his account of the scene and in this way miss the thrust of his argument. He is warning readers to beware of aestheticized readings of Homer, which are guaranteed to produce ethical disavowals.

Auerbach's overarching point about Homer's fairy-tale realism, defined for an elite audience who wish to see the imperturbable stability of their universe mirrored back to them unproblematically, has a particular resonance given the sorts of images of Homer that were popular in Nazi Germany at the time, a world that was wracked by violence. But then, Auerbach sighs, legendary accounts of war like Homer's are constitutionally "unfit" to cope with the complexities of their subject matter. Auerbach knows this firsthand. He points to the experience of "the present (1942) war" (a phrase found only in the German editions) and to the way the propaganda "of National Socialism in Germany" (19) obeys the laws of legend but not of history: it too, like Homer, simplifies reality and catches only its surface reflections. We should not be misled by Auerbach's seemingly reductive attitude toward Homer. His reading is strategic, not final. His ultimate target is not Homeric naiveté but naïve readings of Homer.

## What's Left?

Despite the disenchanted readings of Homer's poetry of war that were produced from Vico onward, the aesthetic fantasy of Homer's world continues to reign among scholars. Critique has been replaced by reparative reading. If warfare is inexcusable in itself, it can be excused from a larger humanistic perspective that judiciously balances the brutality of war against the moral significance that can allegedly be wrung from it. Thus "suffering produces song," and Homer's Trojan War illumines "the pathos of vain human effort" and "the tragedy of human life."[65] Tragic humanism here finds solace in the fact that in war humans confront their mortal limits; they learn to admit the consequences of mortality. A universal "sympathy" is found in this suffering, the value of which is augmented, and seemingly rewarded, by the sheer "heroic" scale of the sufferers and their suffering.[66] On this logic, the final reconciliation between Priam and his son's murderer, Achilles, is the fruit of these lessons learned over the course of the poem, which is now read in a redemptive and reparative light: we all must die; death is a terrible thing; so let's live on, chastened by the prospect.

The trouble with readings like this is that they try to extract value out of something that is devoid of value. It's hard to make killing meaningful and even harder to make it stand for something of universal human significance. It's hard to argue that when I hold a sword to your throat what stands revealed to me and to you is the shared fact of our humanity, let alone our mortality, and that we should therefore count the lesson a good even if the instruction is not. These are consoling readings, and it's not at all clear that consolation is really the thrust of Homer's poetry. While we might want Homer to be affirming the value of human life, of existence for its own sake, or of the origins of humane feelings, it may be that all that his poetry points to is the negation of these things in the context of war. And as much as one might wish the poem to bring to a close the war that surrounds it, it does nothing of the sort. As Achilles says in his own attempt at consoling Priam a few hundred lines from the end of the poem, "There is not / anything to be gained from grief for your son; you will never / bring him back; sooner you must go through yet another sorrow" (24.549–51).

Consolation here comes with an ominous sting, a prediction of what we know is to come. Priam departs from the Greek camp under the conditions of a truce assented to by Achilles, a delay of twelve days that will allow for a proper burial of Hector: "I will hold off our attack for as much time as you bid me" (24.670). And then the city will be razed without a trace, aside from the record of it kept by Homer and, to a lesser degree, by other minor epic poets, and aside from the charred rubble of a citadel that some might wish to identify with Homeric Troy, as if that identification could offer up one last consolation and one final benediction, a ringing tribute to the great glory of the past that has been lost. But in both of Homer's epics we are left not with resolution but with the bitter taste of regret, "regret," as Simone Weil puts it, at "what it is that violence has killed and will kill again" and at the waste that was needed to produce a sense of grief and of grievable life—a high cost, indeed.[67] The *Iliad* is not "a poem of death."[68] It is a poem of war. And Homer, however we choose to understand the name, never lets us forget the difference.

# Acknowledgments

The theme of this book first grew out of teaching and then out of an article that appeared in the journal *Arion* in 2002 with the same title and more or less the same scope as the present book. That essay became a pilot for this study, which I have gradually been developing in piecemeal fashion over the years in the classroom, in public lectures, and in publications. *Homer: The Very Idea* represents a distillation of that earlier work, now in a more reader-friendly form that is meant to be accessible to nonspecialists, students, and specialists alike. To that end, I have sought to pare down the scholarly apparatus to a bare minimum without sacrificing the flavor and richness of the original materials, however recondite or arcane—for it is there that all the interest lies.

For comments, discussion, friendly criticisms, and other sorts of first aid, large or small, pertaining to various aspects of this sprawling inquiry, all of which helped me sharpen my sense of my project and its aims, I wish to thank the following: Mary Bachvarova, Alastair Blanshard, Jonathan Burgess, Shane Butler, Stephen Campbell, Paul Chan, Raffaella Cribiore, Jack Davies, Eric Downing, Andrew Erskine, Marco Formisano, Robert Fowler, Herb Golder, Barbara Graziosi, Mark Griffith, Lorna Hardwick, Laura Jansen, Joseph Koerner, Meg Koerner, Chris Kraus, François Lissarrague, Tony Long, Phil Mitsis, Sarah Morris, Ramona Naddaff, René Nünlist, Robin Osborne, Maria Pantelia, Irene Peirano Garrison, Alex Purves, James Adam Redfield, Brian Rose, Ralph Rosen, Andrew Shelton, Kim Shelton, Susan Sherratt, Henry Spelman, Nigel Spivey, Anthony Snodgrass, Andrew Stewart, Caroline Vout, Emily Wilson, Victoria Wohl, and two anonymous readers for the University of Chicago Press. Bettina Bergmann, Évelyne Prioux, and Volker Michael Strocka helped me sort out a crucial detail in Dilthey's nineteenth-century drawing of the

Pompeian wall painting of Homer and the fisher boys—Homer's eyes—and the question of its faithfulness to the now much decayed original. Daria Lanzuolo of the Deutsches Archäologisches Institut in Rome kindly supplied me with further information about this image. Several years back, Susan Siegfried introduced me to the preparatory sketch, reproduced in chapter 2, of Homer and Orpheus by Ingres, which redeemed for me the latter's overdone and over-reproduced signature work, *The Apotheosis of Homer*. In this sketch, I saw for the first time a visual representation of the idea of Homer that I had been thinking about for several years. It has haunted me ever since. Additional thanks go to Susan for fielding queries about Ingres as I became more familiar with his art, to Brigitte Alasia of the Musée Ingres in Montauban for the same, to the staff at the Library Imaging Services at UC Berkeley for producing two scans at a time when access to the library collections was barred, to Meg Koerner for liaising with William Kentridge to confirm his reading habits and for requesting his permission to reproduce two images from his extraordinary film animation, *Zeno Writing*, to Anne McIlleron of the Kentridge Studio for assistance with these images, and to William Kentridge for his kind permission to use them. Andrew Wein saved me from countless errors while I was preparing the manuscript, and Erin Hogan proved to be an indispensable editor of my prose. James Whitman Toftness and Jenni Fry provided adroit editorial assistance once my manuscript reached the press, and Marian Rogers made copyediting look much easier than it is. Phoebe Garrett assisted with the index. My final thanks go to Susan Bielstein, who was a marvelously patient and encouraging editor and a pleasure to work with at every stage of this project.

The book benefited greatly from presentations at Brown University, Cambridge University, Johns Hopkins University, Swarthmore College, The Townsend Center for the Humanities at the University of California, Berkeley, the University of Toronto, the University of Wisconsin, and, on different occasions, Yale University, in addition to many dry runs made less dry thanks to my undergraduate and graduate students in classes, seminars, and office hours. Final revisions were made possible by a fellowship awarded by the John Simon Guggenheim Memorial Foundation in 2019.

# Notes

## Chapter One

1. Murray (1934), 242 (p. 212 of the 1907 edition).

2. *Divina Commedia*, "*Inferno*," canto 4.88. Statius, Vergil's Christianized successor, replaces Dante in the final cantos of *Purgatorio*, but not even he is permitted to enter heavenly Paradise.

3. Nietzsche (1982), 257. This was Nietzsche's inaugural speech at the University of Basel, entitled "On the Personality of Homer" and published soon afterward as "Homer and Classical Philology."

4. Nietzsche (1982), 258.

5. See Plato, *Ion* 541e and *Republic* 3.398a for the Protean image as applied to the rhapsode and to Homer, a connection that is clinched by the phrase "becomes multiform (*pantodapos*)" in both passages.

6. De Quincey (2001), 18.

7. Hume (1998), 139.

8. For a sampling of some of these, insofar as they are preserved, see West (2003b), 224–93. See also the long list of ascribed titles given by Hesychius of Miletus (West, 431). "Apocrypha" is West's term.

9. On the eighteenth-century developments, see "Homeric Question," in *HE*, to which add "the so-called Homeric Question" (*die sogenannte homerische Frage*) from Joseph Lautenbacher's introduction to Voss (1801), 1:6, the earliest modern occurrence of the phrase that I have found, which presupposes the usage without identifying the source. For earlier developments, see Ferreri (2007) and Demetriou (2015).

10. Once again, Nietzsche proves to be the most perspicacious observer of the tradition: at the time of the poet's canonization, "the word 'Homer' encompassed

a welter of the most disparate things," nor has the confusion lifted since then (Nietzsche [1982], 257).

11. See Haubold (2000), passim, and esp. 146 and 189, citing Simonides fr. 564.4 Page: "Homer and Stesichorus sang to [or "for"] the people."

12. Thonemann (2014); Hunter (2018), 5–21.

13. Hesychius o 718; cf. Achilles Tatius, *Leucippe and Clitophon* 8.9.3, where "Homerize" ("imitate Homer") is made into an obscene pun ("rubbing thighs"); Plato, *passim* (but cf. *Lysis* 212e; *Republic,* books 2–3); Aristotle, *Poetics* 24.1460a18–19.

14. See the Donatian and the Suetonian *Lives of Vergil* in Ziolkowski and Putnam (2008), 190 and 194–95 (§§8, 43–46, 48) for criticisms of his person. For the criticism of Vergil's poetry in later antiquity and beyond, see Hardie (2014), ch. 8.

15. Comparative metrical and literary studies of Indo-European (Vedic), Anatolian (Hurro-Hittite and Akkadian), and Mesopotamian (Akkadian, Sumerian, and Ugaritic) literature hint at this buried rich prehistory prior to Homer. See "Indo-European Background," in *HE*, for a thumbnail overview. For more detail, see Haubold (2002); West (2007); Bachvarova (2016). On Mycenaean dactylic epic, see "Language, Homeric," in *HE*; Horrocks (1980).

16. The stories of the transmission of Homer's poems, wildly divergent in their main lines and details, are reported by various sources from the fourth century BCE to later antiquity (e.g., Ephorus, Heraclides Lembus, Cicero, Plutarch, Josephus, Aelian, the scholia to Dionysius Thrax, and an important scholium on Pindar). The process of the texts' stabilization culminated in Hellenistic Alexandria. For an overview, see "Pisistratean Recension," "Creophylus," "Cynaethus," and "Aristarchus" in *HE*. Thestorides, who was said to have tricked Homer into the process of oral dictation, appears in the pseudo-Herodotean *Life of Homer* (West [2003b], 370–73). Stasinus is said to have earned the coveted poem the *Cypria* from Homer as a dowry gift when he married one of Homer's daughters (*Vit. Hom.* [Tzetzes, *Chil.*] 254.637–40 Allen). (The *Cypria* was detached from the Homeric corpus by the time of Herodotus.) Even the Homeridae seem to have circulated poems that were of rare if disputed Homeric origin (Plato, *Phaedrus* 252b). Further, "Oral Dictated Texts," in *HE*; Janko (1990); Graziosi (2002), ch. 6; Jensen (2011); Martin (2019).

17. See "Athens and Homer," in *HE*; Schironi (2018); Martin (2019).

18. An example of the latter: pseudo-Plutarch tries to make Homer's reticence into a virtue, as though it were a sign of self-discipline and restraint: "Homer was

so reserved as not even to mention his [own] name" ([Plutarch], *On Homer* 1.1; trans. West [2003b]). Almost identically, Dio, *Oration* 53 ("On Homer"), 9–10, who adds, "Like the prophets of the gods, [Homer] speaks *from a place that cannot be seen,* as from some innermost sanctuary, one we are not permitted to enter" (emphasis added).

19. Benveniste (1971), 226; emphasis in original.

20. Most recently, West (1999) and Graziosi (2002), both of whom inherit and expand on earlier accounts such as those by d'Aubignac, Vico, and Nietzsche, but also others to be discussed below. See especially d'Aubignac (1715), 56 on "th[e] false name of Homer" (*ce faux nom d'Homere*) and Nietzsche (1982), 266 on the anonymous compiler of the poems who "sacrificed his name on the altar of Homer."

21. See Burgess (2001).

22. I owe the example of Çatalhöyük to Alastair Blanshard. All three sites belong to the list of UNESCO World Heritage Sites. Hattuşa was added in 1986, Troy in 1998, and Çatalhöyük in 2012.

23. Most recently, Bittlestone (2005). Grotesquely and facetiously, Butler (1922), on whom see chapter 3.

24. The canonical version of this story is found in Hilgard (1901), 29–30 and discussed in Porter (1992), 67–68. For the Near Eastern parallels, see Scodel (1982).

25. Vico (1948), §873; cf. §84.

26. See Vico (1948), §823: "But this does not make Homer any the less the father and prince of all sublime poets." Even Vico's claim that Homer is an idea is evasively hedged by the desire to "affirm him *per la metà,*" halfway (§873). D'Aubignac is less generous: "One can argue that Homer was not a good poet, and even that he never existed" ([Hédelin] [1715], 6). D'Aubignac's controversial thesis appeared posthumously in 1715, but it was already infamous during the last decades of the seventeenth century. Both writers were preempted, however, by La Popelinière (1599), 409: the doubts as to Homer's life are so numerous and so grave, "one cannot be sure . . . when or even if he ever existed." Did Vico know of La Popelinière? Other indications suggest that he may well have. See this chapter, note 29.

27. Epictetus, *Discourses* 2.19.10; trans. Dobbin (2008); cf. 1.28.12. A later echo, even prior to Vico, is Montaigne: "Nothing is so known or accepted as Troy, Helen, and Homer's wars—though they may never have existed" (*Essays* II, 36

[1578–80]; trans. Screech). But this is emphatically a later *echo*, not a novel twist on the ancient tradition.

28. Vico (1948), §875.

29. Vico (1948), §§66, 788, 819, 839, 850, 853–56. A Renaissance predecessor to Vico is La Popelinière, whose compact theory about Homer's orality, illiteracy, and state of civilization (he calls it "savage"), replete with doubts about the veracity of Homer's account of Troy, is so similar to Vico's that one has to wonder whether Vico had any knowledge of this work (La Popelinière [1599], 404–6, 407–9).

30. Wolf (1985), 209.

31. Wolf (1985) 132, 47. Discussion in Porter (2000), 73–76.

32. Quoted in Wolf (1985), 14–15. The Danish scholar Georg Zoëga, a correspondent of Heyne's and later a pupil of Wolf's, anticipated both in 1779 and 1788. See "Wolf," in *HE*.

33. See the introduction to Wolf (1985), 35 for the equivocations. The illustration, made by Ludwig Ferdinand Schnorr von Carolsfeld, is in fact a quotation. The same bust, copied by a different hand (Charles Jervas), adorned the first volume of Pope's translation of the *Iliad* (1715). See further chapter 2, note 57.

34. Truffaut (1967), 98–100. See further Žižek (2008), 183–84.

35. Parry (1971), 240n1, explicitly deriving from Plato's philosophy of Ideas "the [single] essential idea" that is expressed by the Homeric formula (223; see next note); Homer's "Phidian . . . perfection" of an "ideal" (425; cf. 431), which is "the ideal of traditional style" (23) and "an almost Platonic Ideal" (xxv).

36. Parry (1971), 378; emphasis added. The last phrase is a shorthand for Parry's classic definition of the Homeric formula, which captures the essence of Homeric poetry. The expanded version reads, "The formula in the Homeric poems may be defined as a group of words which is regularly employed under the same metrical conditions to express *a given essential idea*" (272; emphasis added). It is doubtful that formulae express anything of the sort. The urge "to hear the voice which tells the *Iliad*," however "simple and impractical" it may be, persists to this day, for the poem "seems to have the persuasive force and coherence of a single, powerful performance, by one poet, whom we have come to call Homer" (Martin [1989], xiii).

37. Hanson and Heath (1998).

38. Porter (2005); The Postclassicisms Collective (2020).

39. See Macintosh et al. (2018).

## Chapter Two

1. Dacier (1711), 1:1.

2. Strategic, but also conventional, if not *de rigueur*. Cf. Jean Samxon's translation of Homer (*Les Iliades d'Homere*, 1530), which is also prefaced with an admittedly differently pitched *Vie d'Homere*. Thomas Parnell would repeat the refrain in "An Essay on the Life, Writings, and Learning of Homer," which prefaced the first volume of Pope's translation of the *Iliad* from 1715 (Pope [1715–20], 1:3).

3. [Plutarch], *On Homer* 1.1; trans. West (2003b), 405. The title is variously transmitted, typically with some combination of *Life* and *Homer*, but is often cited in its most abbreviated version, *On Homer*. I will render it as *Life of Homer* and *On Homer* below, depending on the context.

4. Malcolm Willcock, "Neoanalysis," in Morris and Powell (1997), 175.

5. "To Homer," *Epistolae familiares* 24.12.2 and 42; trans. Robinson (1898), 254, 260.

6. Cf. Philostratus, *Heroicus* 14.4–15.1, where the fame of a person is measured by the number of his statues, in this case a short boxer and wrestler from Cilicia known as the "jumping man," whose "likeness in bronze can be found in many places" (trans. Rusten [2014]).

7. Quoted in Shelton (2005), 229.

8. *Greek Anthology* 16.301; Quintilian 10.1.26; Longinus 13.2, quoted after Boileau-Despréaux (1674), 32, the translation consulted by Ingres (see Siegfried [2009], 206 and 428n43).

9. Siegfried (2009), 195. See chapter 1.

10. Vigne (1995), 176, 179. Calquing seems to have been Ingres's favored method whenever he was working on ancient themes. See Picard-Cajan (1992) for further examples.

11. The Archelaus relief was discovered in Italy in the mid-seventeenth century. A contemporary engraving by Giovanni Battista Galestruzzi (1658; fig. 3.1 below)

later appeared in Cuper (1683), the first major study devoted to the monument, surpassing Athanasius Kircher's brief but important treatment in his *Latium* from 1671. Kircher was probably the source of the relief's modern title. Ingres owned, duplicated, and annotated a copy of Galestruzzi's engraving. See further Ternois (1954/55) on the Archelaus relief and on other borrowings by Ingres, to which add those in the next note and the temple to Homer built by Ptolemy IV in Alexandria as described by Aelian in his *Historical Miscellany* (more on this monument in the next chapter). This source was likewise known to Ingres and copied out by him in one of his many prolific notebooks (Siegfried [2009], 426n28).

---

12. For the feminine personifications, see West (2003b), 411 with n34 ([Plutarch], *On Homer* 1.4); and Clarac (1841), 690 with Clarac (1828–30), no. 733, pl. 226, a line drawing of a fragmentary bas-relief *Apotheosis of Homer* from a sarcophagus held in the Louvre. For the sword and rudder/oar, see Dilthey (1876a), 304, in a discussion of the Pompeian fresco, to which he (1876b) provides the illustration (fig. 3.2 below); and see Pannuti (1984) on the Roman cup that Dilthey ([1876a], 304) also compares with the wall painting. Ingres owned illustrations of the cup. In Ingres's *Apotheosis*, Homer is crowned by Nike (Victory). In the Archelaus relief, he is crowned by the Inhabited World (female) and Time (male). Dacier helped to keep this image alive in the public eye. She gave a detailed ecphrasis of Archelaus's monument, supplemented by a line drawing, in the culminating finale of her *Life of Homer*, where the *Apotheosis* serves as a kind of talisman against and an eternal refutation of Homer's critics, especially the modern variety (Dacier [1711], 1:37–42). Ingres's *Apotheosis* appears to be in Dacier's debt here.

---

13. See esp. *Nathan Admonishes David* (1653). Broos (1993), 275 suggests a parallel with *Jacob Blessing the Sons of Joseph* (1656). The 1663 painting was damaged by fire, which accounts for the cropping, as earlier sketches and a 1773 inventory indicate.

---

14. The source of the cast in Rembrandt's possession is unknown, though it is clearly modeled after the Hellenistic blind type. Extensive discussion in Boehringer and Boehringer (1939), 99–102.

---

15. Richter (1965), 1:50.

---

16. On the practice, see Pliny, *Natural History* 35.9–10, to be discussed below in this chapter; Bernoulli (1901), 1:4.

---

17. The image reproduced in Wolf's edition may well have been drawn after an engraving by Tischbein (Tischbein and Heyne [1801], 10–11) that creates its own *trompe l'oeil* effect: it shows Homer looking out of an arched stone window, his body artfully cropped by the windowsill, as though he were not himself made of the same material as his surround. Tischbein and Wolf reproduce the same

Neapolitan bust that Pope used for his *Iliad* in 1715. However, unlike the later versions, the 1715 frontispiece does not pretend to be anything other than a rendition of a marble bust sitting on a plinth.

---

18. I should note that my sequencing of these images is meant to trace an arc in Ingres's thinking irrespective of their chronology (which in any case is not easily determined).

---

19. A nice detail noticed by Siegfried (2006), 57.

---

20. The original epitaphic inscription reads, "Here the earth conceals that sacred head / marshaller [or "adorner"] (*kosmētōr*) of heroes, the godly Homer (*theion Homēron*)" (trans. West [2003b], 353). Omitting the first verse, Ingres takes the first part of the second verse, turns it into a dedication by changing the case to the dative *kosmētori* ("*to* the marshaller of heroes"), and moves the last two words to the temple's face above, where he reverses them and likewise changes their case to the dative so as to create a second dedication echoing the one below: "*To* Homer, a God" (*Homēroi theoi* [*sic*], an apparent mistake for *Homērōi theōi*). The omission of the first verse is both iconographically necessary (Homer must be visible in the painting) and programmatic (Ingres's Homer is an extrapolation of a sculptural head but also the partial concealment of this fact). In the Greek original, "head" points by metonymy to "the person," and the same logic holds for Ingres, who has turned the bust of Homer into a metonymy for his person and then, by extension, for his afterlife.

---

21. Orpheus was in any case incalculably older than Homer. See Seneca, letter 88.39: "Shall I calculate how much time elapsed between Orpheus and Homer, when I don't have a chronology?" (trans. Fantham [2010]).

---

22. See Ternois (1965), no. 167 and Siegfried (2006) for the details and date of the work. Vigne (2007), 69–70 seems to believe that the painting was begun in 1827 and retouched in 1865, to what extent he does not say, nor does he provide any conclusive evidence to back up the claim.

---

23. The conceit of a transition to stone was already familiar in antiquity, as François Lissarrague reminded me in conversation. A good example is an exquisite Apulian red-figure *loutrophoros* (ca. 330 BCE, attributed to the painter of Louvre MNB 1148 and now at the Getty) that shows Niobe, enframed by a white marble temple, turning to stone. The same white color is spreading upward from her feet and onto the lowest parts of her robe: she is becoming a monument. In the case of Ingres, the direction of the movement—stone to flesh or flesh to stone—is less certain and more fraught.

---

24. See Siegfried (2006), (2009).

25. See Bernoulli (1901), 1–24; 12: "Idealbildungen"; Esdaile (1912) for coins; Richter (1965), 1:45–56: "invented" and "imaginary" portraits of Homer; Zanker (1995), 14–22, 156–71, 194–97, 324–26; Spivey (2016).

26. This portrait is considered the finest and most representative copy of the so-called Epimenides type; see Zanker (1995), 15–22.

27. [Lucian], *In Praise of Demosthenes* 1; trans. MacLeod (1967). Henceforth, references to this translation will be indicated parenthetically in the text by section numbers only. Lucian's authorship continues to be debated.

28. See this chapter, note 25.

29. Zanker (1995), 164–65.

30. Ingres is quoting, with the slightest of modifications, from Bitaubé, *Oeuvres d'Homère* (1822), 1:1, who is in turn echoing Dacier, who is echoing Plutarch. For a facsimile of the first page of Ingres's original MS, titled "Sur la vie d'Homere," see Siegfried (2009), 197.

31. Siegfried (2009), 198.

32. Tischbein and Heyne (1801), 11. Dacier's formulation is much more concise: the ancient images of Homer are all post hoc inventions, because "there was no [authentic] image of Homer to draw on; *they are nothing but idea and fantasy* (*elles ne sont toutes que d'idée & de fantaisie*)." As evidence, she quotes and translates the passage from Pliny (reproduced above) that all modern art historians invoke to make the same point (Dacier [1711], 1:37–38; emphasis added).

33. Tischbein and Heyne (1801), 12–13.

34. See Theagenes 8A1 DK (Tatian, *Oratio ad Graecos* 31.3 Marcovich): "The earliest to inquire into [the facts of] Homer's poetry, his origins, and his *floruit* included Theagenes of Rhegium," who lived at the end of the sixth century BCE. The source of this information is late, but the impulse it documents is credible. The official custodians of the Homeric poems, the so-called descendants of Homer, may well have inaugurated the biographical tradition in the previous century, if not earlier, though popular impulses must have existed too. (See below.)

35. Helen: Schol. *Il.* 3.126–27 and Eustathius on *Il.* 3.125–28; Demodocus: Eustathius on *Od.* 8.45; Odysseus: Pindar, *Nemean* 7.20–27; Dio, *Trojan Oration* 17; and chapter 4.

36. *Ho mē horōn*: Isaac Porphyrogenitus, *Preface to Homer* 11, ed. Kindstrand; Eustathius, Preface, *Commentary on the Iliad* 1:6.19–20 van der Valk, and on *Od.* 2.319. The other meanings appear in the *Lives* and elsewhere.

---

37. Welcker (1865–82), 1.1:117, 121–22; Durante (1976), 194–97; Nagy (1979), 296–300; West (1999), 374; but already, Vico (1948), §852. For parallel speculations about "Meles," see Marx (1925), 407; West (2003b), 310; Nagy (2010), 136 with n3.

---

38. For example, West ([2011], 10) calls it "a real possibility" that Melesigenes was Homer's "actual" name. But this merely begs the question that the tradition had thrown up: *Why the change of name at all?*

---

39. Aristotle: [Plutarch], *On Homer* 1.3; before Aristotle: Critias: fr. 50 DK; Euagon or Eugaeon: *Contest of Homer and Hesiod* 226.20–21 Allen = West (2003b), 320.

---

40. West (1999), 364. The main thesis is already found in Durante (1976); see West, 375–76. That the Homeridae and then the rhapsodes were involved in the early diffusion of Homeric biography is an ancient speculation known to Isocrates (*Defense of Helen* 65), hinted at by Plato (*Republic* 599e), and widely repeated since, e.g., Wilamowitz-Moellendorff (1916), 367; Nagy (2010), 30, 62; and, with cautions, Graziosi (2002), the most thorough exploration of the early reception of Homer to date.

---

41. One wonders if the earliest form that the Homeric Question took was itself a product of the Homeric poems, which display a formulaic pattern for encountering strangers, as at *Il.* 21.50 and more fully, as one might expect, in the *Odyssey*, for example, *Od.* 1.170–71: "What man are you, and whence? Where is your city? Your parents? / What kind of ship did you come here on?" etc. Homer truly *was* a stranger to his later audiences. The elevated version of this, likewise relevant to Homer's identity, is the query, or anxiety, "Are you a god or a mortal?" which is likewise found in both poems (e.g., *Il.* 6.123–29; *Od.* 6.149).

---

42. These identifications appear in the modern British, Dutch, German, and Argentine traditions, with increasing racial vehemence—or counter-vehemence, as in the cases of Horkheimer, Adorno, and Borges. The Jewish connection is already hinted at in the Sibylline oracles, on which see below.

---

43. A convenient foldout chart listing many of the major details of Homer's life according to their several sources may be found at the back of Allen (1924).

---

44. *Planudean Anthology* 296.7–8, trans. Gow and Page (1968), 1:57, modified. The epigram is preserved in [Plutarch], *On Homer* 1.4. Cf. Hesychius, in West (2003b), 427 (§2) for the same logic.

45. The same logic forces La Popelinière (1599), 409 to reach the same conclusion that the dizzying array of biographical possibilities (read: uncertainties) about Homer and the doubts about his authorship of the poems lead one to the brink of utter skepticism: "if one cannot be sure of what sort [of person Homer was], when, *or even if he ever existed,*" what is the use of consulting the poems, our only touchstone, for confirmation of any of these questions?

46. Cf. Hesychius, in West (2003b), 427: "[Homer's] mighty talent made it seem doubtful that he was mortal at all" (trans. modified).

47. Rosenzweig (2005), 88; Santner (2001).

48. Santner (2001), 19.

49. Kantorowicz (1957), 202, 409; "sublime body": Santner (2001), xxi, 36, etc.

50. See Auerbach (1961) for a shrewd reading of this effect.

51. The phenomenon is familiar. See Žižek (2008), 180 for one formulation, which I have mirrored here.

52. Antipater (?), *Palatine Anthology* 7.75.

53. Ennius, *Annales* 1.1–11 (ed. Skutsch); Lucretius, *On the Nature of Things* 1.117–26. Josephus, *Against Apion* 2.14, connects the dots between Homer, Pythagoras, and Apion (to be discussed next).

54. Pliny, *Natural History, preface* 25; 30.6.18; Seneca, letter 88.40.

55. Philostratus repeats the evasive silence of Homer on the question of his identity and (here) birthplace: though Homer knew the answer, he refused to divulge it in part "so that ambitious cities would claim him as their own" (*Heroicus* 44.2; trans. Rusten [2014], modified).

56. Seneca, letter 88.40; trans. Fantham (2010), modified.

57. 9.226–32, trans. Bergin and Wilson (9.166–71, ed. Festa).

58. Chapman's poem *Euthymiae Raptus* accompanied his 1609 translation of the *Iliad.* La Motte's ode *L'Ombre d'Homere* precedes his modernizing anti-Homeric verse translation of the *Iliad.* In it, La Motte calls on Homer's shade for permission to rejuvenate the poet's "ancient visage," which is to say to clean up his tendentious poetic excesses. Homer, conceding these faults, grants La Motte full license to revise his work. Marivaux's flippant *Évocation de l'ombre*

*d'Homere* punctures the modern cult of Homer, not least by recruiting Homer into enthusiastically seconding his opinion. Swift's satire, which briefly recapitulates his *Battle of the Books,* appears in part 3, chapter 8 of *Gulliver's Travels,* under the title *A further Account of* Glubbdubdrib. *Antient and Modern History corrected.* Borges's short story is found in Borges (1962); illuminating comments are found in Borges (2000), 112–13. We will come back to "The Immortal" in chapter 4.

59. West (2003b), 325 (§5).

60. Richardson (2016), 222.

61. Notice how Longinus's text looks more like an easel than a book, as though he were painting a portrait of Homer and not writing about Homer's sublimity—both activities are, to be sure, a matter of *eidōlopoiia*, or the conjuring up of mental images, which is a hallmark of the Longinian sublime.

62. Siegfried (2009), 212.

## Chapter Three

1. See Zeitlin (2001); Kim (2010).

2. Cf. Seneca, *letter* 58.17: "When you hear 'poet' you understand 'Homer'" (trans. Fantham [2010]). The Greek practice begins early on.

3. [Hédelin] (1715), 5–6; Butler (1922).

4. Pindar, *Isthmian* 4.38; trans. after Richardson, "Aristotle's Reading of Homer," in Lamberton and Keaney (1992), 32.

5. Trans. West (2003b), 351, modified.

6. Syagrus: Diogenes Laertius, *Lives of Eminent Philosophers* 2.46 (corrected from "Sagaris") = Aristotle, fr. 21.1 Gigon; Aelian *Historical Miscellany* 14.21; Eustathius, Preface, *Commentary on the Iliad* 1:6.14–15 van der Valk; Corinnus: *Suda* κ 2091.

7. See chapter 1, note 16. I leave aside three further alleged predecessors, mere shadows: Sisyphus of Cos, Oeagrus, and Oroebantius of Troezen.

8. Sappho, fr. 16.1–4 Lobel-Page; trans. Carson (2002), 28; emphasis added.

9. Rosen (1990). See also Seidensticker (1978).

10. Beatings with a *rhabdos*: frr. 6, 10, and 40 West (1989–92); brawling and begging: frr. 39 and 120–21. See Rosen (1990); Hawkins (2016); Lavigne (2017).

11. *Phaedrus* 243a-b; trans. Nehamas and Woodruff (1995).

12. Text of Hansen (1983–89), 1:252, no. 454. The exact date of the cup's inscription is disputed. Suggestions run from the last decades of the eighth century to the early decades of the seventh.

13. Hansen (1976) was the first to notice this possibility. "Humble earthenware" is from Hansen (42). Murray (1994), 54 speculates that the cup attests to a "society dominated by traders rather than aristocrats," and hence is an early index of a more "demotic" Homer.

14. Athenaeus 11.466e and 489b-c. Athenaeus's learned treatise, set in a symposiastic scene, is the (apt) source of much of this lore about Nestor's drinking cup.

15. Cribiore (1996), catalogue nos. 200 (wax tablet: D. C. Hesseling, *Journal of Hellenic Studies* 13 [1892–93]: 296n11) and 209 (ostracon: H. Youtie, *OMich* III [1951], no. 1100 = *OMich. inv.* 9353; image available online at https://quod.lib.umich.edu/a/apis/x-784). "Divine Homer": Aristophanes, *Frogs* 1034 (405 BCE).

16. *Planudean Anthology* 16.301 (Anon.).

17. *Contest of Homer and Hesiod* 237.302–8 Allen = West (2003b), 349.

18. See Brink (1972); Clay (2004), 87–89, 136–43.

19. The relative dates of the monument and the *Battle of Frogs and Mice* are uncertain, which only complicates the iconographical identification of the scroll. For a recent discussion, see Hosty (2020), who accepts the identification with the *Battle of Frogs and Mice*, thus giving the poem a Hellenistic date. For the pejorative meanings of nibbling mice, an ancient trope, see Juvenal, *Satires* 3.207; Lucian, *Zeus Rants* 8 and *The Ignorant Book-Collector* 17; *Greek Anthology* 6.303 (Ariston); Cuper (1683), [iii]; 46; Stewart (1990), 1:218.

20. Homer's association with knowledge of the bounded *oikoumenē* (the geographical world) is a widespread *topos*, above all in the Hellenistic period, when the extent of Homer's geographical knowledge was an object of intense scrutiny, e.g., by Eratosthenes of Cyrene, Crates of Mallos, Strabo, and others. Cf. also Proclus, *Chrestomathy*, in West (2003b), 425. *Chronos* (chronological time) is also generally understood as bounded and noncosmological. Cuper ([1683], [iii], 14–15, 25, and 35) proposed, cleverly but implausibly, that Homer appears in all three registers: first as honored across space and time, then as singing (the

anonymous poet in statue form off to the right), and finally appearing like Zeus (divinized).

21. A striking proportion of the depicted figures are holding books in the form of a roll (and in one case, two rolls) or a tablet. See Smith (1904), no. 2191 for these and other details. Thanks to Andrew Stewart for this reference.

22. Timon: Athenaeus, *The Learned Banqueters* 1.22d (bird cage); Diogenes Laertius, *Lives of Eminent Philosophers* 9.113 (copies). Editorial marginalia: Cicero, *Against Piso* 73; Horace, *Art of Poetry* 447–50.

23. Aelian, *Historical Miscellany* 13.22 is the source of both pieces of information. See Brink (1970), 549–55 for discussion.

24. Lucian, *Charon, or the Inspectors* 7. Charon in fact *misremembers* what he has consumed (8). Lucian is thus producing an accurate, if irreverent, sketch of Homer's posthumous literary reception.

25. Scholium on *Charon* 4 (ed. Rabe).

26. The last named solution was transmitted by the twelfth-century polymath Isaac Porphyrogenitus, in his *Preface to Homer* §14, ed. Kindstrand. See Porter (2021) for a detailed discussion of these and other controversies surrounding the *Contest*.

27. Bakhtin (1981), ch. 1 ("Epic and Novel").

28. Our *Iliad* is, in some ways, Achilleocentric. But it may have emerged out of or against a set of traditions that revolved around Hector. The complexities of the *Iliad* and its divided allegiances (pro-Greek? pro-Trojan?) could be attributed to such a development. See, most recently, Bachvarova (2018).

29. Parry (1956), 4.

30. See Nagy (1974); (1979), 259–64; Martin (1989); Bachvarova (2016). Closer to home, there is the poetry of the Epic Cycle, which is too often understood as exhibiting folkloric qualities that are not present in Homer. Bakhtin is aware that polyglossia "is more ancient than pure, canonic monoglossia" (Bakhtin [1981], 12; cf. 64). He merely refuses to concede this sensibility to epic on formal grounds alone.

31. Aristotle, *Poetics* 19.1456b; trans. Hubbard (1972).

32. *On the Sublime* 9.15; trans. Russell (1972a). Henceforth, references to this translation will be indicated parenthetically in the text by section numbers only.

33. Aristotle, *Poetics* 24.1460a18–19.

34. Longinus here seems to be echoing Menecrates of Nysa, a pupil of Aristarchus, and both are offering extreme versions of what since Aristotle was deemed a palpable difference in tone, intensity, and subject matter between the two epics. When Lucian puts the question to Homer, he indicates, somewhat oddly, that "most" people assumed that the *Odyssey* was composed first. Homer denies this (Lucian, *A True Story* 20.20). D'Aubignac would later use the evidence of Longinus and the ancient Separatists to confirm his own perception that the Homeric poems are "filled with [poetic] faults and weaknesses," which blind veneration and lazy complacency have only worked to "hide" ([Hédelin] [1715], 5–7, 46, 51, 345, 350–51, 356). Two centuries later, Gilbert Murray was still voicing the same misgivings, as we saw at the outset of this book.

35. 61A2–4 DK; Richardson (1975), 69.

36. Translations of all but Ptolemy Chennus may be found in the Loeb Classical Library. A sample of the literary remains of Ptolemy is available in translation at http://www.tertullian.org/fathers/photius_copyright/photius_05bibliotheca.htm (§190).

37. This hardly covers the range of later imperial epic, but it does illustrate how once a paternal lineage is established there is no way to cap it off, let alone control it.

38. See Bryant Davies (2019) for an informed collection of these and other Victorian burlesques (quotation at p. 15).

39. Butler (1922), 143. Henceforth, references to this edition will be indicated parenthetically in the text by page numbers only.

40. See Porter (2013) for discussion with bibliography.

41. Borges is more explicit. He calls Butler's Homer "a Trojan humorist" (Borges [1999], 250). Butler may mean no more than that Homer was an "Asiatic Greek" (214), which is to say a Greek from Asia Minor (263) who identified more closely with the Trojans than with the Achaean invaders. The thought has occurred to others since, e.g., Simone Weil, *The Iliad, or the Poem of Force*, in Weil and Bespaloff (2005), 33; further, note 64 in chapter 4.

42. Sibylline Oracles 3.419–32 (repeated in 11.163–71), 3.819–28 Geffcken; Diodorus Siculus 4.66.6 (repeated by Varro and Pausanias, among others). At 3.419–20 Homer is called a "writer of falsehoods" (*pseudographos*) who "proclaims a false fatherland" (*pseudopatris*). For a sensitive account of the interaction between Homer and the Bible in the third *Sibylline oracle*, see Amir (1974).

43. Photius, *Bibliotheca* cod. 190, 149b22–25; 151a37–b5 Henry. The most recent incarnation of the claim about female authorship is found in Dalby (2006), where it is extended to cover both epics, as in Ptolemy.

44. Cf. Plutarch, *On Affection for Offspring* 496D, which quotes three verses from the *Iliad* and attributes them to a "Homerid," understood there as a *female* rhapsode (a possibility attested nowhere else).

45. Ptolemy and the Sibyl are the foundation of Bryant ([1796]); see esp. 58–65. For the frequent conflation of Homer and the Sibyl in the Renaissance, see Wolfe (2015), 155–67. Bryant further relies on Metrodorus of Lampsacus and Dio Chrysostom. And in general, the early modern sources were quite well informed about Homeric arcana, which enabled them to transmit this information to later readers like Butler.

46. So the partial *Life of Hesiod* in the scholia to Hesiod's *Works and Days* (223.30–38 Allen).

## Chapter Four

1. Trans. Rosenmeyer (2006), 103–5, modified.

2. In Greek tragedy (Aeschylus and Euripides), the Greek fleet assembled at Aulis was delayed by adverse winds en route to Troy. "Aeschines" seems to be playfully reversing this story, perhaps along the lines of Vergil, *Aeneid* 2.108–11.

3. Strabo 13.1.32, 39; Plutarch, *Life of Alexander* 15.5; Arrian, *Anabasis of Alexander* 1.11.7–12.1; Ampelius, *Liber memorialis* 8.10. See Pfister (1909–12); Vermeule (1995); Erskine (2001). The tombs were often late Neolithic settlement mounds redubbed heroic graves, and some were raised by as much as forty feet in the Hellenistic period to enhance their prominence (Rose [2014], ch. 8). Monuments and ruins are made and not found. Homer is one such monument; Troy is another.

4. In antiquity alone, the list of regents who toured the Troad includes Xerxes (480 BCE), Alexander (334 BCE), the Seleucid king Antiochus III (192 BCE), Julius Caesar (apocryphally? ca. 48 BCE), the Roman emperors Hadrian (124 CE), Caracalla (214 CE), Julian the Apostate (355 CE), and, further on in time, the Ottoman sultan Mehmed II (1453 CE).

5. Plato *Ion* 535b-c; trans. Russell (1972b), modified; emphasis added.

6. Cf. Plato, *Laws* 3.658b (cf. 658d) with West (2010), 2; Herder (2002), 40–41, reliving the experience of Homer *and* Ion; Bakker (2005), 70.

7. Plato's position is reversed in *Laws* 3.682a4–5, where bards (Homer in particular), aided by divine inspiration, "frequently hit on how things really happen" (trans. Saunders, in Cooper and Hutchinson [1997]).

8. *Vita Scorialanus* 2.2, 247.10–248.17 Allen = West (2003b), 445.

9. Eustathius on *Od.* 8.45. Proclus made a similar claim (trans. Lamberton [2012], 250–51).

10. On the mixed and often negative connotations of blindness in Greek culture, see Buxton (1980), to which add the following: *Iliad* 6.139; Aristophanes, *Wealth* 87–96; Plato, *Republic* 411d (associated with poetic inspiration), 484c-d (epistemological blindness), etc.; and Plutarch, *On the Principle of Cold* 2 (blindness is a "negation" [or "deprivation"], both "inert and unproductive").

11. E.g., [Plutarch], *On Homer* 1.5.

12. [Herodotus], *Vit. Hom.* 218.552–53 Allen = West (2003b), 403.

13. Philostratus, *Heroicus* 43.11: "Homer knew the names, and he collected the events from the cities which each warrior led, since he traveled around Greece soon enough after the Trojan war that its events had not been forgotten" (trans. Rusten [2014]). Cf. Dio, *Oration* 11.92.

14. See, most recently, Graziosi (2002).

15. Significant qualifications are made by Katz and Volk (2000), 128–29; Liapis (2017).

16. Christodorus, *Greek Anthology* 2.335. The insistence repeats itself all the way into modernity, whether in Robert Wood ([1775], 16, 19, 127, 181, etc.) or in Anne Dacier ([1711], 1:30), for whom Homer could not have been so fine a "painter" of things in the world "unless he had had extremely good eyes."

17. *Odyssey* 1.3; [Herodotus], *Vit. Hom.* 196.69–71 and 83, 206.310–12, 207.329 Allen; [Plutarch], *On Homer* 1.1, 1.8, 2.1; Proclus, *Chrestomathy* 101.19–22 Allen; Schol. *Il.* 17.575–77; Philostratus, *Heroicus* 43.11.

18. Schol. *Il.* 14.226–27, further noting that Homer renders the reader a "witness" of the action.

19. Schol. *Il.* 7.220a1–2; emphasis added; Schol. *Il.* 11.167; cf. Schol. *Il.* 8.66b; Schol. *Il.* 17.674–75: Homer's "research" is an "as-if" kind of research that does not establish objective truths or facts. See further Nünlist (2009), esp. chs. 5 and 8.

20. E.g., Schol. *Il.* 7.445. See Porter (2011) for details.

21. Schol. *Il.* 21.269a. A further index of the unpicturability of the scene is found in Philostratus's description of a painting of Scamander in *Imagines* 1.1.

22. See Schol. *Il.* 4.154 ("clarity" without "vividness"); Schol. *Il.* 11.604c; Grethlein and Huitink (2017).

23. Lucian, *Saturnalia* 6. Cf. *The Dream, or the Cock* 6; *Double Indictment* 1; *Zeus Rants* 39. Cratinus, the fifth-century comic poet, had already mocked Homer's blindness in his *Archilochoi* (fr. 6).

24. Dio, *Trojan Oration* 11.

25. Dio, *Trojan Oration* 92; trans. Cohoon (1932), modified. The remark stings, because it is a pointed reminder of Homer's profession of relative ignorance in *Iliad* 2.486: "We have heard only the rumor [or "report," *kleos*] of it." Dio is holding Homer to his word.

26. Dio, *Trojan Oration* 1–2; trans. Cohoon (1932), modified.

27. Cf. Thucydides 1.20 and Palaephatus's opening to his critique of myth in his *Incredible Tales* (late fourth c. BCE). Earlier (ca. 500 BCE): Hecataeus's blanket dismissal of Greek myths and legends as "ridiculous" ([Demetrius], *On Style* 12).

28. West (2003b), 437: "Others say, however, that Homer suffered [blindness] as a result of the wrath of Helen." Proclus, *On the Republic* 1:176.15 Kroll (trans. Lamberton [2012], 255): "Homer suffered the same fate as Stesichorus."

29. [Herodotus], *Life of Homer*, trans. West (2003b), 361.

30. Philostratus, *Heroicus* 43.11–16.

31. *Roman Life* 5; trans. West (2003b), 437, modified; emphasis added.

32. Confirmation that the anecdote from the *Life* captures the experience of epic reality by Homer and by us is found in the *Iliad* itself. When warriors clash they are "*blinded / in the dazzle*" of their own weapons (13.340–41). The word for "dazzle" is *augē*, the same word that appears in the *Life* but also elsewhere, most relevantly in the description of Achilles's divine armor at *Iliad* 18.610 (evoking wonder in us when we first behold it fresh off of Hephaestus's forge; it flashes and dazzles terribly when he dons it at 19.375–95) and at 22.135 (causing Hector to run in fear from Achilles). Drawing us into the scene from book 13, the next two verses read: "That man would have to be very bold-hearted / who could be

cheerful and not *stricken* looking on that struggle" (emphasis added). Needless to say, the onlooker is in the first instance Homer and in the second instance ourselves. Here, we have evidence of what will be shown in the next chapter, namely, that Homer's poetry is a *self-resistant* poetry that causes beholders to look on and then away (or else askance).

33. Proclus, *Chrestomathy* 6 (trans. West [2003b], 423), broadening the narrower counterargument by Velleius Paterculus, *Compendium of Roman History* 1.5.3: "If any man holds to the view that Homer was born blind, he is himself lacking in all his senses" (trans. Shipley [1924]). For the metaphysical connotations, which are Platonic in origin, see Proclus's discussion of Stesichorus and Homer in Lamberton (2012), 250–55.

34. Lucian, *A True Story* 2.20. The word for "investigated" is *zēteisthai*, the technical term for posing a Homeric problem. Seneca ridicules the vanity of all such Homeric questions in *On the Shortness of Life* 13.2, just as Timon of Phlius, mentioned earlier, made fun of the Alexandrian editions.

35. The *Troica* by Hellanicus (480–395 BCE) is the earliest known treatment of these problems. See Strabo 13.1.42; Trachsel (2007), ch. 2.

36. Eustathius on *Iliad* 2.504.

37. The term *aphanismos* is used of both the Greek wall and Troy. Cf. Aristotle, fr. 402 Gigon = Strabo 13.1.36, 13.1.41; *Rhet. Anon.* 3:158.5 Spengel; Eustathius on *Il.* 4.163–65, 7.452, 12.6, etc. The conceit originates in the *Iliad* (*aphantos*): 6.60; 20.303.

38. The Shield of Achilles mirrors the action of the *Iliad* down to this detail: it shows a city under siege, but not its capture (*Il.* 18.509–12). Other foreshadowings of Troy's sacking and burning, some especially vivid and brutal, include *Il.* 2.414–15; 4.34–36, 164–65; 5.715; 6.57–60; 9.592–94; 11.329; 15.70–71; 21.375–76; 22.410–11; and 24.551, 729–36. The *Odyssey* is built around "backshadowings" of the sack of Troy (one of Odysseus's epithets is "sacker of cities"), but with a reticence identical to the *Iliad*'s.

39. As mentioned, these absences were noticed in antiquity. Dio, in his *Trojan Oration*, bemoans Homer's lack of detail concerning the terrifying fall of Troy and the episode of the wooden horse (the former is omitted altogether, and the latter receives "only a few lines"), which are the very things that readers yearn "most of all to hear." Tongue in cheek, and anticipating Samuel Butler's *Authoress* (see previous chapter), Dio turns Homer's reticence into an argument from silence that Troy never fell and that the story of the wooden horse was a literally incredible lie (*Trojan Oration* 29, 34–35, 128–29).

40. The scene is "forecast" later on in *Iliad* 21 in the battle between Achilles and the river god Scamander, thematically (Scamander, one of the main players in the destruction scenario of book 12, threatens to wash away the memory of Achilles; 21.318–23) and verbally (12.29 ~ 21.314: "timbers and stones," *phitrōn kai laōn*, an exact repetition at the start of each verse).

41. Schol. *Il.* 3–35, etc. See Porter (2011), 12–23. The parallels were recognized early on. Euripides (*Trojan Women* 81 and 1279) uses the same verb for "setting fire" to the Greek camp and to Troy, as is noted by Case (2018), 12.

42. Cf. Catullus 68.89–90: "Troy—O horror!—the common grave (*sepulcrum*) of Europe and Asia, Troy the bitter ash of all heroes and heroic deeds." Cf. Ovid, *Heroides* 1.47–53. The destruction of Troy was a frequent theme in Greek art; see Anderson (1997).

43. Hesiod, *Works and Days* 160; Hesiod, fr. 204.96–10, 118–19 Merkelbach-West (*Ehoeae*, or *Catalogue of Women*) = fr. 155 Most; cf. *Cypria*, fr. 1 ( = West [2003a], 80–83).

44. Diogenes Laertius, *Lives of Eminent Philosophers* 9.41; trans. Hicks (1972).

45. For the general point, see Finkelberg (2005), 150, 162–63, 169. See further this chapter, note 53.

46. The term "systems collapse" was first introduced by Renfrew (1979). See Cline (2014) for a recent and informed account of this event, and Cline (2013) on the collapse of Homeric Troy viewed against this background. On the complexity and depth of the wider problem, which remains unsolved, see Knapp and Manning (2016).

47. Rose (2014), 61, 69–71.

48. Finley (1965), 46.

49. For an early forerunner of this view, see Jebb (1882); (1883), 522; (1884), 451.

50. Scodel (1982); Watkins (1986); West (2007); Sherratt (2010); Bachvarova (2016); Bachvarova, Dutsch, and Suter (2016).

51. See Vergil, *Georgics* 1.493–97, illustrating the general attitude: "And know that a time will come, when in those fields / A farmer, working the land with his curved plough, / Will find javelins eaten with rusty mold, / Or will strike empty helmets with his heavy hoe / And marvel at gigantic bones in the unearthed graves." For the same image, transferred now to Troy, see Ovid, *Heroides* 1.53–56.

52. Aslan and Rose (2013); Rose (2014).

53. Leaf (1900), 158 (on *Il.* 4.52) partially hints at the connection. Kirk (1985), 336 (on *Il.* 4.51–53) rejects it on weak grounds, and West (1988), 159–60 bypasses it altogether. Wilamowitz-Moellendorff (1916), 288 is spot on: "If Hera is the protector of the Greeks, how can she offer up to Zeus her favorite cities—Mycenae, Argos, and Sparta—for destruction? A disturbing prospect to be sure, until one recognizes how precious a piece of evidence it is. . . . Here we find named, in a way that was possible only in epic, the destruction of the old [Bronze Age] splendor, whose memory was preserved in epic."

54. *Cypria* fr. 1, in West (2003a), 80–83.

55. A case in point: the exotic Phaeacians, representing a mythical world, are cut off forever from commerce with the "real" world as punishment for their returning Odysseus back home (*Od.* 13.140–78). The *Odyssey* as a whole marks a departure from the heroic (Iliadic) past and a gradual entry into a more contemporary, familiar, and domestic reality, as Longinus and others since, including Richard Bentley, complained.

56. See Dickinson (2017), esp. 10–11. On "Mycenaeans" as an anachronistic label invented in the nineteenth century, see Sherratt (2010), 10.

57. Kirk (1985), 239–40, 248; Eder (2003); Danek (2004); Sherratt (2010); Dickinson (2017).

58. See esp. Sherratt (2010). The opposition of Greeks and barbarians forms only in the fifth century. See the next chapter.

59. Freud, "Screen Memories" ("Deckerinnerungen"), in Freud (1953–74), 3:301–22. I am stretching Freud's concept somewhat. The ruse of the screen memory here lies less in the "indifference" of the event it uses to cover a greater trauma than in its idealization of the Heroic Age and the pleasure this yields.

60. The operative term for both battles over walls is *teichomachia*. See Schol. *Il.* 12.3–35.

61. Goethe (1887–1919), pt. 4, 33:132 (letter to Johann Heinrich Meyer, 28 July 1820).

62. See Herder (1985–2000), 10:783–85, 484; emphasis added (*Adrastea* 9 [1803]): "What do I care about the current state of Troy or the Trojan plain when I *read* ancient *Homer*? . . . Thanks to Homer, a plain will always lie before Troy for us even if Troy never existed. . . . Whoever travels to the plain of Troy to see the Scamander [river] in person . . . travels in vain"; "What immense power did it

take to make Greece *believe* what it did when it built the greatest part of its history around Homer!" which is to say around Homer's fiction.

63. Lucretius: "Why beyond the Theban war and the doom of Troy have not other poets sung of other happenings as well?" (*On the Nature of Things* 5.326–27; trans. Bailey [1910]). See West ([1988], 159–60), who, however, offers a different answer from that proposed here.

64. Refugees: Finkelberg (2005), 169 (quotation). Similarly, Wilamowitz-Moellendorff (1916), 288. Gradual fusion of local traditions and (nonrefugee) Greek settlers: Bryce (2008); Rose (2014), 45, 69–71.

65. See Hendel (2001), (2021); Na'aman (2011).

66. Theagenes, fr. 2 DK; Metrodorus (see chapter 3 above); Lucretius, *On the Nature of Things* 1.464–82; Epictetus, *Discourses* 2.19.10; Hermias, *Commentary on Plato's Phaedrus* at 243a; Dio, *Trojan Oration* 129.

67. Judgment of Paris: Strabo 13.1.41; Ilium: Strabo 13.1.25, 27, and 42; Great Pine: Strabo 13.1.44; [Herodotus], *Life of Homer* (West [2003b], 378–79); Leaf (1923), 202–6; springs: Strabo 13.1.43, debating with Demetrius of Scepsis on the question; Hestiaea: Strabo 13.1.36.

68. Strabo 13.1.1.

69. Schliemann (1875), 345–46.

70. Jebb (1881), 528: "Dr. Schliemann cannot shake off the opposite belief." Schliemann (1880), 515: "hearsay"; 326: "*débris*" and "poetic license"; 517: "I wish I could have proved Homer to have been an eye-witness of the Trojan War! Alas, I cannot do it!"

71. Korfmann (2000), 32–33; (2002), 221, repeating the claim, now in pursuit of the fabled thermal springs of Troy.

72. West (1995), 217n43; emphasis in original. In identifying the burial mound now called Paşa Tepe with Homeric Batieia, West is in fact following Schliemann (1880), 656–58 ("Pasha Tepeh"). And both are following the ancient tradition of touring places where Homer once stood—or sat. In one *Life*, we learn that "the Neonteichians [in Asia Minor] were still exhibiting up to my time the place where he [Homer] used to sit and give performances of his verses, and they held it in great reverence" ([Herodotus], *Life of Homer*; trans. West [2003b], 365). In the *Contest*, we read how "the Colophonians even point to a spot where they say Homer . . . started his poetic career and composed the *Margites*" (trans. West [2003b], 319–21). Homer's grave was another such tourist attraction. Cyriac of

Ancona reports how, when he visited Chios in 1447 and was directed to "the actual site of Homer's tomb," he "made a little excavation, but found absolutely nothing worth reporting on except solid earth and a pile of stones" (Cyriac of Ancona [2003], 291).

73. Aslan and Rose (2013); Rose (2014). Highly charged and contested reports that stones from the Trojan citadel were removed to remote sites in the Troad already in the Archaic period (Strabo 13.1.38–39), whether true or not, point to the symbolic value of the remains of Troy.

74. Book 2 is given over to the sack of Troy as horrifically revisited by Aeneas, who was an eyewitness.

75. Borges (1962), 105. Henceforth, references to this translation will be indicated parenthetically in the text and notes by page numbers only.

76. The reference is to *Iliad* 2.824–26. Borges returns to these same verses in his essay "The Homeric Versions," in Borges (1999), 70.

77. See Franz Boas, quoted in Lévi-Strauss (1962), 21: "It would seem that mythological worlds have been built up, only to be shattered again, and that new worlds were built up from the fragments." Closer to home, compare Aristotle's remark about the Greek wall, Troy's fictional ersatz: "The poet who created it also destroyed it" (Strabo 13.1.36 = Aristotle, fr. 402 Gigon). Finally, cf. Philostratus, *Heroicus* 25.5, where Homer is called "the founder of Troy, since it is through his lament for it that its fame began" (trans. Rusten [2014], modified).

78. Freud (1953–74), 21:69.

79. Freud (1953–74), 21:69–70; emphasis added.

80. See Jansen (2018), ch. 3. I have learned much from Jansen's splendid work on Borges and Homer, which first introduced me to the connection, and have sought to repay this debt with a reading of my own.

81. "We do not know if Homer existed. The fact that seven cities vie for his name is enough to makes us doubt his historicity. Perhaps there was no single Homer; perhaps there were many Greeks whom we conceal under the name of Homer" ("Blindness" [1977], in Borges [1999], 479). "The Immortal" takes this wisdom to heart, turning a convention of the oral tradition into a fictional nightmare.

82. The internal narrator discusses the origins of the *Iliad* with Vico in 1729: "His arguments seemed to me irrefutable" (116). Two pages later we learn what those arguments were "Vico . . . defended the idea that Homer is a symbolic character

after the manner of Pluto or Achilles" (118n1). In other words, Homer is a shade. (Pluto is the god of the Underworld, and Achilles must therefore be the Underworld Achilles of the *Odyssey*.) An additional irony is that Borges has Vico convince *Homer himself* ("me") that Homer is no more than *un' idea*!

---

83. The dates given in the story confirm the suspicion. Rufus dates his Roman identity (106) to the reign of Diocletian (ca. 300 CE). The City of the Immortals was razed "some nine centuries" (113) earlier (say, 600 BCE). The troglodytic Homer inhabited the City "for a century" (114) before it was razed, before he rebuilt it from its "ruins," and before he became immortal (thus, from around 700 BCE). The Immortals (including the internal narrator now) were "induced . . . toward the end or the beginning of the tenth century, to disperse ourselves over the face of the earth" (115), thereby, it would appear, inaugurating the diffusion of Homer from the Byzantine period onward, first to Europe and from there all across the world.

---

84. Borges (1999), 110–11.

---

85. "Tlön, Uqbar, Orbis Tertius" (1940), "The Secret Miracle" (1944), "Deutsches Requiem" (1946), and "Emma Zunz" (1948), in Borges (1998); "A Defense of the Kabbalah" (1932), "Isaac Babel" (1938), and the entries under "Notes on Germany & the War" (1937–45), in Borges (1999). See Monegal, Santí, and Alonso (1978); Fishburn (1988); Aizenberg (2005); Kristal (2014); Stavans (2016). Thanks to Pedro Hurtado Ortiz for bringing Borges's anti-Fascist activity to my attention and to Luciano Martínez for the reference to Monegal, Santí, and Alonso.

---

86. It is hard to suppress the thought that "The Immortal" is partly a reply to Carlyle, who wrote that "the immortality of the soul is 'old Jewish rags'" (Borges [1999], 414).

---

87. See "A Key in Salonica" (a short poem from 1936 about the Second Temple, which replaced the First Temple that was destroyed in 586 BCE); and the story "The Maker" (1960), in Borges (1998), 293: "a rumor of glory and hexameters, *a rumor of men who defend a temple that the gods will not save*, . . . a rumor of the *Odysseys* and *Iliads* that it was his fate to sing and to leave echoing in the cupped hands of human memory" (emphasis added). The same connections run together in a late interview in which Borges treated the continued "present" existence of Troy "in the past tense" in Vergil (*fuit Ilium* [*Aeneid* 2.325], rendered by Borges as *Troya fuit*) and after Vergil (Borges [2015], 237); see Jansen (2018), 81–83 (quotations). Also relevant is the long-standing association of Troy with labyrinths. The phenomenon is documented from the time of an Archaic Etruscan vase (ca. 600 BCE) to the *lusus Troiae* or Trojan games of *Aeneid* 5.588–95 to the European turf mazes known as "Troy Towns" or "Trojaborgen," dating from the Middle Ages into the nineteenth century, on which see Russell and Rus-

sell (1991). One can well imagine Borges taking a special pleasure in this little-known fact.

88. For the Victorian culmination of this conflation of Homer and the Jewish tradition, the two "Bibles," with a special focus on Troy, see Gange and Bryant Davies (2013).

89. The third Sibylline oracle abounds in Homericisms, as mentioned in chapter 3, and "predicts" *post eventum* the catastrophic fall of Troy, as well as that of cities across Asia Minor, Egypt, Babylonia, Mycenae, and Rome (3.300–66, 413–32, 464–69). In another tradition, according to a suggestion by Felix Jacoby, the wanderings of the Erythraean Sibyl, with whom the Jewish Sibyl was identified in the third oracle (3.814) and by later writers, "were modelled on Homer's" (Lightfoot [2007], 20). Borges knew about the Erythraean Sibyl. See "The Peryton" (*El Peritio*, perhaps meaning "creature of destruction"), in *The Book of Imaginary Beings* (1967).

## Chapter Five

1. This is the modern figure, but the same figure was known in antiquity. See Dio, *Oration* 36.12.

2. Van Wees (1996), 6, quoting and paraphrasing Homer.

3. See *Od.* 16.269, 20.50.

4. Auerbach (1953; repr. 2003), 13. Henceforth, references to this translation will be indicated parenthetically in the text by page numbers only.

5. Goethe (1887), 221–22.

6. Winckelmann (1985), 34.

7. Herder (2002), 52. See Cyriac of Ancona's journal entry from 1447, composed on the island of Chios: "content with the society of fauns and mountain-nymphs and wood-nymphs, and rejoicing in complete and utter enjoyment," Homer was a "lover of perfect goodness and moderation" (Cyriac of Ancona [2003], 291).

8. Tischbein and Heyne (1801), 27–28.

9. Charles Segal, "Bard and Audience in Homer," in Lamberton and Keaney (1992), 29; Schein (1984), 70, quoting E. Vermeule, *Aspects of Death in Early Greek*

*Art and Poetry* (1979); Wofford (1992), 32, quoted by Lovatt (2013), 274n44, to which Lovatt adds, "The story written on and through his body and blood is a work of art for our entertainment" (275). Cf. Feeney (1999), 182 (seconding Wofford) and 188–89: "[We are] ultimately detached by virtue of the fact that we know, in the end, that we are reading a fiction." See also Bassett (1938), 26: "If for the moment we can put reason in abeyance, we are 'enthralled.' The spell of poetry can make the hearer forget both himself and the poet and the real world about him. . . . Its magic power [is] to make the image seem the only reality"—sentences that could easily have been penned by Auerbach, though Bassett is advocating exactly what Auerbach will critique.

10. Thucydides, *Peloponnesian War* 1.3.3–4; 1.6.5–6; Hall (1989).

11. On most counts, some 180-odd Trojan deaths are named as compared to only some 50-odd Greek deaths, though the total number of casualties is left to the imagination. The statistics are from Stoevesandt (2004), 8 with n26.

12. Cf. *Iliad* 4.444; 18.309; *Odyssey* 8.81–82 and 11.537.

13. Fr. 44b, col. 2 DK. It is worth noting that Homer loses his legendary contest with Hesiod on the grounds that he "rehearsed battle and carnage" and not peaceful activities (*Contest of Homer and Hesiod* 233.209–10 Allen = West [2003b], 341). King Panedes's argument is somewhat specious—Homer's peaceful "Golden Verses" (228.84–229.94 Allen = West, 327) speak against it—but it must reflect the hesitancies of an earlier age.

14. E.g., Plutarch, *How to Study Poetry* 29D–30C.

15. Philostratus, *Heroicus* 27.12; trans. Rusten (2014), modified.

16. See Nünlist (2009) for an introduction.

17. Schol. *Il.* 8.487–88; Schol. *Il.* 8.0.

18. Schol *Il.* 8.78; 11.300b1–2. Thanks to René Nünlist for help with the language of the scholium on *Iliad* 8.78.

19. Schol. *Il.* 15.56b. Cf. Schol. *Il.* 12.13–15.

20. Plato, *Ion* 535a-d.

21. Schol. *Il.* 8.350. The translation is a bit free (there are some peculiarities in the Greek that remain puzzling), but it hopefully captures the gist.

22. Schol. *Il.* 10.14–16.

23. Eustathius on *Il.* 4.539–44. Cf. the scholium on the same line (*Il.* 4.541): "Homer created for himself a spectator of the battle, one guided by the gods, so that he might view it *undisturbed* even in the midst of the fighters, and *so that he might behold the spectacle in all its precise detail*" (emphasis added).

24. Eustathius on *Il.* 4.539–44. This is the gist. More literally, the sentence means: "It is no more glorious (*kallion*), grand, or exciting to engage in a battle than it is to narrate one."

25. "Surprize and Applause": Pope (1715–20), 2:321. Cf. Pope, 2:322: "We may first observe that *Diversity in the Deaths of his Warriors,* which he has *supply'd by the vastest Fertility of Invention that ever was.*" "Poetical Beauties": Pope, 1:47 ("Observations on the First Book"). Pope's knowledge of Eustathius came courtesy of his early collaborators, principally Thomas Parnell and David Broome.

26. Schol. *Il.* 1.1a; Porphyry, *Homeric Questions,* ed. Schrader (1880–82), 323, col. 1.20–25.

27. Lucian, *A True Story* 2.20; trans. Harmon (1961), modified.

28. Aristotle, *Rhetoric* 2.3, 1380b27–29.

29. Schol. *Il.* 24.15 = fr. 389 Gigon. The comment is from Aristotle's *Homeric Problems.*

30. Plato, *Republic* 3.391b; trans. Russell (1972b) (The hero's "wrath" is mentioned at 390e.)

31. Gibson (2008), 271, 273, 275.

32. One of Homer's nicknames among Homeric scholars, parallel to "Greek-lover" (*philellēn*), was "Achilles-lover" (*philachilleus* or *philoachilleus*); e.g., Eustathius on *Il.* 1.1 (1:23.27 van der Valk), 11.505, 20.337–39, 23.185–87; cf. the scholia on *Il.* 19.79–80b ("lovers" in the plural). But, as Aristotle shows, this was not the only way of viewing Homer's allegiances. Contrast Burke (1759), 307; Pt. 4, §24: "Achilles . . . can never make us love him." The thought is shared by Murray (1934), 242.

33. *On Literary Composition* 18; trans. Usher (1985); emphasis added. Dionysius is making a contrast with a passage from the historian Hegesias that he quotes a page earlier. There, Hegesias describes Alexander's brutal imitation of Achilles at the expense of his "black-skinned" barbarian adversary Batis, whose body,

dragged alive behind a chariot, is racked with "pain" (18). To a modern reader's astonishment, Dionysius finds all of this offensive on purely *aesthetic* grounds.

34. *On the Sublime* 9.11, 9.13; trans. Russell (1972a). Henceforth, references to this translation will be indicated parenthetically in the text by section numbers only.

35. Jack Goody, *The Power of the Western Tradition*, 44–45 (quotation), as reproduced in Finkelberg (2005), 169. Goody is speaking of the ways in which cultures can collectively forget, and not only remember, the past.

36. I am grateful to Meg Koerner, who organized the exhibit and wrote the accompanying catalogue and who asked Kentridge if he might confirm the suspicion that he meant us to see dactylic hexameters in these images. He responded: "Yes, traces of high school scansion with spondees and dactyl, elision and prodelision." As "prodelision" betrays, those high school lessons were made on Vergil (there is no prodelision in Homer), but Homer is every bit as à propos.

37. For example, death is fatally associated with music in two scenes on the Shield of Achilles (18.493–99, 525–29), itself a magnificent work of art and an instrument of death.

38. One place to look is in contemporary critical race studies. Compare Frederick Douglass's remarks from 1845 on Black slave song as an expression of sorrow, not joy, and as a release, not a pleasure: "I have often sung to drown my sorrow, but seldom to express my happiness" (quoted and discussed in Okiji [2018], 77–83). But see also Lynn-George (1988), 152: "It is above all this relation between destruction and immortal song that the *Iliad* invites its audience to contemplate."

39. Plato extends the paradigm of Achilles in the Homeric Underworld to Odysseus in the Myth of Er. There, Odysseus gladly chooses a life of humble anonymity and neglect over the conspicuous life that he formerly earned at the cost of great suffering (*Republic* 10.620c).

40. Test. 22 DK = Aristotle, *Eudemian Ethics* 1.1325a25–29; Schol. *Il.* 18.107a.

41. Diogenes Laertius, *Lives of Eminent Philosophers* 9.67; trans. Hicks (1972).

42. Vernant (1991), 64, 68. Cf. Jaeger (1934), 32–37, esp. 36–37 on the heroic "exchange of beauty for life" in Homer, which captures "the signature possession of the Greeks, their feeling for life, in the vicinity of which we ourselves feel related by species [or "kind"] and race (*art- und rassensverwandt*)—[namely, their] heroism." Language like this has led to the suspicion that Jaeger, one of the exemplary classicists of his generation, was catering to a National Socialist bias. I am not trying to draw an equivalence between Jaeger, who emigrated to the States in

1936, and Vernant, who was a courageous member of the French Resistance. I am only pointing to an unfortunate coincidence of inherited values.

43. Similarly, *Iliad* 7.424: owing to the gore of battle, it is "hard to recognize each individual dead man" being collected from the battlefield.

44. See Slatkin (2007), 29 for one such tragic and recuperative reading: "however terrible the deaths, . . . they are *sung*" (emphasis added). Posthumanist views, while exciting in their own right (e.g., Purves [2015]), can too easily slight their own ethical implications. For a healthy (because bracing) alternative, see Marg (1976), 9: "The picture we are given [in the *Iliad*] is grim and grisly. Not a hint of breezy conflicts or of soldiers' beautiful deaths. The atmosphere of the battlefield is, rather, eerie." See further a handful of classicists, most notably Lynn-George (1988), van Wees (1996), Buchan (2005), Grethlein (2008), Halliwell (2012), ch. 2, Carson (2019), 20, and, in the parallel universe of tragedy, Wohl (2015), in addition to those writers outside of classics to be discussed at the end of this chapter.

45. Walcott (1990), 313. See also Carson (2019), e.g., 10: "The truth is, / a cloud went to Troy. / A cloud in the shape of Norma Jean Baker."

46. Thucydides, *The Peloponnesian War* 1.6.6; trans. Mynott (2013).

47. Wood (1775), 151, 161, 177–78, 297. A similar ambivalence is expressed by Hume in 1757: Achilles's heroism must be weighed against his "ferocity," Odysseus's "prudence" against his "cunning and fraud"; and a general "want of humanity and of decency" shows itself "even sometimes" in that poetic "genius," Homer (Hume [1998], 152, 9).

48. Scaliger (1998), 268 = *Poetices*, bk. 5, ch. 3, §241a.

49. See Wolfe (2015).

50. Vico (1948). Henceforth, references to this translation will be indicated parenthetically in the text by section numbers only.

51. Nietzsche (2006), 174–75.

52. See this chapter, note 33.

53. Nietzsche (2006), 174 (trans. modified), 179, 181.

54. Nietzsche (2006), 23, 169, the latter from "The Greek State" (1871/72).

55. Nietzsche (1999), 61 (§12); trans. modified. Not only is the language Goethean, but Goethe is explicitly mentioned in this same context.

56. Nietzsche (2006), 174 ("Homer's Contest").

57. Herder (1985–2000), 7:180.

58. See *On the Genealogy of Morals,* "Second Essay," 7, discussing "the primitive logic of feeling" found exemplarily in Homeric Greece: "Was this logic really restricted to primitive times? The gods conceived as the friends of *cruel* spectacles—oh, how far this primeval concept still penetrates into our European civilization! Maybe we should consult Calvin and Luther on the matter" (Nietzsche [2006], 44; trans. modified).

59. Murray (1934), 126 ("Expurgations: The Homeric Spirit"), emphasis added; 130.

60. An important predecessor is Jean Giraudoux's *La guerre de Troie n'aura pas lieu* (*The Trojan War Will Not Take Place,* 1935), known to English-speaking readers as *Tiger at the Gates.*

61. Simone Weil, *The Iliad, or the Poem of Force,* in Weil and Bespaloff (2005), 3.

62. Rachel Bespaloff, *On the Iliad,* in Weil and Bespaloff (2005), 88.

63. Horkheimer and Adorno (2002), 265n61. Adorno was chiefly responsible for this section of the book.

64. "Garrulousness" is from Horkheimer and Adorno (2002), 53. Auerbach (1953; repr. 2003), 4 speaks of what is "broadly [or "expansively"] narrated" (*breit erzähl[t]*).

65. Griffin (1980), 98, 130, 138.

66. Burrow (1993), ch. 1 ("Homer").

67. Simone Weil, *The Iliad, or the Poem of Force,* in Weil and Bespaloff (2005), 30.

68. Griffin (1980), 138: "a poem of death rather than of fighting."

# Further Reading

The literature on Homer is vast. The selection below highlights some of the more essential recent introductory readings that are currently available, most of these in English. Each of these titles contains further leads to the larger bibliography.

## General Reference

Finkelberg, Margalit, ed. 2011. *The Homer Encyclopedia*. 3 vols. Chichester, MA: Wiley-Blackwell.

## Overviews of Homer and the Problem of Homer

Foley, Jonathan Miles, ed. 2005. *A Companion to Ancient Epic*. Malden, MA: Blackwell.

Fowler, Robert, ed. 2004. *The Cambridge Companion to Homer*. Cambridge: Cambridge University Press.

Graziosi, Barbara. 2019. *Homer: A Very Short Introduction*. Oxford: Oxford University Press.

Judet de La Combe, Pierre. 2017. *Homère*. Paris: Gallimard.

Morris, Ian, and Barry B. Powell, eds. 1997. *A New Companion to Homer*. Leiden: Brill.

In addition, there are several learned multivolume commentaries on the *Iliad* and the *Odyssey* available in English, published by Cambridge University Press, Oxford University Press, and De Gruyter.

## Invention and Reception of Homer

Boitani, Piero. 1994. *The Shadow of Ulysses: Figures of a Myth*. Oxford: Clarendon Press.

Ferreri, Luigi. 2007. *La questione omerica dal cinquecento al settecento*. Rome: Edizioni di storia e letteratura.

Ford, Philip. 2006. "Homer in the French Renaissance." *Renaissance Quarterly* 59:1–28.

Graziosi, Barbara. 2002. *Inventing Homer: The Early Reception of Epic*. Cambridge: Cambridge University Press.

Graziosi, Barbara, and Emily Greenwood, eds. 2007. *Homer in the Twentieth Century: Between World Literature and the Western Canon*. Oxford: Oxford University Press.

Hall, Edith. 2008. *The Return of Ulysses: A Cultural History of Homer's "Odyssey."* Baltimore: Johns Hopkins University Press.

Hepp, Noémi. 1961–62. "Homère en France au XVIe siècle." *Atti della Accademia delle scienze di Torino, Classe di scienze morali, storiche e filologiche* 96:389–508.

———. 1968. *Homère en France au XVIIe siècle*. Paris: Klincksiek.

Hunter, Richard. 2018. *The Measure of Homer: The Ancient Reception of the "Iliad" and the "Odyssey."* Cambridge: Cambridge University Press.

Kim, Larry. 2010. *Homer between History and Fiction in Imperial Greek Literature*. Cambridge: Cambridge University Press.

Lamberton, Robert, and J. J. Keaney, eds. 1992. *Homer's Ancient Readers: The Hermeneutics of Greek Epic's Earliest Exegetes*. Princeton: Princeton University Press.

Létoublon, Françoise, Catherine Volpilhac-Auger, and Daniel Sangsue, eds. 1999. *Homère en France après la Querelle, 1715–1900: Actes du colloque de Grenoble, 23–25 octobre 1995, Université Stendhal-Grenoble 3*. Paris: Champion.

Mavroudi, Maria. 2020. "Homer in Greece from the End of Antiquity 1: The Byzantine Reception of Homer and His Export to Other Cultures"; "Homer in Greece from the End of Antiquity 2: Homer after Byzantium, from the Early Ottoman Period to the Age of Nationalisms." In *The Cambridge Guide to Homer, ed.* Corinne Ondine Pache, with C. Dué, S. M. Lupack, and R. Lamberton, 444–72 and 473–89. Cambridge: Cambridge University Press.

Most, Glenn W., Larry F. Norman, and Sophie Rabau, eds. 2009. *Révolutions homériques*. Pisa: Edizioni della Normale.

Rabau, Sophie. 2012. *Quinze (brèves) rencontres avec Homère*. Paris: Belin.

Richardson, Nicholas. 1975. “Homeric Professors in the Age of the Sophists.” *Proceedings of the Cambridge Philological Society* 21:65–81.

West, Martin L. 1999. “The Invention of Homer.” *Classical Quarterly* 49, no. 2:364–82.

Wolfe, Jessica. 2015. *Homer and the Question of Strife from Erasmus to Hobbes*. Toronto: University of Toronto Press.

Zeitlin, Froma I. 2001. “Visions and Revisions of Homer.” In *Being Greek under Rome: Cultural Identity, the Second Sophistic, and the Development of Empire*, ed. Simon Goldhill, 195–266. Cambridge: Cambridge University Press.

## Material Culture and the History of Troy

Cline, Eric H. 2013. *The Trojan War: A Very Short Introduction*. Oxford: Oxford University Press.

———. 2014. *1177 B.C.: The Year Civilization Collapsed*. Princeton: Princeton University Press.

Erskine, Andrew. 2001. *Troy between Greece and Rome: Local Tradition and Imperial Power*. Oxford: Oxford University Press.

Rose, Charles Brian. 2014. *The Archaeology of Greek and Roman Troy*. Cambridge: Cambridge University Press.

Sherratt, Susan, and John Bennett, eds. 2017. *Archaeology and the Homeric Epic*. Oxford: Oxbow Books.

## Visual Culture

Newby, Zahra. 2007. “Reading the Allegory of the Archelaos Relief.” In *Art and Inscriptions in the Ancient World*, ed. Zahra Newby and Ruth Leader-Newby, 156–78. Cambridge: Cambridge University Press.

Richter, Gisela M. A. 1965. *The Portraits of the Greeks*. 3 vols. London: Phaidon Press 1:45–56.

Spivey, Nigel. 2016. "Homer and the Sculptors." In *The Archaeology of Greece and Rome: Studies in Honour of Anthony Snodgrass*, ed. John Bintliff and N. Keith Rutter, 113–51. Edinburgh: Edinburgh University Press.

Zanker, Paul. 1995. *The Mask of Socrates: The Image of the Intellectual in Antiquity*. Trans. Alan Shapiro. Berkeley: University of California Press. (Consult index s.v. "Homer.")

# Works Cited


Aizenberg, Edna. 2005. "Deutsches Requiem 2005." *Variaciones Borges* 20, no. 2:33–57.

Allen, Thomas W. 1912. *Homeri Opera.* 2nd ed. Vol. 5. Oxford: Clarendon Press.

———. 1924. *Homer: The Origins and the Transmission.* Oxford: Clarendon Press.

Amir, Jehoshua. 1974. "Homer und Bibel als Ausdrucksmittel im 3. Sibyllenbuch." *Scripta Classica Israelica* 1:73–89.

Anderson, Michael J. 1997. *The Fall of Troy in Early Greek Poetry and Art.* Oxford: Clarendon Press.

Aslan, Carolyn Chabot, and Charles Brian Rose. 2013. "City and Citadel at Troy from the Late Bronze Age through the Roman Period." In *Cities and Citadels in Turkey: From the Iron Age to the Seljuks*, ed. Scott Redford and Nina Ergin, 7–38. Leuven: Peeters.

Auerbach, Erich. 1953; repr. 2003. *Mimesis: The Representation of Reality in Western Literature.* Trans. Willard R. Trask. Princeton: Princeton University Press. (Original German edition: *Mimesis: Dargestellte Wirklichkeit in der abendländischen Literatur* [Bern: A. Francke, 1946].)

———. 1961. *Dante: Poet of the Secular World.* Trans. Ralph Manheim. Chicago: The University of Chicago Press. (Original German edition: *Dante als Dichter der irdischen Welt* [Berlin: W. de Gruyter, 1929].)

Bachvarova, Mary R. 2016. *From Hittite to Homer: The Anatolian Background of Ancient Greek Epic.* Cambridge: Cambridge University Press.

———. 2018. "Formed on the Festival Stage: Plot and Characterization in the *Iliad* as a Competitive Collaborative Process." In *Homer in Performance: Rhapsodes, Narrators, and Characters*, ed. Jonathan L. Ready and Christos Tsagalis, 151–77. Austin: University of Texas Press.

Bachvarova, Mary R., Dorota Dutsch, and Ann Suter, eds. 2016. *The Fall of Cities in the Mediterranean: Commemoration in Literature, Folk-Song, and Liturgy.* Cambridge: Cambridge University Press.

Bailey, Cyril, trans. 1910. Lucretius, *On the Nature of Things.* Oxford: Clarendon Press.

Bakhtin, M. M. 1981. *The Dialogic Imagination: Four Essays.* Ed. Michael Holquist. Trans. Caryl Emerson and Michael Holquist. Austin: University of Texas Press.

Bakker, Egbert J. 2005. *Pointing at the Past: From Formula to Performance in Homeric Poetics.* Washington, DC: Center for Hellenic Studies, Trustees for Harvard University.

Bassett, Samuel Eliot. 1938. *The Poetry of Homer.* Berkeley: University of California Press.

Benveniste, Émile. 1971. *Problems in General Linguistics.* Trans. Mary Elizabeth Meek. Coral Gables: University of Miami Press.

Bergin, Thomas Goddard, and Alice S. Wilson, trans. 1977. *Petrarch's Africa.* New Haven: Yale University Press.

Bernoulli, J. J. 1901. *Griechische Ikonographie, mit Ausschluss Alexanders und Diadochen.* 2 vols. Munich: Verlagsanstalt F. Bruchmann.

Bittlestone, Robert, with James Diggle and John Underhill. 2005. *Odysseus Unbound: The Search for Homer's Ithaca.* Cambridge: Cambridge University Press.

Boehringer, Robert, and Erich Boehringer. 1939. *Homer: Bildnisse und Nachweise. Vol. 1, Rundwerke.* Breslau: Hirt.

Boileau-Despréaux, Nicolas. 1674. *Œuvres diverses du Sieur D***. Avec le Traité du sublime, ou, Du merveilleux dans le discours. Traduit du Grec de Longin.* Paris: D. Thierry.

Borges, Jorge Luis. 1962. "The Immortal." In *Labyrinths: Selected Stories and Other Writings*, ed. Donald A. Yates, trans. James E. Irby, 105–18. New York: New Directions.

———. 1998. *Collected Fictions.* Trans. Andrew Hurley. New York: Penguin Books.

———. 1999. *Selected Non-Fictions.* Ed. Eliot Weinberger. Trans. Esther Allen, Suzanne Jill Levine, and Eliot Weinberger. New York: Viking Press.

———. 2000. *This Craft of Verse.* Ed. Călin-Andrei Mihăilescu. *The Charles Eliot Norton Lectures 1967–1968.* Cambridge, MA: Harvard University Press.

——. 2015. *Conversations: Volume 2*. Ed. Osvaldo Ferrari. Trans. Tom Boll. London: Seagull Books.

Brink, C. O. 1972. "Ennius and the Hellenistic Worship of Homer." *American Journal of Philology* 93, no. 4:547–67.

Broos, Ben. 1993. *Liefde, List & Lijden: Historiestukken in het Mauritshuis.* Den Haag: Mauritshuis.

Bryant, Jacob. [1796]. *A Dissertation Concerning the War of Troy and the Expedition of the Grecians, As Described by Homer; Shewing That No Such Expedition Was Ever Undertaken, and That No Such City of Phrygia Existed.* [London]: [n.p.].

Bryant Davies, Rachel. 2019. *Victorian Epic Burlesques: A Critical Anthology of Nineteenth-Century Theatrical Entertainments after Homer.* London: Bloomsbury Academic.

Bryce, Trevor. 2008. "Homer at the Interface." In *Anatolian Interfaces: Hittites, Greeks, and Their Neighbours; Proceedings of an International Conference on Cross-Cultural Interaction, September 17–19, 2004, Emory University, Atlanta, GA*, ed. Billie Jean Collins et al., 85–91. Oxford: Oxbow Books.

Buchan, Mark. 2005. *The Limits of Heroism: Homer and the Ethics of Reading.* Ann Arbor: University of Michigan Press.

Burgess, Jonathan S. 2001. *The Tradition of the Trojan War in Homer and the Epic Cycle.* Baltimore: Johns Hopkins University Press.

Burke, Edmund. 1759. *A Philosophical Enquiry into the Origin of Our Ideas of the Sublime and Beautiful.* 2nd ed. London: R. and J. Dodsley.

Burrow, Colin. 1993. *Epic Romance: Homer to Milton.* Oxford: Oxford University Press.

Butler, Samuel. 1922. *The Authoress of the "Odyssey": Where and When She Wrote, Who She Was, the Use She Made of the "Iliad," & How the Poem Grew under Her Hands.* 2nd corr. ed. London: Jonathan Cape. (1st ed., 1897.)

Buxton, R. G. A. 1980. "Blindness and Limits: Sophokles and the Logic of Myth." *Journal of Hellenic Studies* 100:22–37.

Carson, Anne, trans. 2002. *If Not, Winter: Fragments of Sappho.* New York: Alfred A. Knopf.

——. 2019. *Norma Jeane Baker of Troy: A Version of Euripides' "Helen."* London: Oberon Books.

Case, Zachary. 2018. "What's Nietzsche to Euripides? The Aesthetics of Suffering in Euripides' *Trojan Women*." MPhil thesis, Cambridge University.

Clarac, Charles Othon Frédéric Jean Baptiste, Comte de. 1828–30. *Musée de sculpture antique et moderne: Planches.* Vol. 2. Paris: Texier.

———. 1841. *Musée de sculpture antique et moderne, ou, Description historique et graphique du Louvre [etc.].* Vol. 2.1. Paris: Imprimerie Royale.

Clay, Diskin. 2004. *Archilochos Heros: The Cult of Poets in the Greek Polis.* Washington, DC: Center for Hellenic Studies, Trustees for Harvard University.

Cline, Eric H. 2013. *The Trojan War: A Very Short Introduction.* Oxford: Oxford University Press.

———. 2014. *1177 B.C.: The Year Civilization Collapsed.* Princeton: Princeton University Press.

Cohoon, J. W., trans. 1932. Dio Chrysostom, *Discourses 1–11.* Cambridge, MA: Harvard University Press.

Cooper, John M., and D. S. Hutchinson, eds. 1997. *Plato: Complete Works.* Indianapolis: Hackett.

Cribiore, Raffaella. 1996. *Writing, Teachers, and Students in Graeco-Roman Egypt.* Atlanta: Scholars Press.

Crosby, H. Lamar, trans. 1946. Dio Chrysostom, *Discourses 37–60.* Cambridge, MA: Harvard University Press.

Cuper, Gijsbet. 1683. *Apotheosis vel Consecratio Homeri. Sive, Lapis antiquissimus in quo Poëtarum Principis Homeri Consecratio sculpta est, commentario illustratus a Gisberto Cupero.* Amsterdam: Boom.

Cyriac of Ancona. 2003. *Later Travels.* Trans. and ed. Edward W. Bodnar with Clive Foss. Cambridge, MA: Harvard University Press.

Dacier, Anne. 1711. *L'Iliade d'Homere, traduite en françois, avec des remarques.* 3 vols. Paris: Rigaud.

Dalby, Andrew. 2006. *Rediscovering Homer: Inside the Origins of the Epic.* New York: W. W. Norton.

Danek, Georg. 2004. "Der Schiffskatalog der Ilias: Form und Funktion." In *Ad Fontes! Festschrift für Gerhard Dobesch zum fünfundsechzigsten Geburtstag am 15. September 2004,* ed. Herbert Heftner and Kurt Tomaschitz, 59–72. Vienna: Wiener Humanistische Gesellschaft.

Demetriou, Tania. 2015. "The Homeric Question in the Sixteenth Century: Early Modern Scholarship and the Text of Homer." *Renaissance Quarterly* 68, no. 2:496–557.

De Quincey, Thomas. 2001. "Homer and the Homeridae." In *The Works of Thomas de Quincey*, ed. Grevel Lindop and John Whale, 13:3–63. London: Pickering & Chatto.

Dickinson, Oliver. 2017. "The Will to Believe: Why Homer Cannot Be 'True' in Any Meaningful Sense." In *Archaeology and the Homeric Epic*, ed. Susan Sherratt and John Bennett, 10–19. Oxford: Oxbow Books.

Dilthey, Carl. 1876a. "Dipinti pompeiani accompagnati d'epigrammi greci." *Annali dell'Instituto di corrispondenza archeologica* 48:294–314.

———. 1876b. *Monumenti inediti pubblicati dell'Instituto di corrispondenza archeologica/Monuments inédits publiés par l'Institut de correspondance archéologique* 10 (1874–1878), Tav. XXXV.2.

Dobbin, Robert, trans. 2008. Epictetus, *Discourses and Selected Writings*. London: Penguin Books.

Durante, Marcello. 1976. "Il nome di Omero." In *Sulla preistoria della tradizione poetica greca*, 2:185–204. Rome: Edizioni dell'Ateneo. (First published in 1957.)

Eder, Birgitta. 2003. "Noch einmal: Der homerische Schiffskatalog." In *Der neue Streit um Troia: Eine Bilanz*, ed. Christoph Ulf, 287–308. Munich: C.H. Beck.

Erskine, Andrew. 2001. *Troy between Greece and Rome: Local Tradition and Imperial Power*. Oxford: Oxford University Press.

Esdaile, Katharine A. 1912. "An Essay towards the Classification of Homeric Coin Types." *Journal of Hellenic Studies* 32:298–325.

Fantham, Elaine, trans. 2010. Seneca, *Selected Letters*. Oxford: Oxford University Press.

Feeney, Denis. 1999. "Epic Violence, Epic Order: Killings, Catalogues, and the Role of the Reader in *Aeneid* 10." In *Reading Vergil's "Aeneid": An Interpretive Guide*, ed. Christine Perkell, 178–94. Norman: University of Oklahoma Press.

Ferreri, Luigi. 2007. *La questione omerica dal cinquecento al settecento*. Rome: Edizioni di storia e letteratura.

Finkelberg, Margalit. 2005. *Greeks and Pre-Greeks: Aegean Prehistory and Greek Heroic Tradition*. Cambridge: Cambridge University Press.

Finley, M. I. 1965. *The World of Odysseus.* Rev. ed. New York: Viking Press. (1st ed., 1956.)

Fishburn, Evelyn. 1988. "Borges, Cabbala, and 'Creative Misreading.'" *Ibero-amerikanisches Archiv,* n.s., 14, no. 4:401–18.

Freud, Sigmund. 1953–74. *The Standard Edition of the Complete Psychological Works of Sigmund Freud.* Ed. James Strachey et al. 24 vols. London: Hogarth.

Gange, David, and Rachel Bryant Davies. 2013. "Troy." In *Cities of God: The Bible and Archaeology in Nineteenth-Century Britain,* ed. David Gange and Michael Ledger-Lomas, 39–70. Cambridge: Cambridge University Press.

Geffcken, Johannes. 1902. *Die Oracula Sibyllina.* Leipzig. J. C. Hinrichs.

Gibson, Craig A., trans. 2008. *Libanius's Progymnasmata: Model Exercises in Greek Prose Composition and Rhetoric.* Atlanta: Society of Biblical Literature.

Gigon, Olof, ed. 1987. *Aristotelis Opera. Vol. 3, Librorum deperditorum fragmenta.* Berlin: W. de Gruyter.

Goethe, Johann Wolfgang von. 1887–1919. *Goethes Werke.* 133 vols. in 143. Weimar: H. Böhlau.

Gow, A. S. F., and D. L. Page. 1968. *The Greek Anthology: The Garland of Philip, and Some Contemporary Epigrams.* 2 vols. Cambridge: Cambridge University Press.

Graziosi, Barbara. 2002. *Inventing Homer: The Early Reception of Epic.* Cambridge: Cambridge University Press.

Grethlein, Jonas. 2008. "Memory and Material Objects in the *Iliad* and the *Odyssey.*" *Journal of Hellenic Studies* 128:27–51.

Grethlein, Jonas, and Luuk Huitink. 2017. "Homer's Vividness: An Enactive Approach." *Journal of Hellenic Studies* 137:67–91.

Griffin, Jasper. 1980. *Homer on Life and Death.* Oxford: Clarendon Press.

Hall, Edith. 1989. *Inventing the Barbarian: Greek Self–Definition through Tragedy.* Oxford: Clarendon Press.

Halliwell, Stephen. 2012. *Between Ecstasy and Truth: Interpretations of Greek Poetics from Homer to Longinus.* Oxford: Oxford University Press.

Hansen, P. A. 1976. "Pithecusan Humour: The Interpretation of Nestor's Cup Reconsidered." *Glotta* 54:25–44.

——, ed. 1983–89. *Carmina Epigraphica Graeca.* 2 vols. Berlin: Walter de Gruyter.

Hanson, Victor Davis, and John Heath. 1998. *Who Killed Homer? The Demise of Classical Education and the Recovery of Greek Wisdom.* New York: The Free Press.

Hardie, Philip. 2014. *The Last Trojan Hero: A Cultural History of Virgil's "Aeneid."* London: I. B. Tauris.

Harmon, A. M., trans. 1961. *Lucian.* Vol. 1. Cambridge, MA: Harvard University Press.

Haubold, Johannes. 2000. *Homer's People: Epic Poetry and Social Formation.* Cambridge: Cambridge University Press.

——. 2002. "Greek Epic: A Near Eastern Genre?" *Cambridge Classical Journal* 48:1–19.

Hawkins, Tom. 2016. "Bupalus in Scheria: Hipponax's Odyssean Transcontextualizations." In *Iambus and Elegy: New Approaches,* ed. Laura Swift and Chris Carey, 229–52. Oxford: Oxford University Press.

[Hédelin, François, abbé d'Aubignac]. 1715. *Conjectures académiques, ou Dissertation sur l'Iliade: Ouvrage posthume, trouvé dans les recherches d'un Savant.* Ed. [Boscheron]. Paris: F. Fournier.

Hendel, Ronald. 2001. "The Exodus in Biblical Memory." *Journal of Biblical Literature* 120, no. 4:601–22.

——. 2021. "Exodus, Conquest, and Alchemy." In *Biblical and Ancient Near Eastern Studies in Honor of P. Kyle McCarter Jr.,* ed. Christopher A. Rollston, Neal H. Walls, and Ryan Byrne. Atlanta: SBL Press.

Herder, Johann Gottfried. 1985–2000. *Werke in zehn Bänden.* Ed. Martin Bollacher et al. 10 vols. Frankfurt am Main: Deutscher Klassiker Verlag.

——. 2002. *Philosophical Writings.* Trans. and ed. Michael N. Forster. Cambridge: Cambridge University Press.

Hicks, Robert Drew, trans. 1972. Diogenes Laertius, *Lives of Eminent Philosophers.* 2 vols. Cambridge, MA: Harvard University Press. (1st ed., 1925.)

Hilgard, Alfred. 1901. *Scholia in Dionysii Thracis Artem grammaticam. Grammatici Graeci* 1.3. Leipzig: B.G. Teubner.

Horkheimer, Max, and Theodor W. Adorno. 2002. *Dialectic of Enlightenment: Philosophical Fragments.* Ed. Gunzlein Schmid Noerr. Trans.

Edmund Jephcott. Stanford: Stanford University Press. (Original German edition: New York, 1944; Amsterdam, 1947.)

Horrocks, G. C. 1980. "The Antiquity of the Greek Epic Tradition: Some New Evidence." *Proceedings of the Cambridge Philological Society*, n.s., 26:1–11.

Hosty, Matthew. 2020. *Batrachomyomachia (Battle of the Frogs and Mice): Introduction, Text, Translation, and Commentary*. Oxford: Oxford University Press.

Hubbard, M. E., trans. 1972. Aristotle, *Poetics.* In *Ancient Literary Criticism: The Principal Texts in New Translations, ed.* D. A. Russell and M. Winterbottom, 90–132. Oxford: Clarendon Press.

Hume, David. 1998. *Selected Essays.* Ed. Stephen Copley and Andrew Edgar. Oxford: Oxford University Press.

Hunter, Richard. 2018. *The Measure of Homer: The Ancient Reception of the "Iliad" and the "Odyssey."* Cambridge: Cambridge University Press.

Innes, D. C., trans. 1999. Demetrius, *On Style.* In *Aristotle, Poetics; Longinus, On the Sublime; Demtetrius, On Style, ed.* Stephen Halliwell et al., 344–524. Cambridge, MA: Harvard University Press.

Jaeger, Werner. 1934. *Paideia: Die Formung des griechischen Menschen.* Vol. 1. Berlin: W. de Gruyter.

Janko, Richard. 1990. "Dictation and Redaction: The *Iliad* and Its Editors." *Classical Antiquity* 9:326–34.

Jansen, Laura. 2018. *Borges' Classics: Global Encounters with the Graeco-Roman Past.* Cambridge: Cambridge University Press.

Jebb, Richard Claverhouse. 1881. "Rev. of Henry Schliemann, *Ilios: The City and Country of the Trojans.*" *Edinburgh Review* 153:514–47.

———. 1882. "I. The Ruins at Hissarlik; II. Their Relation to the *Iliad.*" *Journal of Hellenic Studies* 3:185–217.

———. 1883. "A Tour in the Troad." *Fortnightly Review*, n.s., 39:514–29.

———. 1884. "Homeric Troy." *Fortnightly Review*, n.s., 35:433–52.

Jensen, Minna Skafte. 2011. *Writing Homer: A Study Based on Results from Modern Fieldwork.* Copenhagen: Det Kongelige Danske Videnskabernes Selskab.

Kantorowicz, Ernst H. 1957. *The King's Two Bodies: A Study in Mediaeval Political Theology.* Princeton: Princeton University Press.

Katz, Joshua T., and Katharina Volk. 2000. "'Mere Bellies'? A New Look at *Theogony* 26–8." *Journal of Hellenic Studies* 120:122–31.

Keaney, J. J., and Robert Lamberton, trans. 1996. [Plutarch], *Essay on the Life and Poetry of Homer.* Atlanta: Scholars Press.

Kim, Larry. 2010. *Homer between History and Fiction in Imperial Greek Literature.* Cambridge: Cambridge University Press.

Kindstrand, Jan Fredrik, ed. 1979. Isaac Porphyrogenitus, *Praefatio in Homerum.* Uppsala: Bloms Boktryckeri AB. Distributed by Almquist & Wiksell International.

Kirk, G. S. 1985. *The Iliad: A Commentary. Vol. 1, Books 1–4.* Cambridge: Cambridge University Press.

Kirk, G. S., J. E. Raven, and M. Schofield. 1983. *The Presocratic Philosophers: A Critical History with a Selection of Texts.* 2nd ed. Cambridge: Cambridge University Press.

Knapp, A. Bernard, and Sturt W. Manning. 2016. "Crisis in Context: The End of the Late Bronze Age in the Eastern Mediterranean." *American Journal of Archaeology* 120, no. 1:99–149.

Korfmann, Manfred. 2000. "Troia-Ausgrabungen 1999." *Studia Troica* 10:1–52.

———. 2002. "Ilios, ca. 1200 BC–Ilion, ca. 700 BC: Report of Findings from Archaeology." In *Omero tremila anni dopo: Atti del congresso di Genova 6–8 luglio 2000*, ed. Franco Montanari, 209–25. Rome: Edizioni di Storia e Letteratura.

Kristal, Efraín. 2014. "Jorge Luis Borges's Literary Response to Anti-Semitism and the Holocaust." *Jewish Quarterly Review* 104, no. 3:354–61.

Lamberton, Robert, trans. 2012. *Proclus the Successor on Poetics and the Homeric Poems: Essays 5 and 6 of His Commentary on the Republic of Plato.* Atlanta: Society of Biblical Literature.

Lamberton, Robert, and John J. Keaney, eds. 1992. *Homer's Ancient Readers: The Hermeneutics of Greek Epic's Earliest Exegetes.* Princeton: Princeton University Press.

La Popelinière, Lancelot Voisin de. 1599. *L'histoire des histoires, avec l'idée de l'histoire accomplie [etc.].* Paris: Jean Hovzé.

Lattimore, Richmond, trans. 1951. Homer, *The Iliad.* Chicago: The University of Chicago Press.

———, trans. 1958. Euripides, *The Trojan Women.* In *Euripides III: Hecuba,*

*Andromache, The Trojan Women, Ion*, ed. David Greene and Richmond Lattimore. Chicago: The University of Chicago Press.

———, trans. 1965. *The Odyssey of Homer.* New York: Harper & Row.

Lavigne, David. 2017. "ΙΡΟΣ ΙΑΜΒΙΚΟΣ: Archilochean *Iambos* and the Homeric Poetics of Conflict." In *Conflict and Consensus in Early Greek Hexameter Poetry*, ed. Paola Bassino, Lilah Grace Canevaro, and Barbara Graziosi, 132–53. Cambridge: Cambridge University Press.

Leaf, Walter, ed. 1900. *The Iliad: Edited, with Apparatus Criticus, Prolegomena, Notes, and Appendices.* 2nd ed. 2 vols. London: Macmillan.

———. 1923. *Strabo on the Troad: Book XIII, Cap. 1.* Cambridge: Cambridge University Press.

Lévi-Strauss, Claude. 1962. *The Savage Mind.* Letchworth: Weidenfeld and Nicholson.

Liapis, Vayos. 2017. "On the Antagonism between Divine and Human Performer in Archaic Greek Poetics." In *Authorship and Greek Song Authority, Authenticity, and Performance*, ed. Egbert J. Bakker, 197–221. Leiden: Brill.

Lightfoot, J. L. 2007. *The Sibylline Oracles, with Introduction, Translation, and Commentary on the First and Second Books.* Oxford: Oxford University Press.

Lobel, Edgar, and Denys L. Page, eds. 1955. *Poetarum Lesbiorum fragmenta.* Oxford: Clarendon Press.

Lovatt, Helen. 2013. *The Epic Gaze: Vision, Gender, and Narrative in Ancient Epic.* Cambridge: Cambridge University Press.

Lynn-George, Michael. 1988. *Epos: Word, Narrative, and the "Iliad."* Basingstoke: Macmillan.

Macintosh, Fiona, et al., eds. 2018. *Epic Performances from the Middle Ages into the Twenty-First Century.* Oxford: Oxford University Press.

MacLeod, M. D., trans. 1967. *Lucian.* Vol. 8. Cambridge, MA: Harvard University Press.

Marg, Walter. 1976. "Kampf und Tod in der *Ilias.*" *Würzburger Jahrbücher für die Altertumswissenschaft* 2:7–19.

Martin, Richard P. 1989. *The Language of Heroes: Speech and Performance in the "Iliad."* Ithaca: Cornell University Press.

———. 2019. "Onomakritos, Rhapsode: Composition-in-Performance and the Competition of Genres in 6th-Century Athens." In *Animo*

*Decipiendi? Rethinking Fakes and Authorship in Classical, Late Antique, and Early Christian Works*, ed. Antonio Guzmán and Javier Martínez, 89–106. Groningen: Barkhuis.

Marx, Friedrich. 1925. "Die Überlieferung über die Persönlichkeit Homers." *Rheinisches Museum für Philologie* 74, no. 4:395–431.

Marx, Karl. 2000. *Selected Writings*. Ed. David McLellan. 2nd ed. Oxford: Oxford University Press.

Mirhady, David, and Yun Lee Too, eds. 2004. *Isocrates II*. Trans. Terry L. Papillon. Austin: University of Texas Press.

Monegal, Emir Rodriguez, Enrico Mario Santí, and Carlos J. Alonso. 1978. "Borges and Politics." *Diacritics* 8, no. 4:55–69.

Morris, Ian, and Barry B. Powell, eds. 1997. *A New Companion to Homer*. Leiden: Brill.

Most, Glenn, trans. 2007. *Hesiod: The Shield, Catalogue of Women, and Other Fragments*. Cambridge, MA: Harvard University Press.

Murray, Gilbert. 1934. *The Rise of the Greek Epic: Being a Course of Lectures Delivered at Harvard University*. 4th ed. Oxford: Oxford University Press. (1st ed., 1907.)

Murray, Oswyn. 1994. "Nestor's Cup and the Origins of the Greek Symposium." *Annali di archeologia e storia antica* 1:47–54.

Mynott, Jeremy, trans. 2013. Thucydides, *The War of the Peloponnesians and the Athenians*. Cambridge: Cambridge University Press.

Na'aman, Nadav. 2011. "The Exodus Story: Between Historical Memory and Historiographical Composition." *Journal of Ancient Near Eastern Religions* 11:39–69.

Nagy, Gregory. 1974. *Comparative Studies in Greek and Indic Meter*. Cambridge, MA: Harvard University Press.

———. 1979. *The Best of the Achaeans: Concepts of the Hero in Archaic Greek Poetry*. Baltimore: Johns Hopkins University Press.

———. 2010. *Homer the Preclassic*. Berkeley: University of California Press.

Nehamas, Alexander, and Paul Woodruff, trans. 1995. Plato, *Phaedrus*. Indianapolis: Hackett.

Nietzsche, Friedrich Wilhelm. 1982. "Homer und die klassische Philologie." In *Werke: Kritische Gesamtausgabe*, ed. Giorgio Colli and Mazzino Montinari, 2.1:247–69. Berlin: Walter de Gruyter.

——. 1999. *Nietzsche: The Birth of Tragedy and Other Writings*. Ed. Raymond Geuss and Ronald Speirs. Trans. Ronald Speirs. Cambridge: Cambridge University Press.

——. 2006. *On the Genealogy of Morality*. Ed. Keith Ansell-Pearson. Trans. Carol Dieth. Cambridge: Cambridge University Press.

Nünlist, René. 2009. *The Ancient Critic at Work: Terms and Concepts of Literary Criticism in Greek Scholia*. Cambridge: Cambridge University Press.

Okiji, Fumi. 2018. *Jazz as Critique: Adorno and Black Expression Revisited*. Stanford: Stanford University Press.

Page, D. L., ed. 1962. *Poetae Melici Graeci*. Oxford: Clarendon Press.

Pannuti, Ulrico. 1984. "*L'apoteosi d'Omero: Vaso argenteo del Museo Nazionale di Napoli*." *Monumenti Antichi dei Lincei*, Serie miscellanea 3.2, vol. 52:43–61.

Papillon, Terry L., trans. 2004. *Isocrates II*. Ed. David Mirhady and Yun Lee Too. Austin: University of Texas Press.

Parry, Adam. 1956. "The Language of Achilles." *Transactions and Proceedings of the American Philological Association* 87:1–7.

Parry, Milman. 1971. *The Making of Homeric Verse: The Collected Papers of Milman Parry*. Ed. Adam Parry. Oxford: Clarendon Press.

Pfister, Friedrich. 1909–12. *Der Reliquienkult im Altertum*. 2 vols. Giessen: A. Töpelmann.

Picard-Cajan, Pascale. 1992. "Ingres et le 'vase étrusque.'" In *L'Anticomanie: La collection d'antiquités aux 18e et 19e siècles*, ed. Annie France Laurens and Krzysztof Pomian, 279–95. Paris: Éditions de l'École des hautes études en sciences humaines.

Pope, Alexander, trans. 1715–20. *The Iliad of Homer*. 6 vols. London: W. Bowyer, for Bernard Lintot.

Porter, James I. 1992. "Hermeneutic Lines and Circles: Aristarchus and Crates on Homeric Exegesis." In *Homer's Ancient Readers: The Hermeneutics of Greek Epic's Earliest Exegetes*, ed. Robert Lamberton and John J. Keaney, 67–114. Princeton: Princeton University Press.

——. 2000. *Nietzsche and the Philology of the Future*. Stanford: Stanford University Press.

——. 2005. "What Is 'Classical' about Classical Antiquity? Eight Propositions." *Arion* 13, no. 1:127–61.

——. 2011. "Making and Unmaking: The Achaean Wall and the Limits of Fictionality in Homeric Criticism." *Transactions and Proceedings of the American Philological Association* 141, no. 1:1–36.

———. 2013. "Homer, Skepticism, and the History of Philology." In *Modernity's Classics*, ed. Sarah C. Humphreys and Rudolf G. Wagner, 261–92. Berlin: Springer.

———. 2021. "*P.Mich. inv.* 2754: New Readings of Alcidamas, 'On Homer.'" *Classical Philology* 116, no. 1: 1–25.

The Postclassicisms Collective. 2019. *Postclassicisms.* Chicago: The University of Chicago Press.

Purves, Alex. 2015. "Ajax and Other Objects: Homer's Vibrant Materialism." In "New Essays on Homer: Language, Violence, and Agency," ed. Sarah Lindheim and Helen Morales, special issue, *Ramus* 44, nos. 1–2:75–94.

Rackham, H., trans. 1952. Pliny, *Natural History, Books* 33–35. Cambridge, MA: Harvard University Press.

Renfrew, Colin. 1979. "Systems Collapse as Social Transformation: Catastrophe and Anastrophe in Early State Societies." In *Transformations: Mathematical Approaches to Culture Change*, ed. Colin Renfrew and Kenneth L. Cooke, 481–506. New York: Academic Press.

Richardson, Edmund. 2016. "Ghostwritten Classics." In *Deep Classics: Rethinking Classical Reception*, ed. Shane Butler, 221–38. London: Bloomsbury.

Richardson, Nicholas. 1975. "Homeric Professors in the Age of the Sophists." *Proceedings of the Cambridge Philological Society* 21:65–81.

Richter, Gisela M. A. 1965. *The Portraits of the Greeks.* 3 vols. London: Phaidon Press.

Robinson, James Harvey, ed. and trans. 1898. *Petrarch: The First Modern Scholar and Man of Letters; A Selection from His Correspondence with Boccaccio and Other Friends*. With the collaboration of Henry Winchester Rolfe. New York: G. P. Putnam's Sons.

Rose, Charles Brian. 2014. *The Archaeology of Greek and Roman Troy.* Cambridge: Cambridge University Press.

Rosen, Ralph. 1990. "Hipponax and the Homeric Odysseus." *Eikasmos* 1, no. 1:11–25.

Rosenmeyer, Patricia A. 2006. *Ancient Greek Literary Letters: Selections in Translation*. London: Routledge.

Rosenzweig, Franz. 2005. *The Star of Redemption*. Trans. Barbara E. Galli. Madison: University of Wisconsin Press.

Russell, D. A., trans. 1972a. Longinus, *On the Sublime*. In *Ancient Literary Criticism: The Principal Texts in New Translations, ed.* D. A. Russell and M. Winterbottom, 460–503. Oxford: Clarendon Press.

———, trans. 1972b. Plato, *Ion, Republic*. In *Ancient Literary Criticism: The Principal Texts in New Translations, ed.* D. A. Russell and M. Winterbottom, 39–74. Oxford: Clarendon Press.

Russell, D. A., and Michael Winterbottom, eds. 1972. *Ancient Literary Criticism: The Principal Texts in New Translations*. Oxford: Clarendon Press.

Russell, W. M. S., and Claire Russell. 1991. "English Turf Mazes, Troy, and the Labyrinth." *Folklore* 102, no. 1:77–88.

Rusten, Jeffrey, trans. 2014. Philostratus, *Heroicus*. In *Heroicus, Gymnasticus, Discourses 1 and 2, ed.* Jeffrey Rusten and Jason König, 102–327. Cambridge, MA: Harvard University Press.

Samxon, Jean. 1530. *Les Iliades de Homere, poete grec et grant hystoriographe*. Paris: Jean Petit.

Santner, Eric L. 2001. *On the Psychotheology of Everyday Life: Reflections on Freud and Rosenzweig*. Chicago: The University of Chicago Press.

Scaliger, Julius Caesar. 1998. *Poetices libri septem: Sieben Bücher über die Dichtkunst*. Trans. and ed. Gregor Vogt-Spira. Vol. 4, Book 5. Stuttgart-Bad Cannstatt: Frommann-Holzboog.

Schein, Seth L. 1984. *The Mortal Hero: An Introduction to Homer's "Iliad."* Berkeley: University of California Press.

Schironi, Francesca. 2018. *The Best of the Grammarians: Aristarchus of Samothrace on the "Iliad."* Ann Arbor: University of Michigan Press.

Schliemann, Heinrich. 1875. *Troy and Its Remains: A Narrative of Researches and Discoveries Made on the Site of Ilium, and in the Trojan Plain*. Ed. Philip Smith. Trans. L. Dora Schmitz. London: J. Murray.

———. 1880. *Ilios: The City and Country of the Trojans; The Results of Researches and Discoveries on the Site of Troy and through the Troad in the Years 1871-72-73-78-79, Including an Autobiography of the Author*. London: J. Murray.

Schott, Andreas Heinrich. 1783. *Ueber das Studium des Homers in niederen und höheren Schulen*. Leipzig: Crusius.

Schrader, Hermann Ludwig, ed. 1880–82. *Porphyrii quaestionum homericarum ad Iliadem pertinentium reliquias.* 2 vols. Leipzig: B.G. Teubner.

Scodel, Ruth. 1982. "The Achaean Wall and the Myth of Destruction." *Harvard Studies in Classical Philology* 86:33–50.

Screech, M. A., trans. 1993. Michel de Montaigne, *The Complete Essays.* London: Penguin Books.

Seidensticker, Bernd. 1978. "Archilochus and Odysseus." *Greek, Roman, and Byzantine Studies* 19, no. 1:5–22.

Shelton, Andrew Carrington. 2005. *Ingres and His Critics.* Cambridge: Cambridge University Press.

Sherratt, Susan. 2010. "The Trojan War: History or Bricolage?" *Bulletin of the Institute of Classical Studies* 53, no. 2:1–18.

Shipley, Frederick W., trans. 1924. Velleius Paterculus, *Compendium of Roman History; Res gestae divi Augusti.* Cambridge, MA: Harvard University Press.

Siegfried, Susan L. 2006. "L'auto-institution de l'artiste: *L'Apothéose d'Homère.*" In *Ingres, 1780–1867*, ed. Vincent Pomarède et al., 55–67. Exhibition catalogue, Musée du Louvre. Paris: Gallimard.

———. 2009. *Ingres: Painting Reimagined.* New Haven: Yale University Press.

Slatkin, Laura M. 2007. "Notes on Tragic Visualization in the *Iliad.*" In *Visualizing the Tragic: Drama, Myth, and Ritual in Greek Art and Literature; Essays in Honour of Froma Zeitlin*, ed. Chris Kraus et al., 19–34. Oxford: Oxford University Press.

Smith, Arthur Hamilton. 1904. *A Catalogue of Sculpture in the Department of Greek and Roman Antiquities, British Museum.* Vol. 3. London: Trustees of the British Museum.

Spivey, Nigel. 2016. "Homer and the Sculptors." In *The Archaeology of Greece and Rome: Studies in Honour of Anthony Snodgrass*, ed. John Bintliff and N. Keith Rutter, 113–51. Edinburgh: Edinburgh University Press.

Stavans, Ilan. 2016. *Borges, the Jew.* Buffalo: SUNY Press.

Stewart, Andrew F. 1990. *Greek Sculpture: An Exploration.* 2 vols. New Haven: Yale University Press.

Stoevesandt, Magdalene. 2004. *Feinde, Gegner, Opfer: Zur Darstellung der Troianer in den Kampfszenen der Ilias.* Basel: Schwabe.

Ternois, Daniel. 1954/55. "Les sources iconographiques de l'*Apothéose d'Homère*." *Bulletin archéologique, historique et artistique de la Société archéologique de Tarn-et-Garonne* 81:26–45.

———. 1965. *Peintures: Ingres et son temps (Artistes nés entre 1740 et 1830)*. Paris: Éditions des Musées nationaux.

Thonemann, Peter. 2014. "Poets of the Axylon." *Chiron* 44:191–232.

Tischbein, [Johann] Heinrich Wilhelm, and Christian Gottlob Heyne. 1801. *Homer nach Antiken gezeichnet*. Göttingen: Dieterich.

Trachsel, Alexandra. 2007. *La Troade: Un paysage et son héritage littéraire; Les commentaires antiques sur la Troade, leur genèse et leur influence*. Basel: Schwabe.

Truffaut, François. 1967. *Hitchcock*. With the collaboration of Helen G. Scott. New York: Simon and Schuster.

Usher, Stephen, trans. 1985. Dionysius of Halicarnassus, *Critical Essays. Vol. 2, On Literary Composition, Dinarchus, Letters to Ammaeus and Pompeius*. Cambridge, MA: Harvard University Press.

van Wees, Hans. 1996. "Heroes, Knights, and Nutters: Warrior Mentality in Homer." In *Battle in Antiquity*, ed. Alan B. Lloyd, 1–86. London: Duckworth, in association with the Classical Press of Wales.

Vermeule, Cornelius. 1995. "Neon Ilion and Ilium Novum: Kings, Soldiers, Citizens, and Tourists at Classical Troy." In *The Ages of Homer: A Tribute to Emily Townsend Vermeule*, ed. Jane Burr Carter and Sarah P. Morris, 467–82. Austin: University of Texas Press.

Vernant, Jean-Pierre. 1991. "A 'Beautiful Death' and the Disfigured Corpse in Homeric Epic." In *Mortals and Immortals: Collected Essays*, ed. and trans. Froma I. Zeitlin, 50–74. Princeton: Princeton University Press.

Vico, Giambattista. 1948. *The New Science of Giambattista Vico*. Trans. Thomas Goddard Bergin and Max H. Fisch. Ithaca: Cornell University Press.

Vigne, Georges. 1995. *Ingres*. Trans. John Goodman. New York: Abbeville Press.

———. 2007. *Ingres: Autour des peintures du Musée de Montauban*. Montauban: Musée Ingres.

Voss, Johann Heinrich, trans. 1801. *Homers Werke in zwei Bänden: Mit einer literarhistorischen Einleitung von Joseph Lautenbacher*. 2 vols. Stuttgart: J. G. Cotta.

Walcott, Derek. 1990. *Omeros*. New York: Farrar, Straus & Giroux.

Watkins, Calvert. 1986. "The Language of the Trojans." In *Troy and the Trojan War: A Symposium Held at Bryn Mawr College, October 1984*, ed. Machteld J. Mellink, 45–62. Bryn Mawr, PA: Bryn Mawr College.

Weil, Simone, and Rachel Bespaloff. 2005. *War and the "Iliad."* Introduction by Christopher Benfey. Trans. Mary McCarthy. New York: New York Review of Books.

Welcker, Friedrich Gottlieb. 1865–82. *Der epische Cyclus, oder die homerischen Dichter.* 2nd ed. 2 vols. Bonn: E. Weber.

West, M. L. 1988. "The Rise of the Greek Epic." *Journal of Hellenic Studies* 108:151–72.

———. 1989–92. *Iambi et elegi graeci ante Alexandrum cantati.* 2nd ed. 2 vols. Oxford: Clarendon.

———. 1995. "The Date of the *Iliad*." *Museum Helveticum* 52:203–19.

———. 1999. "The Invention of Homer." *Classical Quarterly* 49, no. 2:364–82.

———. 2003a. *Greek Epic Fragments: From the Seventh to the Fifth Centuries BC*. Cambridge, MA: Harvard University Press.

———. 2003b. *Homeric Hymns, Homeric Apocrypha, Lives of Homer.* Cambridge, MA: Harvard University Press.

———. 2007. *Indo-European Poetry and Myth*. Oxford: Oxford University Press.

———. 2010. "Rhapsodes at Festivals." *Zeitschrift für Papyrologie und Epigraphik* 173:1–13.

———. 2011. *The Making of the "Iliad": Disquisition and Analytical Commentary*. Oxford: Oxford University Press.

Wilamowitz-Moellendorff, Ulrich von. 1916. *Die Ilias und Homer.* Berlin: Weidmann.

Winckelmann, Johann Joachim. 1985. "Thoughts on the Imitation of the Painting and Sculpture of the Greeks." In *German Aesthetic and Literary Criticism: Winckelmann, Lessing, Hamann, Herder, Schiller, Goethe*, ed. H. B. Nisbet, 32–54. Cambridge: Cambridge University Press.

Wofford, Susanne Lindgren. 1992. *The Choice of Achilles: The Ideology of Figure in the Epic*. Stanford: Stanford University Press.

Wohl, Victoria. 2015. *Euripides and the Politics of Form*. Princeton: Princeton University Press.

Wolf, F. A. 1985. *Prolegomena to Homer.* Trans. Anthony Grafton, Glenn W. Most, and James E. G. Zetzel. Princeton: Princeton University Press.

Wolfe, Jessica. 2015. *Homer and the Question of Strife from Erasmus to Hobbes.* Toronto: University of Toronto Press.

Wood, Robert. 1775. *An Essay on the Original Genius and Writing of Homer: With a Comparative View of the Ancient and Present State of the Troade.* 2nd rev. and expanded ed. London: Printed by H. Hughs for T. Payne & P. Elmsly. (Original ed., 1767; 1st rev. ed., 1769.)

Zanker, Paul. 1995. *The Mask of Socrates: The Image of the Intellectual in Antiquity.* Trans. Alan Shapiro. Berkeley: University of California Press.

Zeitlin, Froma I. 2001. "Visions and Revisions of Homer." In *Being Greek under Rome: Cultural Identity, the Second Sophistic, and the Development of Empire*, ed. Simon Goldhill, 195–266. Cambridge: Cambridge University Press.

Ziolkowski, Jan M., and Michael C. J. Putnam, eds. 2008. *The Virgilian Tradition: The First Fifteen Hundred Years.* New Haven: Yale University Press.

Žižek, Slavoj. 2008. *The Sublime Object of Ideology.* 2nd ed. London: Verso.

# Index